Recruiting and Retaining Lawyers

Innovative Strategies to Attract, Develop and Retain Legal Talent

Consulting Editor **Rebecca Normand-Hochman**
on behalf of the International Bar Association

Consulting editor
Rebecca Normand-Hochman
on behalf of the International Bar Association

Managing director
Sian O'Neill

***Recruiting and Retaining Lawyers: Innovative Strategies to Attract, Develop and Retain Legal Talent* is published by**

Globe Law and Business Ltd
3 Mylor Close
Horsell
Woking
Surrey GU21 4DD
Tel: +44 20 3745 4770
www.globelawandbusiness.com

Printed and bound by Gomer Press

Recruiting and Retaining Lawyers: Innovative Strategies to Attract, Develop and Retain Legal Talent

ISBN 9781911078159

Table of contents

Law firm strategy for recruiting and retaining legal talent — 5
Rebecca Normand-Hochman
Venturis Consulting Group

Collaboration among partners: increasing the odds of productive lateral hiring — 17
Heidi K Gardner
Harvard Law School

The new employer proposition: getting the balance right between the firm's strategy and the expectations of its workforce — 31
Jean-Baptiste Lebelle
Allen & Overy, Paris

Legal education and training: supporting the recruitment and development of legal talent — 45
Tony King
AGK PSF Training Ltd

Equipping partners with the skills and abilities to retain talent — 63
Alison Nolan
Open Consulting

Coaching lawyers through change — 79
Antonin Besse
Besse Executive Coaching and Training

Retaining women lawyers: the need for new perspectives — 99
Ida Abbott
Ida Abbott Consulting

In-house careers — 115
Cecilia Poullain
Natixis Asset Management

Recruiting and retaining talent in first-generation law firms — 125
Anna Grishchenkova
KIAP Attorneys at Law

Managing underperformance — 137
Patrick J McKenna
McKenna Associates Inc

Working with legal search consultants — 147
Guillaume Pican
Page Executive

Case study: designing and implementing a new people strategy 155
Alessandro Portolano
Chiomenti
Gerard J Tanja
Venturis Consulting Group

Alumni and the value of creating strong networks 161
Mahmood Lone
Allen & Overy LLP
Boyan Wells
Retired Allen & Overy partner

About the authors 173

Law firm strategy for recruiting and retaining legal talent

Rebecca Normand-Hochman
Venturis Consulting Group

1. Introduction

The legal profession is going through fundamental changes and finding the right approach to talent has never been so important: talent and leadership issues have become more determining competitive factors of law firm success than ever before. External factors such as globalisation, technology, pressure on fees and the intense competition for talent are coupled with other profound changes such as the younger generation of lawyers' new internal drivers, values and aspirations.

Until recently, it was assumed that there would always be enough good lawyers knocking at the door of every law firm, but in the last decade things have changed. David Maister's vision about one of the main challenges for professional services firms of the future, described in 1997,[1] is now a reality:

> *Most professional service firms' strategic thinking has focused overwhelmingly on the client market place alone. This is about to change. In the next decade and beyond, the ability to attract, develop, retain and deploy staff will be the single biggest determinant of a professional service firm's competitive success.*

The war for talent that the McKinsey authors described in their book[2] 15 years ago is now happening in virtually all industries and the legal profession is no exception. Even where there is locally a high level of unemployment, organisations of all sizes, sectors and cultures across the globe are competing to find and keep the most talented workers. In many jurisdictions, there are more lawyers than the market can absorb, but there are too few people with the 'right' skills: the level of complexity of client work now requires lawyers both to be technically highly specialised and to possess business and leadership skills that were traditionally not part of their expertise. Because of that, what legal talent was and how it could be described even five or seven years ago has drastically changed.

In its wider definition, talent is the sum of someone's natural abilities, competencies, motivations and internal drivers, but it also includes the ability to learn, develop and adapt to change. Because of the role that lawyers play in society, the legal profession can be described as conservative by nature and is not well equipped to adapt quickly to change. The emotional aspects involved in change processes also make many practitioners resent adopting new approaches or mindsets

1 David H Maister, *Managing the Professional Service Firm* (Free Press, 1997).
2 Ed Michaels, Helen Handfield-Jone and Beth Axelrod, *The War for Talent* (Harvard Business Review Press, 2001).

unless it is critical for them to do so: most lawyers feel more comfortable reacting to change rather than anticipating it. However, because of their broad intellectual capacities as well as their strong sense of professional duties and responsibilities, lawyers also have enormous unexploited potential for embracing rapid change when the situation requires them to do so.

These are exciting times for companies and professional services firms across the globe whose history and entrepreneurship culture have led them to take innovative routes to adapt to tough and challenging conditions. But the current levels and pace of change also represent considerable levels of risk which raise concerns about the future. Some law firm leaders and partners even question whether their firms will be able to survive the current drastic changes in market and industry conditions.

The cultural shifts that both external and internal factors produce require firms to align individual and organisational needs and potential in new remarkable ways.

The first part of this chapter provides tools and approaches for some of today's most difficult talent issues:

- recruiting the right talent;
- developing the next generation of lawyers;
- managing performance; and
- building lifetime talent pools.

These are aligned with the most advanced best practice but, at the same time, are tailored to the specific needs and challenges of our profession.

The second part of this chapter provides a couple of case studies of talent initiatives which illustrate how law firms, of whatever size or culture, can become equipped with the tools and mindsets needed to deal with the current changes as well as to anticipate the next (and most probably constant) set of changes that we can expect in the future.

2. Tools and approaches for today's talent issues

2.1 Recruiting the talent that your firm needs

There are different ways to consider how to attract and select the best talent. Some firms have a very structured approach and others have a more informal way of finding the talent that they need. In general terms, the bigger the firm, the more a clearly defined and well-communicated approach it needs to have in place in order to make sure that all partners, practice areas and offices are capable of attracting the talent needed for the firm.

The preliminary step in order to be in a position to attract the talent that a firm needs is to determine what is the employer value proposition which the firm is making to potential new talent joining the firm. This is not the subject of this chapter but ways of designing and implementing new employer value propositions are described in Jean-Baptiste Lebelle's chapter on the subject in this book.

Then, in order to be able to assess the type of talent that the firm needs, best practice is to introduce assessment tools and instruments capable of identifying specific competencies, talents, motivations and internal drivers of potential new talent. Assessing talent and potential ensures not only that lawyers joining the firm are right for their role but also that they fit with the culture of the firm.

It is too often assumed that the type of legal education that lawyers go through and the culture that we are in shape us in similar ways. Assessment tools look at how someone is likely to behave in a given environment. They help better predict performance but also understand the complex interaction between someone's specific mental framework and the environment/culture.

Bahaviours are shaped by three elements as illustrated below:

- our talents (eg, natural abilities, needs, motivations and values, basically defining who we are at a deep level);
- our competencies; and
- the environment.

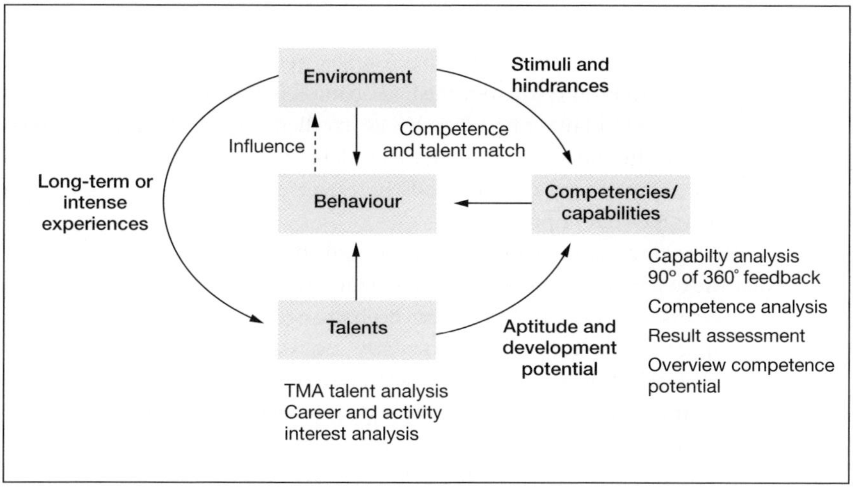

* *Reproduced with the permission of the Human Mobility Group.*

Once what determines specific behaviours is understood and the types of behaviours that are needed for the culture of the firm identified, the talents, competencies and potential that should be sought for particular levels of seniority can be determined.

For junior lawyers, typical talents, competencies and potential needed include:

- the ability to be pragmatic and structured;
- the ability to manage stress and pressure;
- learning and self-development potential;
- social competencies that enable team work and collaboration;
- low need for support.

For senior lawyers and partners, additional typical talents, competencies and potential needed include:

- commercial power;
- client management skills;

- leadership capabilities;
- the ability to mentor and develop others;
- organisational sensitivity.

Being able to recruit people who have the right talents, competencies or potential and who are likely to adopt the behaviours that the firm needs is the foundation of any solid approach to talent in today's law firm. It is surprising to see some of the most advanced international law firms still not taking advantage of the modern tools which can help bring greater predictability and chances of success in the recruitment and onboarding processes.

3. Developing the next generation of lawyers

A traditional assumption that has faded in many firms is that a lawyer's career goal is to become a partner of the firm. The fact that it is no longer the case can be partly explained as an adjustment by the younger generation (and to some extent as a pragmatic response) to the diminished chances for them to make it to partnership. Until recently, if a lawyer had received an excellent legal education, worked hard and was loyal to the firm, he/she had a reasonable chance of making it to partnership. Today, it is no longer the case and the career prospects for nearly everyone have become somewhat unpredictable.

By looking at other professions and industries as well as the research, it is clear that the generational changes in career and life priorities are similar to those in the law profession and that they reflect deep changes in work and society at large and are similar across industries. Particularly interesting academic research shows the generational patterns that can be identified over time, giving a clear explanation of some of the profound reasons that lead new generations to have a different vision of the world from their predecessors.

What the younger generations of professionals are now asking for is a more personalised approach to talent development, enabling them to become the professionals that they are capable of becoming (whether their future is to be a partner in the firm, an accomplished professional somewhere else or to lead a completely different life). They have the aspiration to acquire the skills and abilities to change firm, country or career with agility and confidence.

Some law firms have developed sophisticated training frameworks but what is crucially lacking today is the partners' commitment and ability to support, nurture and develop talent. Some of the talent nurtured and developed will be the partners and leadership of the firm in the future, and a large majority will leave the firm (which doesn't affect the necessity to invest in developing all the talent of a firm).

It was assumed in the past that the best talent would always emerge and that through the process of 'natural selection' the ones who had what it took to become partners would succeed in becoming the future partners or leaders of the firm. This is another assumption that is now no longer true. Not only is the best talent also the most mobile but it is also a category of professionals who know what they are worth and that they are in high demand, and who place quality of life or working conditions as their top priorities. The best talent today will therefore go where their talent is valued and will join organisations that are closest to their values and allow them to have the career and the life that they want.

Developing partners as mentors is one of the most – if not the most – powerful and cost-effective ways to nurture and develop talent in law firms. The research which Harvard Professor Heidi Gardner and I have been pursuing in the last couple of years has focused on understanding how mentoring and collaboration frameworks (as enablers of productive working relationships) can be implemented in law firms and our research clearly shows that there is a huge potential for growing both.

Here are two of the main findings of our work on mentoring.

The first finding is that mentoring programmes don't work in law firms. We've looked at more than 10 international firms in detail and we can say that none of the programmes produce the expected outcomes. What we call 'informal mentoring', whereby relationships develop naturally, tend to be more successful but there are fewer of these.

So what does it mean? It means that, in order to grow productive working relationships, firms have to create the right culture and not a rigid programme (which is much harder of course because culture is to a large extent about behaviour).

The second finding which is relevant here is that the success of mentoring relationships depends to a large extent on the competencies of the partners to mentor and our research shows that there are few partners who have developed these skills.

Mentoring has radically evolved in the last decade and what most partners consider to be mentoring does not coincide with what the younger generation of lawyers expect from their predecessors. Mentoring, like coaching, has essentially moved from being directive (giving advice and telling someone else how to do things) to being non-directive (listening, providing feedback and guidance in a way that raises awareness and self-awareness).

The shift from directiveness to non-directiveness is particularly hard for lawyers to do because of the way in which they are trained and the expert role that they perform for their clients. However, developing these non-directive competencies can not only be the pivotal element of a strong talent development culture, it can also help lawyers of all levels of seniority to develop stronger client relationships, enabling them to identify as well as respond more effectively to client needs.

The competencies involved in mentoring cover a wide spectrum and in alphabetical order they include:

- Accountability
- Adaptability
- Coaching
- Conflict management
- Cooperation
- Courage
- Developing people
- Flexible behaviour
- Initiative
- Insight

- Integrity
- Learning ability
- Listening
- Political sensitivity
- Result-orientedness
- Self-development
- Sensitivity
- Social awareness
- Stress management
- Vision

Until neuroscience showed the ability of the adult brain to learn new skills and competencies and even to adopt new behaviours and mindsets throughout life (neuroplasticity), most law firm leaders were of the view that a limited number of partners actually had the potential to become good mentors. This is changing and there is now a recognition not only of the need for partners to mentor but of the need for them to mentor well.

In the last part of this chapter, there is a case study describing an international law firm which has taken the route of equipping partners with mentoring skills as part of the objective to build the firm's internal capability to support the development of senior talent.

4. Focusing on four radically different performance questions

If you ask partners about what they think of the performance management system in their firm, many will answer that it is time consuming and neither engaging nor helpful in addressing performance issues that need to be dealt with. Traditional performance management systems (whether in law firms or in other professional services industries) tend to be time intensive, more focused on the process than on the outcomes and don't enable real discussions about performance and development to take place.

This was also the conclusion reached at Deloitte a couple of years ago. The firm therefore decided to completely revamp its approach to performance management which is an interesting example for law firms. What follows is largely taken from a case study that *Harvard Business Review* published in 2015 on Deloitte's experiment.

What Deloitte realised is that its process for evaluating the work of its people and then training them, promoting them, and paying them accordingly was increasingly out of step with its objectives. In a public survey that Deloitte conducted, more than half the executives questioned (58%) believed that their current performance management approach drove neither employee engagement nor high performance. They were in need of something more agile, real-time, and more individualised – something focused on fuelling performance in the organisation.

The new system put in place came as a surprise to many: it has no once-a-year reviews, and no 360-degree-feedback tools. Deloitte arrived at a very different and much simpler design for managing people's performance. Its characteristics are:

- speed;

- agility;
- one-size-fits-one;
- constant learning; and
- it is underpinned by a new way of collecting reliable performance data.

Rather than asking more people for their opinion of a team member (in a 360-degree or an upward-feedback survey, for example), Deloitte asked only the immediate team leader – but, critically, a different kind of question. People may rate other people's skills inconsistently, but they are highly consistent when rating their own feelings and intentions. To see performance at the individual level, it asked team leaders not about the skills of each team member but about their own future actions with respect to that person.

At the end of every project (or once every quarter for long-term projects) it asked team leaders to respond to four future-focused statements about each team member. It refined the wording of these statements through successive tests and they clearly highlight differences among individuals and reliably measure performance. Here are the four statements:

'Given what I know of this person's performance, and if it were my money, I would award this person the highest possible compensation increase and bonus' (measures overall performance and unique value to the organisation on a five-point scale from 'strongly agree' to 'strongly disagree').

'Given what I know of this person's performance, I would always want him or her on my team' (measures ability to work well with others on the same five-point scale).

'This person is at risk because of low performance' (identifies problems that might harm the client or the team on a yes-or-no basis).

'This person is ready for promotion today' (measures potential on a yes-or-no basis).

Deloitte defined three objectives at the root of performance management: to recognise, see and fuel performance. It shifted from a batched focus on the past to a continual focus on the future, through regular evaluations and frequent check-ins.

This system made much more sense for Deloitte's talent-dependent business and, since then, many of the most advanced organisations have moved to adopt similar approaches. By early 2015, around 30 large companies, representing over 1.5 million employees, had followed a similar path.

Although law firms are a specific type of organisation, they also share many similarities with other knowledge-intensive organisations such as consulting firms. It is hard not to see the huge benefits that law firms would gain from designing and implementing performance management systems which are capable of assessing individual performance and potential in ways that are engaging and which fuel performance.

5. Building lifetime talent pools

Once a solid recruitment, development and performance management strategy has been designed and implemented, there are additional aspects which firms should add to their framework in order to benefit from the incredible value that their network has. Some associates or partners leaving the firms become clients, others go to competitors (sometimes coming back to the firm at a later stage which a particular international firm calls 'boomerang' talent), and others transition to other careers, potentially recommending their former firm(s) whatever they do.

Firms such as McKinsey have for some time understood the value of creating a strong network of former employees. A few of the most advanced law firms have started to implement similar approaches. The reasons for investing in making that network stronger and bigger as well as the benefits that firms can gain from doing so are discussed in the chapter on alumni by Mahmood Lone and Boyan Wells.

For this part of the chapter, I would like to focus on the opportunity that firms have to improve their talent framework through understanding what motivates a valued professional to leave a firm and how he/she views the time spent with the firm.

Relevant actions resulting from exit feedback analysis fall into two categories:

- Remedial and preventative, for example reducing associate turnover or discrimination.
- Strategic improvement opportunities, for example improving recruitment, induction, management or training, team building, or process improvement.

The aims of exit interviews may include:

- to provide direct indications as to how to improve lawyer retention;
- to give valuable information as to how to improve recruitment and induction of new lawyers;
- to be seen by existing lawyers as a sign of positive culture (they are regarded as a sign that the firm is mature enough to expose itself to criticism);
- to accelerate partners' understanding and experience of people management aspects of the firm (receiving and handling feedback is a powerful development process);
- to help to support the firm's proper HR practices;
- to feed relevant and useful data directly into training needs analysis;
- to sometimes provide the chance to retain a valuable lawyer who would otherwise have left (firms sometimes accept resignations too readily without discussion or testing the firmness of feeling – the exit interview provides a final safety net).

Below are examples of questions which can be used either in face-to-face exit interviews, or to compile exit interview pro forma questionnaires. In interviews, use the word 'why', especially if the first answer is vague or superficial. Questions beginning with 'what' and 'how' are better for getting people to think and convey their thoughts accurately and honestly.

- Why did you decide to leave the firm?
- What is your main reason for leaving?
- What are the other reasons for leaving?
- Why is this important to you?
- Within the particular reason to leave, what was it that concerned you particularly?

- Is there anything that could have been done early on to provide a basis for you to stay?
- Do you have any suggestions for how the firm could manage this situation/these issues better in the future?
- How do you feel about the firm?
- Can you describe what has been good/satisfying for you in your time in the firm?
- What about what has been frustrating/difficult for you in your time in the firm?
- Are there any responsibilities that you would have welcomed that you were not given?
- Tell me how the firm could have enabled you to make fuller use of your capabilities and potential?
- How well do you think your training and development needs were assessed and met?
- What can you say about communication within the firm/your department?
- Can you tell me how you would describe the culture or 'feel' of the firm?
- For recent recruits of less than a year or so: what did you think about the way we recruited you? How did the reality alter from your expectations when you first joined the firm? How could we have improved your own recruitment? How could your induction training have been improved?
- What do you think about the way your performance was measured, and the feedback to you of your performance?
- Do you think that the appraisal system worked well for you?
- Can you make any suggestions to improve working conditions?

6. Case studies

The three short cases studies below illustrate how some of the issues that have traditionally been hard to tackle can be addressed by introducing new tools and approaches.

Case study 1 – Start addressing retention issues by redesigning the recruitment process

As with most professional services firms today, a leading national law firm was experiencing a particularly high level of turnover and we started helping them design and implement a new talent framework in response to that specific challenge. Every company or firm now has to face the challenge that the best talent is also potentially the most mobile (the development of the recruitment and headhunting industry in general facilitating professional mobility on an international basis).

This considerably increased mobility requires law firms to find new ways to engage high-calibre professionals at all stages of their career.

When we looked at the turnover rates as well as the talent framework as a whole, it was clear that the place to start to address retention was by looking at how the firm selected and recruited its people. The firm in question is a firm of the highest reputation that all young lawyers aspire to join as evidenced by the number of applications that the firm receives on a yearly basis. However, the firm has a very specific culture and making sure that the people who are selected don't only have the right skills for their level of seniority but also have a personality and values that fit that specific culture was the obvious first step.

The recruitment process that we designed in this context included, among the usual guidelines to select the appropriate profiles, process to facilitate the exchange of feedback between partners and competency framework for each level of seniority, the following additional elements:

- individual assessments of all candidates and individual tailored feedback provided to every recruiting partner;
- equipping the recruiting partners with the tools and skills to interview and select the right candidates for their department/team.

The ability of partners to understand individual talents, motivations and internal drivers of new lawyers joining the firm enables them to ensure that they are making good hiring decisions. It is also the starting point to enable them to manage the development of their lawyers with the insight and understanding that they need in order to make sure that, despite today's high mobility and competition for talent (especially in the mid-level stage of career), they can significantly improve their ability to engage and retain the best talent.

Implementing a consistent and high-level recruitment process is the first step to address the retention challenges; the next phases are to redesign the performance management system as well as to introduce a mentoring framework to foster the support of individual development and potential.

Case study 2 – Building partner competencies to support senior lawyer development

The recent change in one Magic Circle employer's value proposition led the firm to reframe the way it supports its senior talent. The moral contract between firms and lawyers is no longer that the best talent will be supported to make it to partnership if the business allows them to become a partner but that everyone will be supported to become the professional that they are capable of becoming in a personalised way.

That firm's concern was to be able to better support senior talent and provide them with new outstanding developmental opportunities.

The framework that we designed collaboratively with the firm included the following elements:

- the opportunity for each senior associate to do an individual assessment of their competencies, motivations and potential;
- individual sessions on how they stand on the competencies established by the firm for their level of seniority as well as how these fit with their broader developmental aspirations and objectives;
- matching them with a mentor outside of their practice area in a light but structured mentoring framework;
- tools and sessions to equip mentors with high-level mentoring abilities;
- individual support on request throughout the programme.

The initiative fundamentally shifted the responsibility and ownership of talent development and required a large number of partners of the firm to become skilled, competent and committed to develop talent, support transitions, deal with challenges and encourage individual progression in remarkable new ways.

Case study 3 – Talent integration issues involved in partner/team moves and mergers

The increased partner/team mobility as well as the market consolidation through a number of mergers in some jurisdictions have generated a new type of talent issue: the challenge to integrate talent and provide partners with the environment and the ability to quickly build/rebuild their book of business by using the firm's internal and external resources and network of relationships in a new environment.

The high level of failures in lateral hiring over the years (figures show an average of only a 50% chance of success) demonstrate the complexities of both client portability and organisational maturity and agility to make room to successfully onboard new talent. In mergers, the similar high levels of failure are down to the people and cultural aspects which are the most complex to understand and address when two or more entities need to become one.

Our recent experience in assisting a US firm expanding in one European country consisted of the following initial steps:

- carrying out a strategic review of two local offices in order to establish which of the merger route or lateral hiring of teams route was the most appropriate way to successfully grow the firm in that country;
- carrying out structured interviews of the leadership and partners to identify the individual and collective aspirations and ambitions for the firm;
- assessing the culture and governance of the firm and the potential impact of the growth plans;
- establishing the strategic priorities for the firm and drafting a clear value proposition capable of attracting the best partners/teams or target firms;
- planning the integration objectives and processes to align personal, professional, practice and clients' actions and priorities with a focus on and following progress in the integration phase.

For clarity purposes, the above process has been much simplified. It is intended to show that when the above steps are methodically followed and the 'people and culture' aspects carefully analysed and planned, the chances of any new partner or team joining the firm or merger integration process succeeding become much higher.

Collaboration among partners: increasing the odds of productive lateral hiring

Heidi K Gardner
Harvard Law School

1. Introduction

One of the biggest challenges in today's law firms is recruiting laterals into the firm – and then finding ways to integrate them, retain them, and help make them sustainably productive.[1] Even in historically stable legal jurisdictions, the talent market is heating up and lateral hiring is intensifying. Many of today's law firm leaders agree that the war for talent is at least as brutal as the battle for clients. In this chapter, I draw on years of empirical and qualitative research to show how cross-practice collaboration is one of the essential elements for increasing the odds that a lateral hire will be successful and productive in their new firm.

How, exactly, does collaboration help? Collaborating brings lateral hires up to speed with firm practices, allows them to get to know their colleagues' areas of expertise (and vice versa), and, most important, builds trust between lateral hires, their colleagues, and new clients. The trick, of course, is making sure that your firm is set up to foster this kind of lateral–incumbent collaboration. Supported by my extensive empirical research at Harvard University, this chapter will outline how firms can foster collaboration between newly hired and existing partners by using specific systems in the pre-hire, recruiting and onboarding phases. Doing so will increase their chances of making their lateral hiring more successful.

2. The need for a fix

Let us begin with some sobering facts: in the legal sector, the chance of a laterally hired partner staying more than three years is generally no better than a coin toss.[2] One study of leading law firms in London yielded some truly abysmal statistics: fully 20% of lateral hires were no longer with their firms one year after joining, and an estimated 50% had left within five years. The reported average cost of each of these failed hires was something north of £100,000, but most experts in the field suggest that the actual cost of those failed hires – consider, for example, the opportunity costs of partners' time spent interviewing and onboarding them – was closer to double that figure.[3]

For more than a decade, I've been studying issues related to leadership, teamwork

1 'Laterals' can include anyone who has some successful experience in the workplace – in other words, anyone who is not fresh out of school – but I tend to use the word to describe relatively senior people.
2 Press, A, "Special Report: Big Law's Reality Check", *The American Lawyer*, November 2014.
3 "Lateral Damage: Failed Hires Cost London Dear", *The Lawyer*, February 2012.

and talent development in professional service firms. First, while on the faculty at Harvard Business School and now at Harvard Law School, I've amassed a database comprising millions of data records across multiple law firms, including a decade's worth of their time-sheet, personnel and financial records. Statistical analyses reveal patterns in the data that can be difficult for the human mind to detect. Together with my research team, we marry these quantitative findings with insights from hundreds of in-depth interviews with lawyers, law firm leaders and clients as well as thousands of research surveys.

We can now demonstrate empirically that collaboration is essential to ensuring that lateral hires can become successful and productive, post-move. And collaboration has to happen quickly. According to the data I've analysed, if laterally hired partners are to be successful at their new firm, they have to be sufficiently integrated with incumbent partners and clients within the first 18 months, if not sooner. Specifically, two things need to happen in that short time: laterals need to have had the opportunity to work on at least a couple of the firm's incumbent clients (on pitches, if not actual projects), and they need to get at least a couple of long-term partners to help on client work they generate (either clients they have imported or brand new ones). If either is missing, they are at a higher risk of leaving; if neither happens, they are very likely to leave the firm by their three-year anniversary, as illustrated in Figure 1.

Figure 1: Collateral and lateral hires: two paths

Illustration of empirical research findings based on four domestic and international law firms

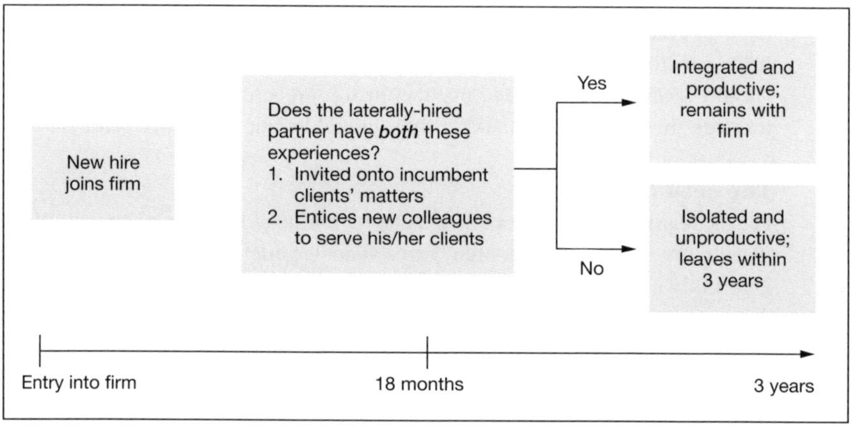

And note that our analyses are what researchers call a 'conservative test': we only report the findings that are statistically significant across multiple firms. Partners in two firms outside my dataset – one law and one accounting firm – have told me that analyses of their own firms' data reveals that the critical window for achieving collaboration is as short as six months after a laterally hired partner joins their firm! Clearly, firms need a well-designed plan, flawless execution and clear accountability processes if they expect to help laterals achieve two-way collaboration in such a short time after entering a new firm.

3. Origins of the war for talent

Why are laterals such a key focus today? Talented problem-solvers with specialised legal expertise are essential for helping the most attractive clients solve their most compelling legal problems. In many such cases, those problems cannot be addressed by a single legal specialist, no matter how talented he or she may be. In fact, many cannot even be addressed by a single practice within the firm. Multiple bases of expertise may have to be called upon – in many cases, from more than one firm.

BP, for example, had to call in legions of lawyers from several firms for the litigation and mitigation that followed the disastrous oil spill of 2010, when the Deepwater Horizon oil rig exploded and sank in the Gulf of Mexico. Within two years, BP's legal fees alone had exceeded $1.73 billion.[4] A tour of the website of Kirkland & Ellis LLP – the Chicago-based firm that leads the BP defence team – hints at the complexity of that assignment, including (to cite just one chapter in a much larger story) the sale of major assets in Texas to help pay for the settlement of claims. According to a press release, that sale alone required the participation of three practices within the firm: antitrust and competition, corporate and energy.[5]

Client demand for solutions that are both deep and broadbased leads to some predictable distortions in the labour market, as multiple firms try to build up whichever practice group is most in demand at the moment. Take cyber security. Across most economic sectors, clients are deeply troubled by either the threat – or the actual experience – of having their data and systems compromised. This issue reaches all the way up to the board level, and experts who can credibly advise on these risks open the doors to client c-suites and boardrooms. The predictable result: every law firm playing in this particular game wants to have the best cyber security experts in their stable, rather than someone else's.

So today's law firms are increasingly engaged in a war for talent – a war that is being fought on a number of fronts. In many places, increased partner mobility has fostered the emergence of a free-agent mentality. Encouraged by growing legions of headhunters, experienced legal talents today have a keen sense of their value in the marketplace, and face far fewer cultural taboos about jumping ship for a more lucrative offer. In some of the hottest markets, it is not unusual for professionals with an in-demand specialty to receive three or more calls every week from recruiters or competitors.

Layered on top of this is the breakdown of the former gentlemen's agreements that divided up the legal landscape into what might be called 'spheres of influence'. In the legal field – as well as in many other professional fields, including accounting, engineering and consulting – the entrance of international firms into previously domestic markets has fuelled competition for top-end partners. For example, when

---

4 See "The Case of the Century", in the 24 February 2012 issue of the *Financial Times*, online at www.ft.com/cms/s/2/8bf50a04-5dc1-11e1-869d-00144feabdc0.html.

5 See, for example, "Kirkland, V&E help BP unload assets to Marathon", online at www.kirkland.com/sitecontent.cfm?contentID=230&itemId=10458. The partner firm in this and other BP-related transactions was Vinson & Elkins, which called upon its M&A, real estate, and environmental practices.

US firms began their push into London, stories abounded of City lawyers doubling or even tripling their income by joining the first wave of partners to sign up with those newcomer firms.

This trend is also visible in formerly stable localised markets like Phoenix, Bogota, Munich and scores of other cities around the world. For example: The arrival of firms like Greenberg Traurig and Mayer Brown in Mexico and Garrigues in Colombia caused some local senior associates to be offered two to three times their then-current salary (as well as additional perks like preferred parking, flexitime and increased vacation days). Reportedly, many professionals who jumped ship did not even try to negotiate a better deal with their then-current firm; they simply announced that they were leaving. Not surprisingly, this caused significant initial salary inflation in these two markets, and forced local firms not only to embrace more sophisticated and institutionalised talent processes, but also better articulate the general value proposition of working at a local firm. It may not be enough: most firms in these jurisdictions feel that there is a 'new normal' when it comes to salaries and that more poaching will continue. Indeed, many authorities on the issue predict that full-scale lift-outs of firms' entire practice groups are the likely next phase.

4. A case in point

Some top-tier firms think that, in the intensifying war for talent, they are predestined to win. Lesser firms may have to scramble and scrap – their reasoning goes – but we can rely on the power of our marquee name to help us fight off poachers and keep our franchise intact.

As it turns out, though, this is not necessarily true. The high-end US legal community was stunned when, in early April 2016, Scott Barshay, the legendary M&A practice co-leader at the super-elite Wall Street law firm of Cravath, Swaine & Moore, abandoned his firm for a rival.[6] Barshay had just wrapped up an amazing year at Cravath, serving as lead adviser on $292 billion in M&A transactions, which amounted to about a third of the firm's total activity in that area.

Admittedly, the firm he moved to – Paul, Weiss, Rifkind, Wharton & Garrison – was also a premier firm – just not quite so much as Cravath. In the first quarter of 2016, Paul, Weiss ranked first in both global and US private equity buyouts and exits by deal value. In the previous two years, the firm had advised on more than 65 deals valued in the billion-dollar-and-up range.[7] Nevertheless, in 2015 the firm's M&A rankings were a mere number 20, in contrast to Cravath, which ranked second. Industry observers suggested that, all in all, Barshay was the most significant defection from Cravath since the late 1990s.[8]

---

6 The story is online at www.americanlawyer.com/id=1202753959278/Top-Cravath-Deal-Lawyer-Scott-Barshay-Jumps-to-Paul-Weiss?slreturn=20160318100839.

7 See a related press release on the Paul, Weiss website at https://www.paulweiss.com/practices/transactional/private-equity-transactions/awards-and-rankings/paul,-weiss-ranked-1-in-private-equity-by-mergermarket.aspx?id=21707. The 65 deals reference comes from another press release at https://www.paulweiss.com/practices/transactional/corporate/publications/scott-barshay-joins-paul,-weiss-as-global-head-of-ma.aspx?id=21671.

8 Cravath has certainly lost senior partners in recent years, but mostly to career changes, rather than flat-out defections. See, for example, http://abovethelaw.com/2016/04/a-deeper-dive-into-scott-barshays-move-from-cravath-to-paul-weiss/.

On the face of it, the parting was amicable. In a written statement, Barshay lauded the co-heads of the Cravath M&A department that he was leaving behind. "While I've very much enjoyed practicing law at Cravath," Barshay elaborated, "Paul, Weiss's wide range of highest quality practices and extraordinary lawyers will be invaluable in serving the needs of our clients."[9] But he also hinted at what was missing at Cravath: a full suite of practice groups. No doubt compensation and other issues were part of Barshay's calculations as he considered making his momentous move.[10] But for the purposes of this chapter, we will put the spotlight in the same place that Barshay did in his statement. Most of Cravath's 470-plus lawyers are focused exclusively on high-end M&A activity and related litigation. In contrast, Paul, Weiss has a very different profile, with 1,000-plus lawyers working in a wide variety of practices.

In other words, Barshay was moving toward cross-practice collaboration.

5. The risks of lateral hiring

As Barshay's case illustrates, laterals are hot – and for good reason. By 'acquiring' Barshay, his new firm brought in a star who had built his own M&A practice that was as big as their entire firm's existing M&A operation. Their ambition seemed to be to double their M&A business by hiring a sole individual.

Will that big gamble pay off? The jury in that case will remain out for the foreseeable future, but statistics suggest that – in lateral moves like Barshay's – success is far from guaranteed.[11] The problem is that, in and of itself, the strategy of accumulating stars and hoping for the best simply does not work very well. In fact, after spending vast sums to build and buy stables of thoroughbreds and extend their geographic reach and practice breadth, today's premiere law firms have reached a sobering conclusion: all that talent cannot be harnessed for competitive advantage or profit enhancement unless they find a way to get partners to collaborate. To maximise the worth of those expensive individuals, firms must integrate their partners' diverse and distributed knowledge in a way that clients value. But research in the legal sector and elsewhere shows that knowledge-based firms are generally quite poor at integrating laterals in a way that makes them more productive.

For example, the Wharton School's Matthew Bidwell – in a study of lateral hiring aptly named 'Paying More to Get Less' – looked at six years of personnel data from the US investment banking branch of a financial services corporation. He found that, despite external hires generally having more education and experience than internal hires, external hires performed significantly worse for the first two years of their employment than workers who were promoted to the same job from within the organisation. Furthermore, he discovered that lateral hires were far more likely than internal workers to leave their job – either because they quit, or because they were

9 See www.americanlawyer.com/id=1202753959278/Top-Cravath-Deal-Lawyer-Scott-Barshay-Jumps-to-Paul-Weiss.

10 It is worth noting in this context that Cravath has a pure 'lockstep' compensation model, whereas Paul, Weiss's modified lockstep plan allows major rainmakers to make substantially more money. See www.americanlawyer.com/id=1202753959278/Top-Cravath-Deal-Lawyer-Scott-Barshay-Jumps-to-Paul-Weiss.

11 Notably, Barshay took nobody from Cravath with him to Paul, Weiss.

fired. Despite all these shortcomings, Bidwell concluded, external hires cost the firm 18% more money in salaries than did their internally promoted colleagues.[12]

Most firms recognise that it takes several years to bring an experienced hire up to speed – even to reach the level of performance they displayed in their old firm, let alone to become even more productive. Compelling data demonstrates that professionals who switch firms are likely to fall off quite significantly, in terms of performance, and that it takes them between three and five years to climb back to their former level of productivity.[13] In reality, as mentioned above, most laterally hired lawyers who are struggling to become productive in their new firm simply do not stick around for so many years.

In addition, lateral hiring may cause tremendous upheavals in the compensation system, given that firms generally need to pay much more for an individual brought in from the outside in order to compensate them for the risk of changing firms. In US law firms, for example, the pressures associated with lateral hiring can lead to enormous disparities in compensation between partners within the same firm. Although the median spread between the highest- and lowest-paid partners inside a US firm is 10 to 1 (already quite a gap), that ratio swelled as high as a staggering 23 to 1 in one firm where lateral hiring was rampant.

Finally, the biggest risk might be the dilution – or worse – of a firm's culture. Sometimes the addition of employees with different perspectives can be hugely beneficial for firms, opening up new ways of thinking, which in turn open up new opportunities.[14] But unless you are deliberately seeking and hiring candidates with a specific, diverse set of characteristics, you are leaving the evolution of your culture to chance by hiring people who come from firms with cultures radically different from your own.

6. Critical action steps for improving lateral hiring

So that is a formidable list of risks. Reflecting that sobering field of obstacles, some industry leaders, such as the law firm of Wachtell, Lipton, Rosen & Katz, have effectively prohibited lateral hiring in an effort to husband their resources and preserve their unique culture. Even that venerable firm, though, has made a few notable exceptions – for example, when it hired 90-year old Robert Morgenthau, whom the New York Times described as "a legendary former prosecutor with a Rolodex as extensive as the Dead Sea Scrolls".[15] So even the wary firm can embrace a lateral, in the right circumstances.

Assuming that your firm concludes that the potential upsides to hiring laterals outweigh the downsides, there are a number of steps you can take to better your odds with laterals. They fall into three phases that correspond to the pre-hire, recruiting and onboarding stages: an analytics-driven business plan; a structured assessment of

---

12 Bidwell, M, "Paying More to Get Less: The Effects of External Hiring versus Internal Mobility", *Administrative Science Quarterly*. September 2011 vol 56 no 3 369–407.

13 Groysberg, B, *Chasing Stars: The Myth of Talent and the Portability of Performance* (Princeton University Press, 2012).

14 When the US Army opened up its front lines to female soldiers in Afghanistan – even in limited ways – it suddenly acquired the ability to interact with the 'other half' of the local population.

15 John Eligon, "3 Weeks into Retirement, Morgenthau Takes a Law Job", *New York Times*, 21 January 2010.

a candidate's collaborative capabilities; and post-hire mentoring and accountability processes, as illustrated in Figure 2. Let us consider each in turn.

Figure 2: Critical steps for integrating lateral hires: 3-stage process for hiring success

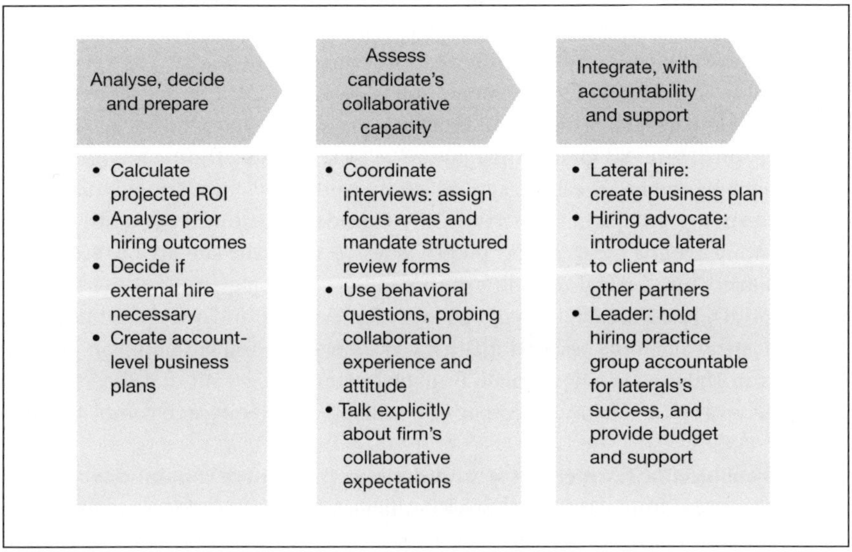

6.1 Analytics-driven business plan

First things first: You need a robust, data-based analysis that forms the business case for each lateral hire. Many firms kid themselves that they already have such a system in place, but most of the plans I have reviewed are more about arguments than analyses – which is not surprising, given that they were written by lawyers who had had neither been supplied with data nor trained to perform quantitative analysis. Instead, engage your financial and business development experts to collect and dissect both internal and market data to calculate anticipated returns on investment (ROI) for each proposed candidate. More specifically, analysts should work with partners in both the proposing practice group and adjacent ones to understand a range of realistic scenarios, and then calculate how sensitive the initial, projected ROI is to these differing assumptions.

Whether to hire and how many to hire should be based not only on these financial models, but also on strategic factors, such as expanding business opportunities, new offices in specific geographic markets, partner turnover, and newly developed (or growing) practice or sector-focused groups. For each of these factors, you need to analyse current capacity and utilisation to reveal whether the emerging market needs can be covered by an internal, existing resource. Set the bar high to convince yourself that a lateral is the only option.

Also scrutinise the organisation's readiness to absorb a new partner. Is the practice group appropriately leveraged? If you hire a lateral partner, will she have adequate associate support for her business? Has that office or practice just hired a cohort of other laterals that are taking up all the onboarding attention and energy? Your ability to answer these questions ties directly to your ability to help a newly hired partner succeed.

I also encourage firms to 'run the numbers' in another way: Which practice groups or even individual partners have successfully built a team through lateral hiring? Gather and review your lateral hiring data from the last five years or so, with a specific focus on: who pushed for or sponsored the request; and how well each of those laterals fared, once hired. You may well find a strong correlation between certain partners' or practices' attempts and success rates, in which case you should reward them by giving their future requests greater legitimacy. In contrast, your analysis might reveal pockets of 'churn and burn', that strongly suggest that the offending groups fail to strategically consider their hiring requests, use the wrong hiring criteria, or lack the proper ways to integrate laterals once they arrive – a subject that we will return to shortly.

If you do decide – based on convincing evidence and a sound strategic plan – that a lateral hire is the best option, then you should require a business plan to that end. The plan should include specific client objectives, along with a named individual who accepts accountability, with specific deadlines for initiating and completing the actions.

6.2 Structured assessment of a candidate's collaborative capabilities

Some law firms already have well-established processes for assessing a candidate's merits – especially their technical, legal capabilities and often their reputation with clients. If those processes are actually getting the results you want, then do not short-circuit the procedures that have proven themselves over time at your firm. Use them – but also consider augmenting them with additional techniques that can help you collect evidence about a candidate's suitability to become the kind of partner who can truly leverage your firm's full set of expertise in order to solve clients' most complex, high-value problems. In other words, you must assess a candidate's collaborative capacity.

One important, basic technique is to use multiple interviews in order to mitigate the risk of bias from a single opinion. Some firms put interviewees through dozens of interviews with staff members and partners, in multiple geographies and offices.

Merely setting up multiple, unstructured interviews is basically a waste of time, however, because they may or may not unearth critical issues; partners outside the candidate's area of expertise will only walk away with vague impressions of cultural 'fit'. Instead, to make the use of multiple interviews productive requires significant coordination within the firm, both before interviews – in order to figure out which situations and competencies each interviewer will focus on – and afterward, to cover gaps and probe possible weaknesses. For example, in one consulting firm that I have worked with, as interviewers meet with a particular candidate, they feed back their points of view and make suggestions about issues that can be probed in subsequent interviews. Eventually these interview notes should be mined to reveal competency gaps where the successful candidate needs to improve, setting the stage for a plan of integration and training for the prospective employee.

In the interview process itself, the current best practice is to use behavioural questions, rather than hypothetical ones. Candidates should be asked to describe particular situations they have faced, how they handled them, their personal emotional response, and what they learned from the experience. For example: "Can you provide me with an example of when you made a bad decision?" Follow-on questions might include, "How did you feel? Did you take steps to rectify it? Did you take the hit or try to minimise the fallout?" Interviewers keep digging based upon how the candidate responds to each question.

The objective is to break the candidate out of predictable and standard responses, thereby enabling the interviewer to gain more insight into candidates' problem-solving approaches and emotional intelligence – skills that are essential for the kind of client service that involves unearthing complex problems and forming teams to tackle them. The theory is that the best predictor of future behaviour is past behaviour, in similar circumstances that were either recent or reflected long-standing behaviour patterns. Interviewers need to unearth the evidence before they can evaluate it.

Obviously, this kind of interviewing is new for most lawyers. It requires training and practice, which many partners will resist. But consider this: many of the same probing, listening, analysing and empathy skills that are essential for interviewing are the same ones that skilled lawyers use with clients to uncover and understand complex business issues. So the partners who become excellent spotters of collaborative candidates are the ones who are better equipped to discover client opportunities where those candidates' expertise could be useful.

How can you directly assess a candidate's actual collaborative capabilities themselves? My advice is to get the issue on the table well in advance of the interview. If you are using a search firm, make sure they are extremely well briefed on your demands for collaboration, and are prepared to pre-screen candidates for this quality. Candidates should know that they will be closely questioned about their teamwork experiences, both as leaders and followers, and that they should not bother to apply unless they have a strong track record with demonstrable outcomes. Anyone who is weeded out by these kinds of statements is well weeded out.

Once the candidate is in the chair, first use the kinds of behavioural questions described above to explore their past experiences with collaboration. Table 1, below, lists additional key competencies associated with strong collaborators, with sample prompts that the interviewer can use to probe. Next, tackle collaboration head-on with the candidate. Describe the firm's expectations for collaboration, with as many specific, successful examples as possible. Be clear about how collaboration will be measured and rewarded, both financially and otherwise. Candidates need to know how much the firm cares about origination versus execution, and exactly how those activities are tracked. Explain the extent to which the firm values and rewards non-billable activities like mentoring, marketing activities, firm management, recruiting, *pro bono* work, and so on. Again, clarity helps to weed out non-collaborative candidates through self-selection. This is a very efficient way to weed.

Table 1: Key collaborative competencies to test with candidates

Key collaborative competencies	Sample interview prompts to elicit example
• Adaptability • Conflict management • Initiative and follow-through • Integrity • Learning motivation/curiosity • Listening and probing • Networking • Perseverance • Persuasiveness (leading without authority) • Political sensitivity	• Tell me about a situation when you teamed up with colleagues to solve a really tough client problem. – Follow-on: How did you find the right expert? How did you know they were capable? How did you convince them to join the effort? What role did you play after the team was formed? • Describe a time when you needed a colleague's input on client work, but that person did not respond to requests. What did you do? • Give me an example of a time when you uncovered an opportunity to serve a client with a multi-practice team. What ultimately happened?

Remember, the goal is to find candidates who are able not only to produce revenue, but can do so by drawing on others' capabilities and contributing their own expertise whenever possible. To put a finer point on it: if you want your partners to collaborate, you cannot hire jerks; you have to hire people who work well with other people.

6.3 Post-hire mentoring and accountability

Most firms already have a nominal 'buddy system' for incoming hires, but far too few of those programmes actually work. To create the highest chances of a lateral hire being successfully integrated, you need to take some specific steps to ensure that mentoring happens (in multiple directions, as we discuss below), and that all parties are held accountable for delivering post-hire collaboration within the first 12 months:

- Work with laterals immediately upon their entry to the firm to develop a strategic client service plan, which identifies specific opportunities for them to involve incumbent partners. Leaders should facilitate those introductions, and make it clear to incumbents that they are expected to participate. Incumbents may be inclined to distrust the newcomer ("she came in here with that other firm's clients; I'll be damned if I'm going to share my clients with her"). That resistance has to be rooted out and worn down.
- Assign a peer mentor for the new hire who will help her learn the cultural norms – the kinds of issues that HR staff will not be able to acquaint them with, such as people who serve as 'honest brokers' in the firm to help connect partners for client or other work. Ideally, this mentor will be someone the

new hire met and connected with during the recruiting process so that they have already established a level of interpersonal trust.

- Gain commitment from a few specific people in the hiring group (practice, office, or ideally, both) who are responsible for introducing the newcomer to several pre-determined accounts or other kinds of strategic contacts, as outlined in the pre-hire business plan. And you should require them to report on progress – to you, or at least their practice leader (whose feet you then hold to the fire), not to a functionary in HR. Again, the key here is specificity and accountability, rather than a vague hope that partners will do the right thing in the midst of all their other pressing concerns.
- Use competency grids to assess the collaborative and mentoring abilities of both the newly hired partner and those in the surrounding practice. (If you do not have these tools, your professional development staff needs to source or create them.) Anyone scoring less than 'very strong' on these assessments needs support because their deficiencies may likely prevent them from properly integrating.
- Provide a budget for laterals to visit colleagues (even for exploratory conversations) and set the expectation that they will use the full budget (appropriately) within the first six to eight months. You should not wait until the end of the period to follow up. Expect laterals to report back to you with opportunities they have uncovered, and when, how and with whom they are taking action.
- Hold formal internal road shows for laterals to present their client work to offices, practice groups, and sectors. Make sure the leader of that group has spoken with the lateral ahead of time, so that he or she can: suggest specific people or account opportunities that the lateral can reference during their presentation; and ensure that the highest potential collaborators attend the road show.
- Make it clear to hiring groups that their ability to hire future laterals will depend on how successfully they integrate each newcomer. You might not be able to see immediate financial results, but you should be able to track activity: how many partners have used the newcomer's expertise to develop joint pitches, to create new IP such as white papers or conference presentations, or to visit clients? When partners do create these opportunities, be sure to celebrate them across the firm. Recognition for good behaviour not only encourages more partners to engage in it, but also helps spread the newcomer's reputation as a collaborative, value-adding asset within the firm.

At the end of this rather long list, it is probably worth putting in a plug for good citizenship within your firm. Good citizens in the senior ranks of your firm typically believe that 'what goes around comes around'.[16] In other words, they are willing to

16 Research supports the idea that 'givers' are often more successful than more self-centred individuals who operate on a strictly *quid-pro-quo* basis. See Grant, A. *Give and Take: Why Helping Others Drives Our Success*, Penguin Books.

contribute – their time, contacts, and knowledge – generously, without calculating direct returns. They act in the belief that building up their colleagues' capabilities is the right thing to do and trust that they may ultimately benefit from this in an indirect way. They do not keep score or mentally track reciprocity.

In this ideal state, lawyers who feel that they can contribute to a newly hired lateral's progress in a certain context naturally reach out to that person, without necessarily expecting that it will promote their own career or advancement. Professionals in that type of culture know that, by involving colleagues from other departments/offices in a client's matter or providing guidance to a colleague, it will ultimately best serve their clients' or their firm's interests, without calculating whether it will benefit their own interests or career.

All of the techniques cited above for setting the stage for post-hire collaboration have to do, at their heart, with culture. There is really no other way to sum it up: A commitment to collaboration is a commitment to a collaborative culture. As you venture into this new, complicated, and rewarding realm, watch for signs of cultural chafing, and fix what needs to be fixed.[17]

7. Conclusion

The focus of this chapter has been on collaboration as a means of bolstering the success of lateral hires. But it is worth noting that collaboration is crucial across your firm more broadly.

Collaboration between partners in law firms is essential for developing and maintaining competitive advantage. As clients' problems become increasingly complex, firms have been responding by creating more narrow practice areas and encouraging their partners to specialise. As a result, professionals' expertise is now dispersed across different practice groups and offices.

But think back to the environmental disaster faced by BP, cited earlier in this chapter. The only way that a law firm could address the legal issues swirling around the Gulf Horizon oil spill was to get its experts to integrate their highly specialised knowledge into a joint solution that would be superior to any single contributor's potential.

At risk of stating the obvious, superior solutions pay off. While financial costs and benefits have not been the focus of this chapter, our research over the last decade clearly shows that when professionals do successfully collaborate, their clients are stickier and more profitable.[18] The more practices that are involved in serving a client, the greater the annual average revenue the client generates. Clients might view any given lawyer as fairly fungible, but they find it difficult to find substitutes for entire cross-practice teams.

Further, cross-specialty work is likely to be less subject to price-based market

---

17 Note that culture is typically the outcome or by-product of many of the formal systems and structures in a firm, and strongly related to the type of people employed. See Jay W Lorsch and Emily McTague, "Culture is not the Culprit", *Harvard Business Review*, April 2016.

18 Gardner, H K *Smart Collaboration: How Professionals and Their Firms Succeed by Breaking Down Silos* (forthcoming, 2016), Harvard Business Review Press, Boston. Gardner, H K "When Senior Managers Won't Collaborate: Lessons from Professional Service Firms", *Harvard Business Review*, March 2015.

competition. Whereas clients view single-specialty legal expertise as a commodity that can be bid out and sourced based on price, they know that cross-specialty work is more sophisticated and harder to accomplish effectively. They are willing to pay for it. As the CFO of a major multinational told me, "Margins rise with complexity."

And it is collaboration, by and large, that enables you to embrace and overcome complexity, on behalf of your client.

The word 'culture' is badly overused today, but it speaks to a central issue in this chapter. Any lawyer who walks into a new law firm quickly perceives the level of formality, support or competition that exists between people in that environment. It is an instinctive sense that we develop through experience, because we have to adapt to a particular culture in order to be able to work within it.

Our research shows that it is culture that enables, encourages, or prevents mentoring and collaboration more than processes; processes only support culture when they are aligned to that particular culture.

"Within a few days of having integrated my new firm," recalls a senior associate at one firm, "I knew that the types of professional relationships in that firm didn't foster the support and collegiality that their values proclaimed to. It was obvious that I would have to walk my way through that environment and create my own circle of support and guidance in order to develop well."

In today's competitive marketplace, your firm's ability to attract, integrate and ultimately retain lateral hires is a critical competence. Done right, it allows you to boost collaboration across your firm. Of course, 'right' requires strong leadership, sustained efforts, and strong commitment from your partners at all levels to collaborate with the newcomers.

Increasingly, the alternative to collaboration is pretty dire. Conversely, the money and energy your firm puts into fostering high-level collaboration – including the recruitment and retention of key laterals – will almost certainly pay you back many times over.

The new employer proposition: getting the balance right between the firm's strategy and the expectations of its workforce

Jean-Baptiste Lebelle
Allen & Overy, Paris

1. Introduction

1.1 Loyalty to the workplace: an old-fashioned notion?

Today, if you ask partners, they seem to be convinced that organisational loyalty is a key factor in the success of their team. But in the meantime, they also think that this loyalty is an old-fashioned concept akin to the obligation of a vassal to his 'liege lord' under the feudal system ... and that they will not be able to find the same level of loyalty that existed in their perception of a golden age.

It is true that implied moral lifetime contracts expired a long time ago. The days of spending a career with one firm, becoming a partner and retiring by the age of 55 with a gold watch and a generous pension are long gone. Lawyers now focus on their career rather than loyalty to their employers. In a world full of opportunities no one could object to such behaviour, and building a career is a respectable goal especially in entrepreneurial professions such as lawyers. But does this mean that looking for employee loyalty is futile? Are all associates largely disillusioned with the very idea of loyalty to their firms? I don't think so ...

Years ago, I used to work as a headhunter for major law firms in the Paris market. In order to find potential candidates for my clients, I had many discussions with the most talented young lawyers, especially around their expectations of getting a new position in a well-established law firm. I noticed that loyalty was very important for some of these people. Of course, the career outlook was no longer the same with many new opportunities arising from the growing presence of international law firms in Paris, but some of the potential candidates that I was trying to recruit remained very loyal to their firm. Over time, I was able to classify law firms: there were those where people were always eager to discuss new opportunities and others where people always said that they were fine, thank you very much.

What made this difference? Of course relationships within the team and moreover the relationship between the associate and their partner are crucial. But if some law firms are better than others, there is also a more global explanation that lies in the specificities of particular firms which operate to build more loyalty.

Partner behaviour is influenced by the general culture and values of the firm. Some of these environments are more suitable for developing bonds of loyalty between employers and employees. The best kind of loyalty is when both parties benefit. So, in that kind of law firm, there is an understanding between the associate and his manager; perhaps not a formalised agreement, but one which is always clear and honest. How can we define, build and make this promise real? This chapter seeks to answer that question.

To be perfectly clear, loyalty is not blind faith to the employer. Loyalty means that the relationship between the employee and the firm is based on a clear level of expectation and an understanding that open and honest discussion on that premise is possible. Leavers can still be very loyal to their firm and continue to work as a client or play an ambassadorial role in the labour market. Leavers should not be treated as somehow disloyal. And some of the senior employees within a firm may be very disloyal to their employers in their day-to-day behaviour. So it is important to understand that people should not simplistically be regarded as just either inside or outside the firm.

2. The employer value proposition

For many lawyers, the term 'employer value proposition' (EVP) may not sound familiar, but, as we have seen, the desire to create a solid deal between the firm and its people is nothing new. In many firms, there is not necessarily an EVP as a formal policy, but it can be found in employer brand propositions or other in-house project names.

The EVP could be defined as the 'people deal' or the 'employment deal', a clear promise to help employees meet their needs in exchange for their daily efforts to help the firm to succeed. Basically, it is the reason why an employee is willing to continue to work for the same firm despite other market opportunities, and why the overall work experience seems superior to that at other firms. This 'people deal' characterises a firm in its market and differentiates it from its competition (this is a difficult but fundamental element). It is the foundation of an organisation's reputation as a place to work. More than ever, with the development of social networks, reputation is difficult to handle without an honest approach and EVP has an important role to play.

The term EVP refers to the marketing notion of unique value proposition (UVP). Therefore, marketing tools and techniques are used in order to build an EVP. UVP and EVP are two sides of the same coin: one is designed for clients, the other for the workforce. These two value propositions should be coherent, appealing and reflect reality.

This unique set of offerings, associations and values should positively influence target candidates and employees in order to increase people engagement, attract and retain top talent, and ultimately improve financial performance. A clear employer proposition should be able to define the loyalty that will benefit both parties.

We can classify EVP into five categories:

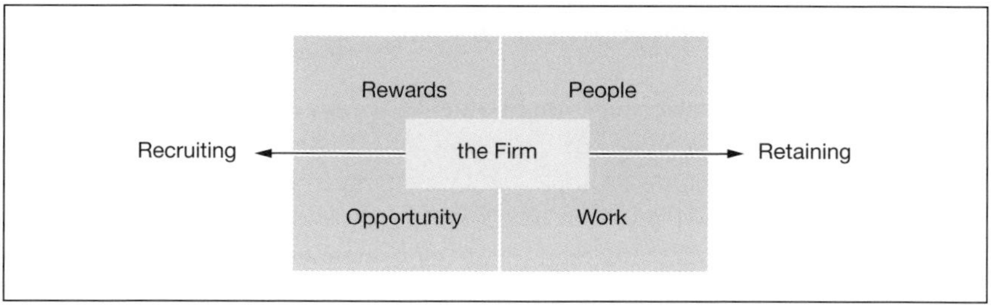

An EVP should be tailored on the basis of all these categories to meet the value expectations of the targeted talented people.

2.1 EVP and the legal services sector?

EVP should be important to the legal services sector because of the particular features of the sector. Law firms are characterised by a very fast-track career and recruitment of highly qualified and talented people. For a structured career path that almost guarantees a solid lifetime income, the law is right up there with accounting and consultancy. But there is a downside to this: the 'up-or-out' model is also inherent in the sector, even if it is not always openly acknowledged.

These characteristics, which can also be found in a consultancy firm, contribute to a high attrition rate among associates. It is very important to take care of future leavers who represent the overwhelming majority of the workforce. In a major law firm, given the pyramid structure and the up-or-out model, more than 90% of the workforce have a future outside the firm. Different studies and data (eg, Above the Law, NavForward promotion statistics) point out the correlation between prestige (and the profits per partner focus) and partnership promotion rate, but overall associates in the top major law firms tend to have something between a 1 and 16% chance to make partner according to the 2015 NavForward survey. The rest will never attain partnership status. This huge majority could become clients or business providers and thus play an important role in building a strong reputation in the legal working market. Some firms, following the McKinsey model, have successfully managed to turn their loyal alumni base into a loyal client base.

EVP is clearly a useful tool in this regard and may communicate to potential candidates the benefits of joining a firm where ultimately it is incredibly difficult to become a partner.

Secondly, with the development of real human resources teams in major law firms, it is normal that firms in the legal services sector consider EVP to be part of their people strategy. It is about time that law firms used advanced HR tools such as the EVP that have been successful in other sectors. Some law firms are more advanced in that transition and are able to work with an HR professional as a real business partner and not merely as administrative support staff. This evolution is also inherent to the growth and the sector concentration of the legal profession.

2.2 Observations on the legal business sector

(a) *Legal service providers operate in a fiercely competitive world*

The legal business sector has undergone an extraordinary evolution over the last 30 or 40 years to become a complex and very competitive market. All jurisdictions have seen the increased presence of US and English law firms. These two models are spreading all around the world and the competition to get a piece of the cake is fierce. The success of these law firms revolves, of course, around their very specific model; but the battle for talent is also an important element. Top law firms are always looking to recruit the best legal talent on the market and furthermore they also absolutely need to retain their most valuable people. In the legal business sector, human resources constitute invaluable assets that should be preserved above (almost) all.

The number of headhunters and recruitment agencies in the legal services sector is a very good indicator of the battle for talent that law firms are facing. Maybe more than in any other sector, lawyers from top law firms are solicited by these entities almost every month and even at the very beginning of their career. Some headhunters are trying to play the part of career coach (just like a sports agent) for the most brilliant lawyers and promise to be very adept at identifying any opportunities that might lead to their desired goal. In some cases, these headhunters may be the only people that talk honestly about career opportunities and development with lawyers. If loyalty to such people is more important than to the firm where the lawyers work, that constitutes an important danger to retention. Changing from one firm to another can be very easy, especially when there are no distinctive features between law firms.

(b) *A solid reputation is no longer enough for recruiting and retaining top talent*

Law firms were also of the belief that their reputation and branding was enough for recruiting and retaining top talent. Making any other effort could be seen as a sign of weakness. Some of the well-established law firms will, inevitably, not see the need. They will think that what they are already doing is good enough for recruiting and retaining their talent. That kind of attitude is impossible to maintain in the context of an intensifying battle for talent. If you do not take it seriously then you will face many difficulties in the future. Once it was enough to use reputation among clients to communicate with candidates. Some firms use the same brochure for their clients and for their candidates. But now there is a need to adapt your reputation to a new kind of audience and to many different media.

When your prospective candidates are looking for an opportunity, they can use more resources than ever before to help them to decide whether your firm is the right fit. They can learn from your career website but they also usually do some research on the internet and can access information from many sources including employee reviews, social media and websites like 'glassdoor'.

(c) *Building a new employer proposition as a key factor of success*

One of the most powerful answers to recruiting and retention issues is to have a unique employer proposition. Some law firms, inspired by the most advanced professional services firms, have developed a clear employer offer and have successfully increased their attractiveness and retention rate.

McKinsey & Company has developed a concept to help companies remain competitive in the labour market. This concept is built around "Five Elements of a Successful Talent Formula". The second of these five elements is about EVP. For McKinsey, to "create a winning EVP that brings scarce talent through the doors, and keeps them there" is crucial. This is clearly a key factor for success given the present 'war of talents'. The benefits of having an EVP are now clearly established, especially for a professional services firm that is facing the same issues of recruiting and retaining key talent. Having an employer proposition that is consistent, unique, true and relevant to top talented lawyers, is clearly a competitive advantage. Developing and making the EVP come alive in day-to-day behaviour will increase the talent pool, motivation and engagement. In addition a well-thought-out and executed EVP allows firms to source more deeply within the labour market and increase access to passive candidates without having to work with expensive headhunters in an increasingly difficult talent market.

EVP will also help to prioritise your people agenda by focusing efforts and commitments on the most relevant actions.

(d) *The legal sector has been a late developer*

As we have seen in the introduction, if you consider the specifics of the legal services sector, it is obvious that there is an overwhelming need for a comprehensive HR strategy. In spite of this, for many years, lawyers thought that they were able to deal with HR strategy without the help of HR professionals. Fortunately, times have changed and major law firms have now hired top talent HR professionals in order to develop a better and coherent people strategy. But the sector has been slow compared to other professional services firms and the time has come to fill the gap to avoid being overtaken by competitors.

For example, the consulting sector is well advanced and some of its best companies have a very solid HR strategy, including an EVP. Global management consulting firms can be seen as very good examples, given that they operate in an environment that shares many cultural and economic similarities.

(e) *The emergence of a multigenerational workforce*

For many, many years, the EVP was not very formalised and it was often about making a lot of money, working hard and become a partner. That was the promise of the major law firms and it was well received by future lawyers.

But that model is no longer efficient. Furthermore, it contributes to a problem that affects most law firms today: poor diversity in the work environment. Although wider society has faced enormous transformation, law firms have tended to keep their models unchanged. It is strange to think that one of the top talent recruitment sectors has been very late in developing, when compared to other professional services companies.

The EVP of a firm must be different from the traditional offering, but the promise around money and partnership should not be forgotten. If the remuneration policy is not the only driver to take into account, it certainly remains an important part of the equation. To be frank, if you aspire to a career as a business lawyer, one of your motivations will definitely be the money that you will make. It is not that law firms are full of greedy professionals who are just thinking of how they can bill more from their clients, but money is still an important incentive. In all the surveys about criteria and motivation, salary is always one of the top three criteria in terms of importance, as well as contributing to low satisfaction rates when it falls below the market rate.

The money issue should not be absent from the EVP. Having a fair and transparent remuneration policy is an important part of the people deal and it certainly contributes (along with other elements of the EVP) to staff motivation and loyalty. Furthermore, the conditions for access to partnership have to share the same transparency requirements.

(f) Becoming partner is not the only form of success

Given that partnership is no longer the carrot it once was, and with the arrival of new generations into the legal services business, many things have changed significantly. Even if candidates who wish to make a career in major law firms are perfectly aware of the level of involvement that is necessary, they are also more eager to get the balance right between their professional goals and their private life.

A clear example is that (in the associate's mind) becoming a partner is no longer the only way to have a successful career in the legal business sector. People are aware that it is more difficult to access partnership in a law firm than it used to be. Nowadays, in the eyes of most associates, there is nothing wrong with giving up, quitting, going in-house, going to work in a 'boutique law firm', or doing something else entirely. Not becoming partner is no longer seen as a failure among associates. In fact there are some who believe that becoming partner will inevitably lead to disaster in their private life. For this new generation, an alternative career path has become a real possibility in some firms. But partners should understand that leavers are not 'traitors' or 'failures' and that joining a big law firm is also the promise of a springboard for launching a career.

(g) How the 'free-agent mentality' of lawyers could be fought by an EVP

The term 'free agent' was originally coined to describe the shift in major league baseball that allowed players to switch teams on their own. When you read about all the movement in the specialised press you could sometimes think that you are reading the sports section of a newspaper.

So, is the sector full of mercenaries ready to offer their skills to the firm offering the most money?

It is true that lawyers usually have a more developed sense of freedom and independence than other professions. However, although the free-agent mindset might be regarded as a positive (free agents deliver high-quality services and think like entrepreneurs – traits which constitute qualities in a lawyer), there is also the risk to the firm that it could harm client relationships.

How can such a free-agent mentality be avoided? By taking advantage of the EVP. The more you define a clear promise, the more loyalty you get. By engaging your top people and making them feel that they have a vital role in your firm's future, you can substantially reduce the chances that your rising stars will seek greener pastures. If you succeed in setting a deal where both parties are benefiting, then you can be much more confident in your ability to retain people with high potential.

(h) The employer proposition should be redefined

Millennials are demanding different things than previous generations of lawyers used to demand (see the chapter on "Leading millennials" in *Leadership for Lawyers* (Henrik Bresman, Heidi K Gardner and Samantha Sheehan)). Partners should understand that their mindset when they were young lawyers seeking opportunities was not the same as that of young lawyers today. Millennials do not expect a career for life and they want a clear understanding of what differentiates one firm from another.

Major studies regarding the millennial generation are helpful in understanding the mentality of the new generation of lawyers. But it is also important to keep in mind that this new generation of lawyers is not exactly the same as the employees described in other areas. Graduate lawyers joining a large law firm are usually perfectly aware of the global sector value proposition: a demanding work environment, involving travel and long working hours in return for a good salary, great experience, opportunity and professional development. So even if these new graduate lawyers share some values with the millennial generation described in many articles and studies, they also have a common approach with their colleagues from previous generations. The EVP of a law firm should be tailored to this very specific population.

However, the work–life balance issue is becoming increasingly important for legal services firms. This is not only because law firms have made (or must make) efforts on gender balance but because we know that it is more a generational issue than a female issue. Research shows that millennials have a different relationship with work. Although new joiners are focused and ambitious people like their predecessors, they are unwilling to put their private lives on hold for their career. It is futile to condemn such behaviour and try to recruit only the most dedicated lawyers. The only solution to the problem of how to attract, recruit and retain the brightest and best people to your firm is to understand their expectations and adapt your model to these changes.

The current trend to develop wellbeing programmes in law firms is part of the answer and is expected by the current generation. Furthermore, this is a win/win situation since people will be more dedicated and efficient if their work environment is designed to meet their needs.

3. Building a new employer proposition

3.1 How to build the new employer value proposition

If you take a look at the career pages and the recruitment brochures of the leading law firms, you will find a succession of almost identical statements, that are totally interchangeable and homogenous. Even the images and titles of such materials are usually very similar. If you put yourself in the shoes of a new graduate seeking a good position, it is almost impossible to distinguish between these law firms.

If you focus on the firms that propose a formal EVP, you will find many similar words or concepts, such as 'global', 'innovation', 'opportunities'. These concepts are part of the 'global EVP' offered by major law firms. These propositions are already known to your potential candidates. Broadly, they know that embracing a career in a major law firm will give them the opportunity to work on challenging and innovative assignments with a global approach. They already know the huge amount of work they will need to undertake. They also already know that in return the pay will be good.

Rather than helping them stand out, what law firms do when they talk about who they are is blend in and sound the same. Large law firms share around 80 or 90% of common values. So in order to be distinctive, why not focus on the different 10 or 20%?

This is why your EVP should focus on your own identity and values. Otherwise your EVP will be broadly the same as that of your competitors. So, should your EVP focus on those obvious promises? Do you have to remind people that you are a law firm much like a number of others, or do you need to put the emphasis on what will be different within your firm?

When you finally identify the differentiating features that could be included in your EVP, another problem could emerge: the EVP must accurately reflect the reality of your people experience. All too often, it is easy to devise an appealing EVP that could attract the best talent, but when it comes down to reality people are disappointed and the attrition rate rises.

Building your specific EVP and emphasising what is different and unique about your firm needs a methodical approach in order to collect insights from your people, create the EVP and implement it at every career step.

Even if you are not starting from scratch, building an effective EVP is not a simple process. It requires time and energy from different parts of the firm (partners, associates, HR and marketing/communication) in order to research, identify and understand the key elements of your EVP. It clearly won't happen overnight; Rome wasn't built in a day.

Example of a method for building an EVP

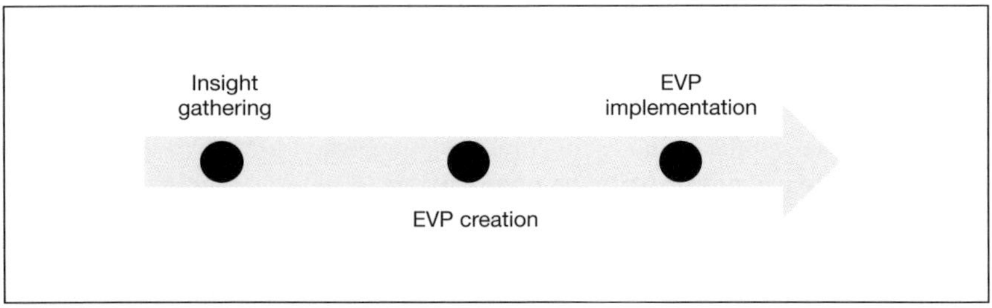

(a) *Insight gathering*

The first step is to gather all the insight needed to provide input into the reflection. You will have to explore both internal opinion and data from outside the firm (eg, reputation in the labour market, social media feedback, candidates' experiences etc). It is important to collect an overall and honest view of the firm.

In this step you will have to:

- define what kind of law firm you want to be and what sort of talent you want to attract;
- use insight survey data to help you develop a formal EVP (an onboarding and exit survey will be very useful);
- gather information from the market (ie, competitors and candidates);
- find out how to appear different from competitors;
- understand the expectation of your targeted candidates.

(b) *EVP creation*

Secondly, you will have to create (or adapt) your EVP using all the data collected. It is important to have an EVP that reflects the reality of the firm but that shows it has the potential to reach another level. You just have to get the balance right between the reality of the firm, the strengths that you can be proud of and the reasonable ambition that you should have for the future. You should:

- align the EVP with the firm's reputation;
- include and align your remuneration strategy with your EVP; and
- design customised EVPs for partners and support staff.

(c) *EVP implementation*

The final and most delicate step is implementing the EVP. Do this by communicating efficiently both inside and outside the firm, delivering your EVP promises and measuring the results in order to improve or adapt, if necessary. Here you should:

- test your EVP in order to ensure its credibility;
- effectively communicate the EVP to everyone in the firm;
- deliver on EVP promises; and
- measure your progress and results and improve or adapt your EVP.

3.2 Using new ways of working

Flexibility in the workplace is not optional or a choice that you should make in your HR policy; it is just a reality. People no longer work within a specific time frame before becoming free to do something else. The working day could start with an email very early in the morning and last until very late in the evening. But the working day will not follow a set timetable, especially for lawyers.

This flexibility is facilitated by all the IT technologies that enable lawyers to work anywhere without major difficulties. It is important to understand that we are facing a huge technological revolution and are being influenced by these disruptive innovations and generational changes, and forced to adapt very rapidly. One of these changes is in lawyers' relationship to work. This is why these new ways of working should be included in the EVP. The firms that will be able to adapt their working models to this new reality will have a huge competitive advantage. Until every law firm has adopted this flexible model, there is room to use it as a differentiator in the EVP.

3.3 A specific employer proposition for partners

When we think of lawyers' careers in large law firms, we usually focus on the early years and think that this first period of six or seven years is the most important and decisive for the overall success of a career. It is usually during this period that a graduate fresh from university, who is fully equipped with technical skills, can develop into a brilliant lawyer with management and client skills. But when you take a look at the full picture, this is only the very beginning of the career and lawyers spend almost 80% of their work life as a partner (for those who manage to stay in big law firms).

This is why when fee earners make partner they should continue to be engaged and motivated by a clear promise. The EVP might change and be tailored to the specific partner's driver engagement (ie, the key drivers of partner engagement; a positive attitude held by the partner towards the firm, its strategy and values). But this promise should not disappear. The EVP should still be needed to support their progression and to build trust and strengthen commitment. Furthermore, a specific partner EVP would be very useful regarding the opportunities to develop into new areas by attracting senior lateral partners. All the findings regarding how difficult it is to retain our best associates apply also to partners, while everybody knows that losing high-quality people could affect a law firm in many ways and in many areas.

Becoming a partner is usually a very *intuitu personae* process, depending on the partnership selection process (internal or lateral); but if an associate is eager to access this position it is because there is a promise. This promise need not always be engraved in marble but it has to be in the very DNA of a law firm.

Just as marketing professionals segment their customer targets into different categories, the firm's workforce can be segmented into different groups: partners, associates and support staff. These groups all care deeply about culture, values and work environment, but they will differ in their expectations. So, for increased efficiency, it will be necessary to customise the EVP for these workforce segments.

4. Experience the EVP every day

4.1 The importance of partner commitment and effort

Now it is done, you are proud of your EVP, it is a magnet for recruitment and candidates are eager to join your firm. But promises should not bind only those who want to believe them; there's nothing worse than failing to deliver the value proposition that you have announced to your people. Many firms have failed with that step and EVP has become just another useless HR programme. Furthermore, frustration and demotivation will cause more trouble to the organisation than having no promise at all.

The first thing to do is to be sure that partners understand that creating an EVP demands commitment and effort and making the EVP live and breathe. If the partners do not think that this is important for the firm, and that the EVP is a powerful tool which can be beneficial for recruitment and retention, then the battle is already lost. Some education is needed for every partner to understand that EVP will provide many benefits if there is commitment from their side. Without the full involvement of the partners, it is impossible to deliver on that promise. They must understand that in order to deliver on the promise of the EVP, they must reflect it in their day-to-day behaviour.

4.2 Understanding the new generation's expectations and the role of the EVP in firm strategy

A lot of work is required to change the mindset and to be sure that partners understand how important the EVP is in the firm's people strategy. With a short-term vision, it could be difficult to be convinced that EVP will be a solution to some people issues. Partners should understand that an EVP is part of a more global HR strategy that should only be judged with hindsight.

Changing partners' mindset mostly involves changing their view of their team. With a little distance and by trying not to project their own value system or expectations, they should try to put themselves in their associates' shoes. In order to help partners understand the new generation's expectations, firms can develop some specific training or workshops with millennial specialists, for example. A powerful method which can help to promote awareness is to conduct an annual survey with specific questions on driver engagement. The results of such annual surveys should be analysed carefully, generation by generation, and communicated to the partnership. But the most important thing is to encourage partners to take the time to listen carefully to their associates and overcome any overly simplistic vision of the generation gap.

4.3 The role of HR

We have seen how it is important to have a real people strategy and how the EVP is a key factor for success. I certainly believe that the time when lawyers thought that they were able to handle every aspect of a firm's management is behind us. Big law firms are now fully staffed with professionals in their key functions such as finance, marketing and business development and, of course, human resources. These professionals could bring a fresh insight to the legal sector, along with the *savoir faire* that is already used successfully in other sectors.

HR's role is certainly key to the EVP. The HR function must be involved at the earliest stages of the implementation of the EVP. This is not because HR will have a better understanding of workforce issues, their expectations or the atmosphere within the firm, but more because the HR professionals will have a complementary vision to that of the partner. The more the HR team is regarded by all parties as a trusted adviser, the more they can bring added value to the thinking. One of their tasks will be to open partners' eyes (if necessary) to the importance of the people strategy. Partner education is necessary to share the same vision and to deliver the EVP.

Then we could define the role of the HR team by a simple statement: to deliver the Employer Value Proposition. As HR are involved in many of the important steps of a career, whether recruitment, onboarding, annual appraisal, the promotion process, partnership or departures, they should be very cautious and try to make real the promise given to the workforce in the EVP.

4.4 Making the employer proposition consistent with the firm's strategy, its business case and the client model

The EVP should feature as part of an integrated and more global strategy. During the creation stage of the EVP, it is important to ensure that the HR strategy and the firm's strategy are coherent. The EVP should be aligned with the business case of the firm. It is pointless to make great claims in relation to work–life balance if associates are in fact being asked to bill more than 2,000 hours a year. It would be much more effective to underline all the initiatives that make an associate's life easier in achieving the billing requirement.

It is during the testing phase that it is important to challenge whether the value proposition matches the firm's strategies and the realities of life in the firm. At this point, the full involvement of different teams (not only fee earners) will be required to ensure that all the different strategies are in line with the EVP.

4.5 The need for a culture of open and honest discussion

If the promise is clear and both the partners and HR are fully committed to delivering that promise, then the atmosphere of dialogue within the firm will be decisive. EVP is ultimately about building trust between the firm and its people. The EVP is a promise made to potential candidates who sometimes do not know much about the firm. If you want to deliver that promise, you have to encourage a culture of open and honest dialogue. If your people do not feel secure enough to be able to discuss how they think this promise is delivered, then you will face difficulties.

Encouraging discussion can be accomplished in a variety of ways. Forming peer advisory groups is one of the most effective for changing behaviours and culture in relatively short order.

Open and honest discussion is also about courage. We all have many excuses to postpone a difficult discussion with an associate, but ultimately things will only get worse if they are not confronted. Honesty means that no matter how difficult the message is, you will treat your people with respect and honesty without avoiding difficult conversations. Most of us probably have examples of people who were ultimately thankful to have been informed clearly about their career perspectives.

4.6 All employees should be able to explain the firm's EVP

One of the main factors of success for the EVP is to have a clear and coherent dialogue at every level of the firm. The EVP must be shared with your workforce and the clearer your EVP statement, the easier it will be to communicate the value your firm offers. If the message shared with partners, associates, new joiners and job candidates is consistent, then your EVP will come across as both genuine and consistent.

So, communicating your EVP to your entire staff is an essential step, even before disseminating it to the outside world of the legal business sector. All the functions of the firm should understand what EVP means for the firm and how it makes it different from potential competitors. In turn, this will allow you to test the impact of the EVP and to make any necessary adjustments.

5. Conclusion: putting the employer proposition at the heart of HR strategy

The battle for new talent is not going to end soon. The most successful law firms will be those that can win this battle and use innovative approaches designed to achieve the right balance between their strategy and the expectations of their workforce. For many law firms, this is a huge cultural change. Changing the way partners look at their associates and understanding their expectations is fundamental. EVP is a central element in that cultural change and should be placed at the heart of the people strategy. Furthermore, the need for a solid EVP specific to partners is important in an environment where lateral hires are so strategic.

The first step is not necessarily the most difficult, but partners must adapt their mindset to this new reality. If they are able to be agile and adapt their business model to meet the continuing demands of their clients and the economic environment, they should be able to do the same with their people strategy. Once this first step is achieved, they should be more confident in working together with their HR team.

If the EVP is an important part of the people strategy, then partners should be evaluated for their capacity to deliver this promise. If you are not taking this dimension into account in the annual review process then it will be very difficult to implement an EVP successfully. The retention rate and more specifically the retention rate of staff with high potential (with all the explanation and precautions necessary) could be used as an indicator by which partners are assessed. Some voices will always say that the only criterion for partner evaluation is client satisfaction. But surely clients will be satisfied when they deal with a motivated team that is stable and enthusiastic when working on their matters? Is this criterion not a very good sign of the sustainable performance of a firm?

To change mindsets, the surrounding structures (rewards and recognition systems) must be in tune with the new behaviour. Otherwise, the necessary change will not be achieved. The overall change-management process can be used to transform attitudes and behaviour towards the partnership.

There is now an opportunity to rethink firm loyalty. Building a new employer proposition is a long-term vision that will actively prepare firms for future success in the hyper-competitive and fast-changing environment of the legal sector.

Legal education and training: supporting the recruitment and development of legal talent

Tony King
AGK PSF Training Ltd

1. Introduction

All lawyers around the world will go through a process of acquiring academic legal knowledge at the start of their careers. For the vast majority, that process involves studying for a law degree with the topics covered determined by the faculty of the teaching institution at which they are studying, the regulatory authorities of their home jurisdiction or a combination of the two. In a minority of countries, that process might be via some form of conversion course (such as the Graduate Diploma in Law in England and Wales) and it is even possible to qualify as a lawyer without a degree (notably, in England and Wales where would-be lawyers can follow either the Chartered Institute of Legal Executives route or the new apprenticeship process).

The law in all jurisdictions is constantly changing to reflect different economic or societal demands. While those changes may not affect every single lawyer in a particular jurisdiction, it is a rare individual whose legal practice is not affected by some form of change at regular intervals throughout his or her career.

Therefore, learning the law is not something which ends on graduation or admission to the register of lawyers (or the equivalent), rather it is a career-long process. As a result, education and training is an activity in which all lawyers need to engage from before they enter the profession to the time they retire.

This will come as no surprise to the readers of this chapter or their colleagues in their law firms. Equally, it will be understood by most, if not all, of the likely recruits to those firms.

The quality and extent of training offered by firms is becoming an increasingly important part of the way firms differentiate themselves (and make themselves attractive) in the recruitment market. It may not overtake factors such as the firm's reputation or the nature of the firm's client base (which determines the work the firm does). However, it may tip the balance when the potential recruit is considering which of a number of firms (which to an outsider may look very similar) to apply to for a job.

While developing knowledge and skills will be important to any lawyer whatever stage their career has reached, it is particularly important to younger lawyers early in their careers. Therefore, a well-thought-out and comprehensive training programme (within the limits of the firm's budget and resources) plays a significant role in attracting talent particularly, but not only, at the 'junior end' of the profession.

Its role is just as significant in retaining talent. If lawyers do not feel they are developing both as lawyers and managers of their part of the legal business in which they work, they can become frustrated. They will either leave, or their productivity will decline.

Providing training is not an altruistic activity. It is essential to the business of the firm that the people working in it are fully capable of performing their allocated roles. They also need to have the knowledge and skills to adapt to the constantly changing demands of a dynamic business, such as a successful law firm. Perhaps most importantly for the long-term health of the firm, the partners need to ensure that they develop associates who will become the next generation of partners, taking the firm on into future decades.

With this in mind, this chapter will look at the types of legal education and training in which would-be qualified lawyers need to engage at different stages in their careers (and so what a firm needs to consider offering).

The chapter will look (in sections 5, 6, 7 and 8) at the needs of and approaches for:

- students;
- new entrants to practice;
- associates (from juniors to seniors); and
- partners.

The specific training lawyers (whether qualified or not) need at different stages in their careers will be informed by the generic knowledge or skills all successful lawyers need to acquire and develop. This is considered in section 2.

Before looking at those issues, some caveats.

First, the readers of this chapter will come from a very wide range of jurisdictions and will practice in a wide variety of law. Therefore, it is not possible to be specific on, in particular, the detail of the legal rules which need to be studied at any particular point in an individual lawyer's career. Instead, this chapter will focus on the skills which that lawyer may bring to bear in order to stay up to date or develop his/her knowledge.

Nevertheless, it may be possible to divide the practices of lawyers around the world into the following four broad headings:

- private client contentious;
- private client non-contentious;
- commercial client contentious; and
- commercial client non-contentious.

However, there are myriad specific practices which can legitimately sit under each of those four headings.

Secondly, it is not possible for this chapter to examine the qualification processes in all jurisdictions around the world. Therefore, there have to be some assumptions made or generalities expressed.

Thirdly, the chapter assumes that the readers will be working in law firms, rather than in an in-house legal department, a governmental body or a non-profit organisation. While the points made may, in fact, be relevant to individuals working in those organisations, the particular structures of those organisations and the environments in which they operate may mean some of the points made are less relevant.

Finally, the environment in which the firm operates will have an impact on the training lawyers working in that firm may need. 'Environment' here means how the firm practices law in the macro sense.

The firm could be a local, regional or national firm which practices exclusively in its home jurisdiction. In that case, the training will focus on the law and practice in that jurisdiction. However, much business is done on a cross-border or even global basis and the law firms which service those types of clients need to have some knowledge of law and practice outside the borders of their home jurisdictions. What that knowledge will be will depend on the particular nature of the firm's practice and a simple illustration of it is the need to be aware of the different approaches in common law and civil law jurisdictions. There are many more.

For all firms, whatever their practice, their business strategy will also inform the firm's environment. The training needs of the lawyers in a firm which takes on complex commercial transactions will be different from those working in a firm doing commoditised work (which can cover debt collection, certain property transactions or personal injury claims).

Technology also contributes to the environment. Email is the obvious illustration but it goes far beyond that, from in-house financial management systems through knowledge management systems to the use of social media.

It is not the purpose of this chapter to look at environment in more detail than this. However, it should be borne in mind when adapting the general guidance in this chapter to the specific needs of an individual firm.

2. The business and professional knowledge and skills all successful lawyers need

Knowledge of the law and the approach to practice (whether that is practice in the sense of how deals are done or cases managed, or in the sense of how a practice may be organised to deliver profitable service of the right quality standard to clients) is not all that is involved in being a successful lawyer.

A law firm is, of course, a business but being a lawyer means being a professional. There may be a number of ways of defining a professional but the definition must include being ethical. There will be regulatory definitions of ethics in many jurisdictions, but being ethical is also a state of mind.

The expectation is that any would-be entrant to the legal profession will have a clear personal moral code which they will apply in any given situation when deciding on the correct behaviour. That moral code needs to be overlaid by whatever regulatory code may apply to the individual.

Explaining or reinforcing the ethics of the local profession will be very important when it comes to the training of young lawyers. However, it is equally important to more senior lawyers, especially when any new legislative/regulatory ethics-related obligations are introduced, of course. That situation aside, more senior lawyers will constantly gain more experience of the wide range of ethical issues a busy practice can throw up and of how to deal with them appropriately.

Being ethical will complement the lawyer's legal expertise by giving reassurance to clients and so supporting the development of the lawyer's practice.

It is implicit in what has gone before that, aside from any other knowledge or skills, a successful lawyer must be a good manager. He or she needs to be able to manage or contribute to managing the firm's:

- business;
- clients;
- people.

The nature of the managerial responsibilities of an individual lawyer will depend on his or her role at any given time. For a very junior lawyer, his or her contribution to 'management' may be relatively limited – say, ensuring accurate time recording or working well with his or her secretary. For a senior partner, the managerial responsibilities could be considerable – setting strategy, managing the firm's finances, building strong relationships with clients and managing teams of people.

Linked to this, many firms have developed competency structures which identify the knowledge and skills which lawyers need in order to be effective, with each skill broken down into the skills/knowledge/behaviour expected under each heading of lawyers at different stages of their careers. This approach is sometimes described as a 'progressive competency framework'.

For example, if one of the skills the firm has chosen for its competency framework is communication, that might be defined for junior lawyers as being able to communicate clearly in letters or emails and to be able to give an oral report of a piece of research clearly and concisely. In contrast, for a senior partner, communication may include the ability to construct an effective pitch when seeking to win work from an important client.

Firms which put competency frameworks in place will have tailored those frameworks to the particular needs of the firm. However, there will be a lot of commonality between such frameworks.

Many will divide competencies between lawyerly competencies and managerial competencies. Without intending to be prescriptive, a list of headings for a competency framework might look like this:

- 'lawyerly' skills
    - legal issue analysis;
    - knowledge of the law;
    - legal problem solving;
    - drafting.
- 'managerial' skills
    - business/financial understanding;
    - client management;
    - commercial problem solving;
    - people management/leadership;

- communication skills;
- networking.

The internet will be a source of a wide variety of illustrations of competency frameworks, whether tailored for legal practice or not. However, one helpful framework is the competence statement prepared by the Solicitors Regulation Authority of England and Wales. This statement underpins the SRA's regime of continuing competence for the purposes of continuing professional development of all English and Welsh solicitors with current practising certificates (see www.sra.org.uk/solicitors/competence-statement.page).

One important point to note about the competence statement is that, unlike many competency frameworks, it is not progressive. That means it has been written on the basis that a lawyer, of whatever level of seniority, can read it and apply it to his or her particular circumstances when deciding what steps to take to maintain competency in their particular area of specialisation. Nevertheless, it is a helpful list of skills, both lawyerly and managerial, which will help anyone new to competency frameworks understand how they are constructed.

Before turning to the specific legal education and training which lawyers, whether qualified or prospective, would benefit from at different stages of their careers, one final general question is, What are the best methods of helping individuals develop whatever knowledge or skills they need to perform their roles?

In this regard, there is a useful trainers' maxim – the '70:20:10' rule. Obviously, this is intended to be indicative, not prescriptive. However, it means that looking at the sum total of knowledge which any individual has acquired at whatever stage they have reached in their career, some 10% was acquired through some sort of formal training (whether a substantial course such as a degree or any other shorter, formal training courses). Then, 20% of the individual's knowledge has typically been acquired through supervision, mentoring, coaching or other guidance; while the remaining 70% has been gained by 'doing the job'.

Many lawyers recognise this as a rule of thumb and it can be applied to whatever skill the individual is trying to develop. Therefore, for example, during the early years of a lawyer's career, he or she will rely heavily on formal classroom training when it comes to acquiring the legal technical knowledge needed for his or her particular area of practice. That knowledge will be honed by guidance from the more senior lawyers with whom the individual works. Over time, the individual will become 'expert' and thereafter will refine their knowledge in the light of the changing circumstances in their practice. That may involve formal classroom training but, for the most part, it will be a matter of keeping up to date and building on the existing knowledge base.

The same approach applies to managerial skills. Obviously, would-be lawyers will have developed the basics of some of the managerial skills, sometimes to a very high level, before they start their legal studies. For example, any would-be lawyer will have developed communication skills (both written and oral) to a high degree by the time they leave school. However, other managerial skills (eg, business understanding) will be new topics to them, certainly at the start of their legal careers, and maybe after qualification too. Such knowledge may be picked up on the job, but it can also be acquired through formal classroom training.

For example, a lawyer who is an expert in his or her particular area of legal practice may need to return to the classroom to understand the core concepts of a relevant business skill (say, law firm finances).

This is not to say that, for example, a partner who is taking over the management of a group or an office needs to go back to university to acquire an MBA. That individual will, by reason of having worked for several years in a law firm, have a sound understanding of the managerial issues he or she will face in their new role. However, an insight into best practice (perhaps through a relatively short course) can be a sound foundation for them to develop their abilities on the job.

3. Students

In headline terms, students are no different from any other lawyer in that they must develop both their lawyerly knowledge/skills and their managerial skills.

Assuming the individual student is studying for a law degree in his or her home jurisdiction, the bulk of the individual's efforts will be devoted to acquiring a sound foundation in that jurisdiction's laws. What particular topics the individual will study will depend on any regulatory requirements, the range of topics offered by the faculty with which the student is studying and the student's individual choice (assuming there are optional subjects available which complement any compulsory topics the student has to study).

It is leaving hostages to fortune to list topics which students should study but most, if not all, law degrees will cover core topics such as the law of obligations (contract and tort), land law, criminal law and constitutional law. There will, of course, be additional core subjects in particular jurisdictions and the list of potential optional topics a student could study could be very long indeed.

While (hard earned) knowledge of hard legal facts is extremely important, merely rote learning those facts is not enough as rote-learned information can soon be forgotten.

Following on from this, students should understand that the academic knowledge they are acquiring in the course of their degree will have direct relevance to their work as practising lawyers and this will help with the retention of that knowledge. Many degree courses are very effective at putting the law into a practical context, whether by reason of the approach to teaching (which in a number of jurisdictions includes clinical education – see below), or by using practitioners to teach part or all of particular courses.

It is reasonable for students not to make the connection between their legal studies and legal practice if they have not experienced law in real life. However, it is important that the system prevents students from saying, as one student did, 'I didn't realise that my contract course would inform the whole of my practising career; I thought it was no different from the geography course I studied at school.'

Another way of looking at this issue is that the students should be taught to think like lawyers. This means, in addition to knowing the law, bringing to bear analytical skills to identify the issues and any areas needed for research, applying the fruits of that knowledge/research to the issues with which they are faced and proposing legally effective solutions. It goes without saying that coupled with this is the ability to communicate clearly and concisely, whether in writing or orally, the conclusions they draw at each stage of this process. These skills, if honed well on their university courses, will form a very sound foundation for the future careers of would-be lawyers. (It is, of course, true that not every law graduate goes on to become a practising lawyer. However, these skills should stand them in good stead whatever their career path after they graduate.)

Teaching on degree courses may deliver this outcome, but 'clinical education' has been introduced in a number of jurisdictions which is an excellent way of achieving the same objective.

'Clinical education' is where the teaching institution runs a law clinic for people in the locality. Students then advise these real life clients on their issues (under the supervision of a suitably qualified lawyer). The topics on which the students may advise will be many and varied but typically they include issues such as employment, landlord and tenant and debt. As unqualified individuals, the students may not be able to take the advice they give very far (so there will be processes in place for passing the law clinic's clients on to qualified lawyers as and when appropriate). However, this type of approach is very effective at developing the student's skills of interviewing, researching, problem solving, advising and communicating.

Whether or not clinical education is available in any particular jurisdiction, students can obtain similar experience by work experience (of whatever length) in a law firm.

This section has so far assumed that the student is studying only for an undergraduate degree (or a JD or equivalent in the jurisdictions where that is the route to qualification). However, many law graduates will go on to study for a higher and more focused degree, typically, a master's degree.

The attitude to master's degrees varies from jurisdiction to jurisdiction. In some jurisdictions a master's degree is expected; in others, it is the student's choice. Whatever the jurisdictional view may be on master's degrees, they are obviously an excellent way for the student to develop a much deeper knowledge of particular areas of law. The arguments in favour of undertaking that course of study are compelling if the topic is going to be the basis of the student's future practice. The arguments in favour may be less compelling from a future utility viewpoint if the student is either uncertain of their future area of practice or is studying the topic out of intellectual interest (not that that is objectionable). However, any study of law at this higher level will help further hone the student's legal skills and so the individual can derive benefit from the expenditure of effort come what may.

Whether the student wishes to take on the financial burden of such courses is a decision for the individual and should be taken in the light of the possibility that having the higher degree will not necessarily improve the individual's employability.

While many students will only ever study in their home jurisdiction, there is a trend in some jurisdictions for students to undertake a master's degree in a different country and even in a different language (eg, German lawyers undertaking LLMs in the United States). Beside the benefits of living and studying in a different country and therefore getting to know another culture, this path can give a unique insight into the approach to lawyering in a different jurisdiction as well as opening up a wider range of employment prospects.

Following on from the points already made, helping students appreciate the nature of the environments in which law is practised will help them develop their skills on a broader base.

That broader base should include their managerial skills which, in addition to the 'thinking like a lawyer' skills, will include personal organisation, team working (depending on the nature of their degree course) and communication skills.

It is right that students should focus their efforts on what is required by their degree courses and not be overly focused on the direction their career may take subsequently. However, having regard to the different demands and pressures they may face in practice will make the transition from student to junior lawyer less of a shock. clinical education may help with this and some jurisdictions (notably, but not only, England and Wales at the moment as the qualification process there is under review) require students to complete a 'bridge' course designed to help them make the transition from academic law to practical law.

Much has been made in this chapter of the need for lawyers to acquire both legal technical knowledge skills and managerial skills.

Picking that up in the light of the 70:20:10 rule, should students complete a heavy management course before embarking on their practising careers? There are pros and cons to this in that an MBA-type course can be an excellent basis on which to build a managerial career. However, one issue to be borne in mind is when will a student use the knowledge gained on such a course? Typically, junior lawyers will be involved in handling client work rather than the management of the law firm. Having the academic knowledge gained on an MBA will put in context the way the law firm in which they work is managed. However, some may be frustrated by not being able use that knowledge to any great extent. Furthermore, if they reach a position where they are involved in the management of the firm, the knowledge gained on the MBA may be a distant memory albeit one which can be resurrected relatively easily.

An alternative view on the timing of taking an MBA is to wait until the individual is closer to taking on managerial responsibilities. However, for most lawyers that is when they are senior associates or partners, at which point it is much more difficult for them to take a substantial period of time out from their practices.

4. New entrants

In some jurisdictions, new entrants are required by the local regulators to go through some form of pre-admission traineeship of whatever length and subject to whatever experience requirements.

The advantage of this is that the new entrants can gain experience of (usually) a range of areas of practice under the close supervision of an experienced senior. They can be socialised as an ethical professional by watching their seniors deal with the range of issues (legal, practical, ethical and interpersonal) which regularly cross the desks of practitioners. It can also allow both the new entrants and their employers to take an informed view of the area of practice in which the individual will specialise going forward.

There are many jurisdictions around the world where the new entrant may arrive fully qualified (eg, having gained the required law degree) and will go into a field of practice in which they will stay for the rest of their careers. There are some firms in those jurisdictions which adopt some form of traineeship because of the business benefits they derive from it, including the socialisation of the new entrant (see above).

Whichever approach is adopted in the particular jurisdiction or firm, the new entrant needs to acquire or develop the legal knowledge to practice the relevant area of law.

On top of that, the new entrants may need support to help them with the transition into a working environment. With that in mind, it is common to organise some form of induction programme which will explain issues such as:

- the organisation's strategy;
- the organisational structure;
- the roles and responsibilities of a new entrant.

Some new entrants struggle to adapt to a client service environment. They may need guidance on how to change their written style from one which is suitable for academia to one which is suitable for an office. They may also need guidance on how they contribute to the financial health of the business (through accurate time recording) or their professional/ethical obligations (such as the duty of confidentiality etc).

Come what may, they should be given clarity as to the expectations the firm has of them (perhaps through the combination of a competency framework and an effective performance management structure including whatever training support the firm may offer). With that, they will understand both what they have to do and also what support they can ask of the firm.

It is not the purpose of this chapter to describe performance management structures in detail. However, regular review/appraisal meetings, at which objectives tailored to the needs of both the firm and the individual are set and subsequently monitored, will maximise the contribution of the individual and the developmental benefits for that person.

5. Associates

The term 'associate' covers a number of discrete stages in a lawyer's career in the run-up to being considered for partnership. As a result, 'associate' is a portmanteau word for any qualified lawyer who is not yet a partner. While 'associate' is a commonly used term, it is not the only word used to describe non-partners. They may be assistants, senior associates, directors or counsel depending on the firm's culture and their seniority.

Again, associates need to strike a balance between acquiring/developing their legal technical expertise and developing their managerial skills.

Associates will go from acquiring legal knowledge (as junior associates) to becoming expert (as senior associates, directors or counsel). Similarly, they will develop their managerial skills. The balance of acquiring new knowledge will shift between acquiring legal technical skills (which will predominate in the early years of their careers) and managerial skills (which will become increasingly important in the later years of their careers as associates).

What does this mean in practice? The detail will depend on the particular nature of the lawyer's practice – the balance between legal/practical knowledge and managerial skills may be different as between a tax lawyer and a litigator. Nevertheless, to use a generic illustration of a transactional lawyer, in the early years of his or her career, most of the training effort will go into learning the law and practice relevant to the particular type of transaction on which the lawyer's practice focuses. The skills which need to be developed will be those of a junior lawyer which will be drafting, personal time management, understanding the clients and their business sector and so on. Suggesting an arbitrary percentage split between these two aspects of the lawyer's development may not be helpful. Nevertheless, approximately 75% of the lawyer's effort should be devoted to becoming an expert in his or her area of specialisation, with the remaining 25% devoted to developing the necessary skills.

That split will change over time so that once the lawyer achieves a level of seniority, the split may be closer to 50:50 or even with the skills development predominating.

To elaborate, once the lawyer is an 'expert', he or she must ensure they are up to date with the relevant law and practice. That may largely be done on the job, but there will always be a need for some additional training (whether through courses, reading cases or journals, discussion with colleagues and so on).

The range of managerial skills to develop will broaden. The lawyer may need to learn how to manage and motivate teams, how to build client relationships, how to manage the finances of his or her practice, how to determine the future strategy for the practice and so on. These can be learned by much the same methods as the legal or practical knowledge is honed.

The lawyer may work out what developmental steps he or she needs to take on their own initiative. However, some guidance from the firm is needed as the key to ensuring that an associate, of whatever level, contributes effectively is clarity regarding the firm's expectations of that individual. Therefore, the desirability of the benefits of a performance management structure come into play.

Focusing on the managerial skills in more detail, a typical junior associate will initially be an 'individual contributor' (eg, amending parts of a transactional document or creating a minor document needed for the transaction). Over time, he or she will become a team leader, responsible for taking a transaction forward with the help of a team of more junior associates (albeit all under the supervision of a partner).

As the associate becomes more senior, the role of training is to reinforce the message that being a successful lawyer is a combination of legal knowledge, practical skills and managerial skills.

An issue with some associates is that they see their role as being that of 'legal execution'. Doing the legal work to the quality standard required in line with the client's instructions is, of course, extremely important. However, that might be a somewhat narrow contribution if either the firm wants the associate to contribute more widely to the development of the business, or the individual has aspirations to become a partner (ie, a business owner).

This issue can arise for a number of reasons. The associate may enjoy being a 'pure' lawyer and so not be interested in the wider business aspects of the firm. Alternatively, it may be a result of the training, mentoring or guidance they have received as they have gone through their career to date.

There is a tension here in that in many firms the senior associates are described as the 'engine room' of the firm. They do high-quality work very profitably, leaving the partners free to manage the business and the relationships with the clients as well as overseeing the legal work their teams do. If associates focusing on legal execution fits the business model of the firm and suits both sides (ie, the partners and the associates), there can be no objection.

However, if the senior associates do not understand or have not developed the wider managerial skills the firm needs, how will they be effective partners? Returning to the point about clarity of expectations, the partners need to decide what they require, particularly from their senior associates, and train them accordingly.

If they want the associates to focus on legal execution, the partners will need to provide them with appropriate training or support on managerial issues once they become partners. It is, after all, certainly true that there will be associates who make it to partner by virtue of their very high level of legal technical knowledge.

If the partners want the associates who become partners to make that transition seamlessly, they need to be clear as to the expectations of future partners. They then need to provide the necessary training, mentoring and guidance to prepare the associates to become partners.

The issue to avoid is a disappointed would-be partner candidate who says 'I thought all that was needed was for me to do the work the partners had brought in; I didn't know I was supposed to develop the business myself.'

There is an issue here about identifying the individuals in whom the firm should invest this particular effort. In some firms, it may be crystal clear who the future partner candidates are. However, in others (notably, but not only, larger firms) there may be a pool of talented senior associates from which the partner candidates will be chosen.

Whichever situation the firm finds itself in, it is probably better to develop the managerial skills of all the senior associates rather than selecting a chosen few for special treatment. This is not a hard and fast rule; it will depend entirely on the culture of the firm and the nature of the senior associate cohort. However, making a selection too early could deny the firm the benefit of a talented associate if the process excludes someone who will blossom with some additional guidance or support. On the flip side of that, the firm may find its investment does not bring a sufficient return if one of the chosen few is a talented lawyer but someone who does not ultimately develop the managerial skills the firm needs in its future partners.

What form should the support given to these senior associates take? Again, it will depend on the structure of the employing firm. In a large firm, the support may be a formal training structure. However, the 70:20:10 rule must not be overlooked. Training courses will take the associates only so far; any classroom training needs to be supplemented by mentoring guidance from the partners. It should be followed up with the associates handling business issues for real.

In a smaller firm, the support may be provided entirely on an informal basis by the partners for whom the individual works, mixing the mentoring guidance with the real-life experience explained above.

Whatever is the appropriate structure in the circumstances, the assumption will be that the associate's legal technical knowledge is at the required standard albeit that it will need to be continually updated and developed.

On the managerial skills side, the associate will need training and/or guidance on what is expected of a partner in the firm. In headline terms, this will be the ability to manage the firm's business, clients and people but what does that mean in more detail?

Managing the business means understanding the firm's strategy and how the associate can support it. At this stage in the associate's career, he or she should be well aware of how the firm positions itself in its particular market and the type of clients for which it wants to act, and have some appreciation of the financial realities of the firm (within whatever limits of confidentiality the partners may wish to impose). Armed with this information, the associate should be encouraged to develop a personal business plan designed to position them, within a reasonable time frame, as a credible candidate for partnership. In brief, that personal business plan will cover:

- the associate's 'unique selling point' (ie, whatever area of legal knowledge or practise the firm sees as the associate's principal contribution to the business);
- the associate's target clients (whether clients with whom the individual already has a strong working relationship or ones where the firm wants the associate to help with the development of the relationship);
- the associate's competition (namely, the external law firms which possess the same or similar knowledge as the associate and/or have strong relationships with the associate's target clients);
- the associate's resourcing plans for the work (which will involve the associate analysing the work to be won along with a work allocation plan to show who the associate needs to work with in order to deliver work of the right quality);
- the associate's expectations as regards the likely revenue stream the work will generate.

Picking up a couple of points from this list, in some firms, the competition may be the associate's peers. Whether that is articulated either by the firm or the associate is a matter for the culture of the organisation.

On the resourcing plan, the associate should understand that, save in exceptional circumstances, the firm probably will not give him or her additional resources in the form of, say, a dedicated junior associate until the work has been won. This may mean that the associate carries a heavy burden in the initial stages of implementing the personal business plan. However, that may be informative to the firm in terms of the individual's longer term capabilities.

In terms of managing the clients, the role the associate will play in this will depend on the firm's approach. At the very least, the associate should understand:

- how the firm decides which clients to act for or target;

- how the firm wins work from its target clients (so, for example, the approach to differentiating the firm from its rivals, the firm's approach to servicing its clients, the firm's policy on billing methods etc);
- how the firm delivers work of the required quality profitably (which should be meat and drink to the associate although the associate should be encouraged to think of ways of making the practice even more efficient/ profitable);
- how to maintain a strong relationship with clients between mandates.

On managing the people the associate's prime responsibility will be leading and managing his or her team. However (and depending on the approach in the firm), an understanding of manpower planning, recruitment processes and performance management approaches will stand the associate in good stead for when he or she has to deal with these issues as a partner.

While this would inform all three general areas of management, understanding risk and how the firm's professional obligations are managed is an important tool in the associate's toolbox. At this stage in the associate's career, he or she should be very familiar with the professional standards rules but they may need guidance on how the firm deals with particular situations. For example, the associate will be very familiar with the conflict rules. However, he or she may be less clear on how the firm deals with a conflict situation in a way which is both ethical and maintains strong client relationships with all parties.

This knowledge could be delivered in a series of classroom sessions. However, it could more effectively be achieved by the associate having discussions with the partners for whom he or she works; first, to understand how they deal with the range of management decisions they come across and, secondly, to support the associate in implementing the personal development plan.

This two-pronged approach to the associate's development (maintaining his or her legal technical knowledge and developing his or her wide-ranging managerial skills) should help make the transition from associate to partner relatively smooth. Depending on the culture of the firm, progress achieved in these areas may help with the promotion decision itself.

6. Partners

As with lawyers at the earlier career stages, partners need to maintain and develop their legal technical skills and their managerial skills. Again as with associates, a competency framework for partners looking at both development strands will give clarity to partners in terms of where they should focus their efforts. Equally, some form of partner appraisal/review will ensure partners are kept on track. Clearly, how formal this process will be and what is the focus of any discussions will depend on the nature/culture of the firm. A highly formalised structure may be wholly inappropriate in many instances.

For partners, much of the development they undergo will be similar in principle to that which associates undergo albeit tailored to the more senior role of partner.

This section will focus on the stages in the career arc of a partner and the development which is needed at each stage.

6.1 New partners

Assuming the new partners have had support (eg, with the implementation of personal business plans) prior to promotion, they should be in a good position to develop a strong partner-level of practice after they are promoted. If they have not had that support prior to promotion, the support can be given at a 'New Partner Course', supplemented by subsequent training or guidance.

Typically, the focus of new partners is to build their personal practices. Some firms will have laid the foundation for this when the new partners were associates. In others, they will have been the number two to the partner who, most likely, was their sponsor as they went through the partnership selection process. Whatever position the individual new partner finds him- or herself in, they need to establish themselves in their particular market as the 'go-to' expert. Insofar as guidance is needed, it is often on how the new partner can raise his or her profile, distinct from the profiles or reputations of other partners. Going on from that, they may need support in developing strong personal relationships with their clients.

As always, this may be through formal classroom training, but guidance from mentors within the firm whenever possible is more effective. Needless to say, a combination of training and guidance, coupled with the opportunity to learn on the job (with feedback) is ideal.

6.2 Client relationship partners

Once a partner has established his or her personal practice, they will develop ever stronger relationships with their key work providers. That is entirely appropriate but both the firm and the individual partner need to take a view on whether that is the best way the partner can contribute to the health of the firm. It may well be that the firm and the individual feel that the individual partner is well placed to develop a deeper institutional relationship between the firm and the client organisation.

For example, the individual partner may have a very strong relationship with the general counsel at the client organisation. That relationship may produce a steady flow of work but what happens if the general counsel leaves and is replaced by an individual with a strong working relationship with a rival firm? Articulating the reason for the wish to institutionalise the relationship may be counter-productive if it is expressed to the current general counsel but, with sensitivity, this can be managed. The objective should be for the individual partner to develop strong relationships with other key decision makers in the client organisation (say, at board level) and ideally introduce colleagues to the institutional relationship.

Aside from the obvious advantage of deepening the relationship between the firm and the client organisation, this approach has the advantage that, for example, it can help junior partners develop their personal practices by sharing the relationships between partners.

There may be a degree of persuasion needed by the individual partner's own managing partners to agree to this change. However, that aside, support in the form of client relationship and management guidance should result in success.

6.3 Management partners

The term 'management partners' is intended to cover a partner with any form of internal management responsibility. This could be responsibility for a particular project, a group, a firm-wide practice area, an office or even the firm as a whole. This particular stage could be subsequent to the client relationship partner stage, or be concurrent with it.

A successful fee-earning partner will have developed many of the skills needed for the management roles which could come under this heading. Line fee earning partners will be experts in project management, strategy, team leadership and so on. However, it is one thing to use these skills on a client matter, but perhaps another when managing one's colleagues.

Some individuals who take on these roles may be able to draw on the knowledge gained from formal management courses they have completed in the past (say, an MBA). However, that knowledge may be rusty and need updating.

It is probably unrealistic to expect anyone who is in the running for this type of management role to take significant time off to attend a formal training course. However, the bigger the role, the more justification there is for a substantial training programme. While this is not universal, many partners taking on significant management roles (eg, managing partner of the firm) may attend substantial executive management courses at business schools (of anything between one and three months in length), or at least attend a focused management course covering the key issues, albeit in a much shorter time.

All this is predicated on the choice of individuals to take on these roles being subject to some planning process. A situation to avoid is where partners say, 'Our leaders tend to emerge and we go from emergency to emergency.' Clearly, volunteers for these management roles are better than 'pressed men' but the holder of the role can have a very significant impact on the business so the decision has to be the right one. Drawing on information from partner evaluations, soundings from other partners etc will all help in making the right choice.

6.4 Retiring partners

All partners will eventually leave the firm, and managing that process well is important for the health of the firm.

Whatever the reason for the retirement and whenever it happens in the partner's career, the firm should have regard to minimising any adverse impact the departure will have on the firm's business.

If a partner has a very strong relationship with a particular client, his or her retirement may mean the client is lost to the firm (whether because the retired partner takes that relationship to a new firm or, the partner having 'properly' retired, the client has no sense of connection with the firm). For this reason, institutionalising client relationships is very important and if that approach is not already in place, steps to secure the relationship after the partner's departure need to be taken.

While this may not be relevant in every case, the retiring partner may need support from the firm. If the firm has a fixed retirement age, it may be appropriate to offer retirement support in the form of guidance on finances, work opportunities (paid or *pro bono*) etc.

Equally, the retiring partner (assuming he or she is not going to a rival firm) is a valuable resource. He or she will have an 'institutional memory' in relation to both client relationships and legal practice. The retiring partner may be keen to stay in touch with the firm, albeit on a different basis from that which has been the case to date. As a result, the retiring partner may be an invaluable resource who can act as:

- a mentor to existing partners;
- a contributor to the firm's knowledge management systems;
- a trainer of the lawyers (of whatever seniority);
- a link to client organisations;
- an ambassador for the firm in the wider world.

Whether training is needed on any of these issues would depend on the individual, but planning ahead to take advantage of the opportunities is clearly vital.

7. Conclusion

The law is a knowledge profession and as such every conscientious practitioner working in it knows the importance of acquiring and maintaining their legal knowledge.

A lawyer's initial academic legal studies offer a foundation on which they build their future careers. However, the knowledge acquired on a law degree may go out of date or not be directly relevant to the area of practice in which the lawyer eventually specialises. Therefore, the legal knowledge gained from academic study must be complemented by developing 'lawyering' skills.

For example, the speed of change in many areas of law (whether driven by new approaches to practice, or legislation) means that lawyers may have to reinvent themselves in the course of their careers. One illustration of this is where a tax lawyer specialising in a particular tax faces the 'death' of his or her practice when the government abolishes that tax. In that case, the tax lawyer needs to find some complementary area of tax on which to base a new practice. Similarly, after the financial crash of 2008/2009, lawyers who specialised in securitisation reinvented themselves as restructuring lawyers. The ability to be flexible is a vital skill for a lawyer and needs to be developed.

Even if the change to a lawyer's practice is not dramatic, few cases are identical and so the lawyer always needs to be adaptable in terms of addressing the particular needs of the client in the particular circumstances.

Legal technical knowledge must be complemented by knowledge of practice and managerial skills. What those complementary skills will be will depend on the particular practice and role of the individual. However, it is important that lawyers develop on all these fronts, at an appropriate rate, throughout their careers.

Self-aware lawyers will understand their own strengths and areas for development which need to be aligned to the business objectives of their firm. The nature of some firms is such that the alignment is self-evident, but in others the organisation needs to give guidance to the individual lawyer.

While this can be done very effectively by informal conversations between the lawyer and his or her supervisor, a clear competency framework and performance management structure linked to the firm's overall strategy will give helpful clarity on these issues.

Finally, lawyers tend to be individualistic and an overly structured approach could be more damaging than beneficial. Not only must the lawyers be flexible; so (within reason) must the firm.

Not every lawyer wants to be a partner and so is there scope for non-partner roles? (These might be roles as technical experts in a fee-earning capacity or professional support lawyer roles developing the firm's knowledge management system.)

Not every lawyer wants a long-term career with the law firm for which they work or even a long-term career as a lawyer. It is true that investing in the development of a lawyer who moves to a rival firm after a few years could be seen as training the competition. However, not training lawyers because of that risk means the existing team may not be as effective as they could be. Furthermore, giving lawyers good training means they are likely to be good leavers and may prove to be work givers in future, especially if they move to client organisations.

Learning and development is not a one-off exercise at the start of a lawyer's career; it is career-long. It is not just a matter of learning the law; it is a matter of seeing the law as a business and managing it as such. It is not a matter of relying on classroom training; education and training can be delivered just as effectively by experienced seniors mentoring or coaching their junior colleagues.

An effective education and training structure running from a would-be lawyer's academic studies through to the retirement of a very experienced partner in a law firm will ensure the lawyer develops the right skills in the right way at the right time, so benefiting the firm's clients and in turn supporting the financial health of the firm. It is essential, not a 'nice to have'.

Furthermore (and as was mentioned in the introduction to this chapter), a carefully thought-through training structure cannot only encourage talented would-be recruits to apply to the firm; it can also be a significant aid to retaining those talented lawyers in the firm. If the lawyers see there is a clear development path (based on, for example, the firm's competency framework giving clarity on the firm's expectations of its lawyers at different stages in their careers, reinforced by the performance management systems and mentoring guidance from the partners), the lawyers will be encouraged to stay. They will be able to see the range of legal and managerial skills they will develop over time which they would miss out on if they left too early.

There is no question of locking in associates; nor should they be misled about their prospects. However, retaining an effective associate even for one year longer than might otherwise be the case will add to the firm's bottom line.

Developing the next generation of partners not just to be excellent lawyers but also great managers will secure the future of the firm.

Equipping partners with the skills and abilities to retain talent

Alison Nolan
Open Consulting

This chapter focuses on the skills and qualities partners need to develop strong partner–lawyer relationships. These relationships are at the heart of a firm's ability to attract and retain talent at all levels, from graduates looking for a manager/mentor who will enable them to learn and progress, to lateral hire partners needing to integrate and collaborate with existing teams so as to establish and grow their practice in the new firm.

Before we know what skills it is most important to develop and how we should do that, it is important to be really clear what matters most to the people we want to retain.

1. What do lawyers want?

There seems to be a growing disconnect between what lawyers entering the workplace expect from their careers and the expectations of the senior lawyers and partners who manage them. Lawyers who have been qualified for one or two years may want to move on not only for more money or more regular hours, as has been the case in the past. They see a world of possibilities their seniors did not imagine for themselves (entrepreneurial peers creating their own companies, including the wealth of opportunities opened up by new technology), and the prospect of partnership is not necessarily seen as a prize worth waiting for. There is an increasingly urgent need for the traditional world of the law firm to provide an environment where millennials want to be – a working environment which makes them feel valued as individuals, recognised for their contribution, and supported in their development. There are processes that a firm can deploy which can help. Many firms are increasing their focus on diversity, flexible and agile working policies, or considering creative ways to engage millennials, such as shadow boards or reverse mentoring. But the key is often in the relationship with the immediate manager – people do not leave jobs, they leave people.[1]

So what do associates want from the partners they work for, and what really motivates them to want to stay with that person? A recent survey in my own firm brought some interesting results. We asked groups of lawyers at different career stages a similar question. Groups of junior and senior associates were asked:

> *Which characteristics and behaviours do you most value in partners, which make you want to continue to work for him or her?*

1 Buckingham, M and Coffman, C, *First, Break All the Rules* (Simon & Schuster, 2001).

And we asked groups of new and experienced partners:

What characteristics and behaviours do you think associates most value in partners, which make them want to work for him or her?

The differences between the groups were plain. At the junior end, the most commonly occurring themes concerned:

- the personal interactions with the partner (particularly approachability, encouragement, making people feel valued, showing concern, interest in others' opinions, recognition, and care for others' wellbeing);
- the partner's ability to manage himself or herself (calm, patience, consistency, resilience, positive attitude);
- to a lesser but significant extent, the ability to give clear instructions and regular and helpful feedback.

Overall, the most frequently occurring characteristic by far was 'approachability'. Typical comments included:

- "I appreciate when a partner values my time as highly as his or her own, doesn't keep me waiting for no reason, and takes the time to explain things clearly."
- "They are interested in who you are, beyond what you do in the firm."
- "He genuinely asked for and listened to my views, explained our strategy, and truly valued my contribution."

The single most frequently occurring phrase used by this group was 'taking the time', as in partners taking the time to greet, explain, listen to, thank, and give feedback to team members.

In the senior associate group, the focus of responses begins to shift. While personal interactions are still important, they are less so than for the more junior group. There is also an increase in the number of items relating to:

- coaching, mentoring, providing stretching work opportunities and career development;
- team work, personal qualities (such as honesty, fairness, integrity), and professional expertise.

Typical examples include:

- "Interest in my development and professional growth."
- "Capacity to help others grow in responsibility and autonomy."
- "Sharing their knowledge and information with others, always be open for discussion."

When it came to analysing experienced partners' responses, the emphasis was on:

- coaching and mentoring;
- leadership;
- personal interactions;
- personal qualities.

Overall a picture emerges in which partners and senior lawyers are much better matched in terms of expectations than our group of millennials with either senior lawyers or partners.

For the group of new partners surveyed, there seems to be a spike in the importance of leadership and the harder qualities of technical and client-related expertise, perhaps reflecting the particular challenges for that group during the transition to partnership.

Results of survey of most valued characteristics in partners (thematic analysis)

Theme		Typical items	Junior lawyers	Senior lawyers	New partners	Experienced partners
			Percentage of total responses by group			
1	Personal interactions	Approachable, Encouraging, Empathy, Recognise individual achievements, Concern, Respect, Values contribution, Makes others feel valued, Friendly	47%	23%	15%	15%
2	Self-management	Calm, Patient, Resilient, Consistent, Polite, Positive, Organised	19%	7%	4%	5%
3	Clarity and feedback	Regular feedback, Clear instructions	17%	0	0	6%
4	Teamwork	Trust in team, Involvement of team, Cooperative, Delegates, Generous with time	8.5%	11%	8.5%	6%
5	Personal qualities	Honesty, Fairness, Integrity, Trust, Openness	4%	11%	6%	14%
6	Leadership	Leadership, Charisma, Inspiration, Passion, Enthusiasm	2%	7%	23%	16%
7	Technical/ intellectual competence	Knowledge, Professionalism, Intelligence, Expertise, Skill as a lawyer, Competence	2%	11%	17%	6%

continued on next page

Theme		Typical items	Junior lawyers	Senior lawyers	New partners	Experienced partners
			Percentage of total responses by group			
8	Coaching and mentoring	Coaching, Shows interest in developing people, Mentoring, Providing opportunities, Assisting career progression	0	16%	4%	20%
9	Drive and ambition	Ambition, Drive, Commanding respect, Confidence, Initiative	0	4.5%	6%	1%
10	Clients and business	Successful, Ability to generate work, Client handling	0	9%	15%	9%

What does this tell us? There is clearly a gap between what partners think is important about their leadership style, and what is actually important to individual team members. This is not to say that one is right and the other wrong, but it highlights the need to help partners flex their approach to managing and developing their people so as to engage with differing needs, particularly across the three generations we currently have in the workplace.

We also conducted some in-depth interviews, including with partners who have a reputation as leaders within the firm. The best partners know what they need to do to retain talent. One said:

Be a role model. Associates know if we are good and fair, if we care about them or just ourselves, they watch the partners all the time and form their own opinions. A partner has to work hard himself, be good at the job, be fair and generous, in short, lead by example. With these qualities a partner is usually successful, and associates love to work for successful partners.

Another said:

If a partner can maintain trust and communication with her associates, retaining talent doesn't have to be learnt in a hard way.

2. Partners as everyday leaders

Not all partners perform so well in their role as leaders. Partners are role models for others, whether they think about it or not and, as the partner quoted above makes clear, team members notice how partners behave. Skills-based training, such as delegation, giving feedback, coaching and mentoring go part of the way. But I would suggest there are two more fundamental elements underpinning all of these, which are crucial for retaining talent:

- emotional skill (how we make people feel);
- conversational skill (how we help people think).

2.1 Emotional skills

Daniel Goleman sets out clearly the anatomy of emotional skills in leaders, an abbreviated version of which is set out below. Goleman argues that "... the primal job of leadership is emotional", creating a positive emotional climate in which people can be their best. This resonates with many of the themes and specific items in our internal survey.

Goleman's leadership competencies[2]

Self-awareness

Emotional self-awareness: Leaders recognise their own feelings and how they affect their performance. They are attuned to their guiding values, candid and authentic.
Accurate self-assessment: Leaders understand their own strengths and limitations. They are willing to learn and welcome feedback.
Self-confidence: Leaders play to their strengths. They have presence and self-assurance.

Self-management

Self-control: Leaders can manage their own difficult emotions or impulses, staying calm and clear-headed under stress or crisis.
Transparency: Leaders are open to others, live by their values and show integrity. They openly admit their mistakes.
Adaptability: Leaders are able to juggle competing demands and are comfortable with ambiguity. They show flexibility in adapting to change.
Achievement: Leaders have high personal standards and drive for continuous improvement. They set clear, stretching and attainable goals.
Initiative: Leaders have a sense of their own ability to control their own destiny. They seize or create opportunities rather than simply waiting.
Optimism: Leaders bounce back from setbacks, seeing opportunity rather than threat. They see others positively and expect the best from them.

Social awareness

Empathy: Leaders are attuned to the emotions of an individual or a group. They listen well and see others' perspectives. They are able to get along with people from other cultures or backgrounds.
Organisational awareness: Leaders are politically astute, able to work well within social networks and power relationships. They are alert to the unspoken rules that create organisational culture.
Service: Leaders foster an emotional climate that keeps people on the right track with clients. They monitor client satisfaction closely and make themselves available when needed.

Relationship management

Inspiration: Leaders have a compelling vision or shared mission, which they are able to articulate in a way that inspires others to follow. They embody in themselves what they ask of others.

---

2 Goleman, D, Boyatzis, R and McKee, A, *The New Leaders* (Time Warner, 2003).

Influence: Leaders are persuasive and engaging. They know how to build buy-in from key people.
Developing others: Leaders show genuine interest in helping others develop. They understand others' goals, strengths and weaknesses, and give timely and constructive feedback.
Change catalyst: Leaders recognise the need for change, challenge the status quo and find ways to overcome barriers.
Conflict management: Leaders are able to draw out all parties, understand different perspectives and redirect energy towards a common ideal.
Teamwork and collaboration: Leaders generate an atmosphere of friendly collegiality. They are respectful, helpful and cooperative. They build team spirit and identity. They create relationships beyond mere work obligations.

If ever there was a misnomer, it is the term 'soft skills' applied to the ability to develop emotional intelligence and apply it in the workplace. Developing emotional intelligence and the presence of mind required to learn and apply those skills requires persistence and a real intent to learn. The model is straightforward and easy to grasp at an intellectual level. Introducing and embedding these skills is challenging, and some successful approaches are outlined in section 4 below.

2.2 Conversational skill

The working world in which we all operate is made up of a network of multiple conversations. It is through this medium that relationships get built, and work gets done. And this applies just as much to developing client relationships as it does to leading teams. The firms that can seriously improve the quality of conversations will have genuine competitive advantage. Clients are people too, and the skills that partners build in the context of being leaders of teams are just as valuable in developing client relationships.

There are a number of well-known approaches, variously called courageous conversations,[3] dialogue,[4] creating a thinking environment,[5] fierce conversations[6] and more. All of them require time and practice, but mastering these skills puts partners in a position consistently to have conversations that enable people to do their best thinking, build trust within which feedback can be given and received, and engage with others as equals, regardless of role and seniority. There are some key principles that link these approaches:[7]

- *listening,* with attention and without interruption – not simply waiting for one's turn or preparing a response;
- *respect for the other perspective,* including a real curiosity to understand, and a sense of equality at a fundamental level;

3 See www.hr.com/en/articles/thought-leaders-david-whyte-on-courageous-conversa_eaj1hqw2.html.
4 Isaacs, W, *Dialogue and the Art of Thinking Together,* (Doubleday, 1999); Dixon, N M, (1998) *Dialogue at Work: Making Talk Developmental for People and Organizations,* (Lemos & Crane, 1998).
5 Kline, N, *Time to Think,* (Cassell Illustrated 1999).
6 Scott, S, *Fierce Conversations,* (Piatkus, 2002).
7 Isaacs, W (see above).

- *suspending opinion*, and the assumptions that lie behind it, allowing time to consider one's own perspective critically; being prepared to show our thinking in a way that lets others see and understand it;
- *speaking your truth* based on what needs to be said.

Imagine these principles applied to an appraisal conversation, or an important decision that needs to be made as a group. In practical terms, we can devise workshops to teach skills related to giving feedback, having difficult conversations, coaching and mentoring, and these are useful because they give people frameworks for planning or managing a conversation, and a space to rehearse and practice. But conversations, whether in or outside of work, really come to life when we connect with one or more of these principles at a deeper level.

3. Why is this difficult?

Research into personality type shows significant differences between the average lawyer personality and that of other professionals and managers.[8] These differences may be instrumental in making them great lawyers, but their personal style does not always make them natural leaders, particularly when you take into account the kind of qualities and behaviours that the new generation of lawyers values most. In particular, there is a tendency to score lower on emotional stability (staying steady in the face of pressure) and emotional sensitivity or warmth (including social sensitivity, tact and perceptiveness). Looking at potential 'de-railers', the lawyer population as a whole scores relatively highly on the scales that measure qualities which, particularly under pressure, cause people to distance themselves from others. These scales describe people who are typically quite tense, sceptical, risk-averse, reserved and autonomous.

As one partner said to me:

The lawyer personality is against you. It's hard to relax when you're all about finding and fixing problems. It's tense and stressful and you're walking on eggshells, so sometimes you're not willing to take time because you're just trying to get through the day.

Psychometric tests (such as Hogan HPI and HDS) offered as part of coaching or development programmes can be very helpful to lawyers to understand how to work on improving the way they interact with others, and to develop emotional intelligence and skill.

A number of lawyers have pointed out to me that lawyer training tends to exacerbate the tendency to value logic and analysis over other qualities. To quote Ali Hall, a US ex-lawyer, now an Associate Fellow at the University of Oxford: "The training at law school makes you prize and value logic, analytical and critical thinking above all else. There is no reward for empathy and compassion. You have the feeling side beaten out of you – it's not measured or prized." It's important to emphasise that when we are asking lawyers to develop their emotional skills, we are not devaluing the intellectual skills they already have in abundance.

---

8 See www.peterberry.com.au/files/hogan_white_papers/understanding_lawyers_why_we_do.pdf.

Most lawyers have not had the benefit of the kind of incremental learning of management skills that most corporates take for granted. Legitimacy for lawyers lies in legal and client expertise, not in management expertise, which is sometimes treated with suspicion or disdain. For this reason skills development for lawyers needs to be genuinely embedded in their practice and explicitly linked to the real-life context.

The good news is that there are tried and tested ways of designing development programmes that minimise the effect of lawyers' natural scepticism, and maximise the effect of their drive to perform well and to learn from other professionals and from each other.

4. Designing development programmes that work

Designing the right programme for your partners in your firm is an art, not a science. But there are some principles that will help you. There are three levels we need to think about in making sure that learning on workshops or programmes gets transferred into action in the real world of work:

- the individual;
- the programme design;
- the working environment.

4.1 The individual

Probably the most important, and the most intractable of the three. We all know the partners who sign up first for every learning opportunity, as well as those who have no belief in the potential of 'off-the-job' learning to benefit them, their clients or their practice. Carol Dweck[9] writes about people having a 'fixed' or a 'growth' mindset. Do they want to be proved right, or do they seek out experiences that will stretch them, but at which they might fail? Developing a growth mindset as a cultural norm can take time. As well as being willing to take a risk and learn something new, partners need to believe that this effort will be worth their while, and that the culture of the firm and the individual climate of groups of partners within it will support the change they are trying to make. Fortunately we can manage the design of the programme in a way that encourages partners to be willing participants. First of all, it is important to engage with partners upfront to make sure that we are basing our programme design on their reality, not ours.

(a) Do the research

Don't assume that you know what potential participants on your programme or workshop think – ask them. By spending time upfront having a structured conversation with as many of your participants as possible, before you design the programme, you achieve three things. You give yourself the best chance of designing a programme that will resonate with people. You start to build the relationship with your audience, so that they arrive in a positive frame of mind. And when they arrive on the programme, by showing them how you have built in their real concerns, you

9 Deck, C S, *Mindset* (Ballantine Books, 2008).

engage them as full participants in the programme. In particular, asking people to describe their challenges in the area or topic you are working on will give you real-life examples to base the workshop on.

4.2 The programme design

(a) Link development to strategy and values

One of the keys to developing people in organisations is aligning personal values to organisational values. There has to be an overlap, something that an individual can genuinely develop in themselves which also resonates with where the firm wants to go. That is why buying in a 'sheep dip' programme or product rarely works. Start with what is aspirational in your strategy or your values. Where's the real stretch for the firm? What do you need partners to be doing differently? In the context of retaining talent, what does the talent have to say? Gathering 360 feedback for partners can be a great way for individual partners to work out what they are doing well, and what people are noticing about them that they may not be noticing themselves. Pulling out themes from 360 can give some clear pointers for where partners in the firm might need some help to improve their skills; especially so if you design 360 specifically around your strategy – what behaviours do you need from partners, to support your strategy?

(b) Design solutions to real problems

Before you start to design a learning or development intervention, always ask the question, What problem are we trying to solve here? This keeps learning closely aligned to strategy, makes it focused and means you have a reasonable chance of measuring success over time. Lawyers respond to reason; they are not by nature particularly attracted to personal development for its own sake; nor do they have much disposable time. At an individual level, this applies to many sorts of 'just in time' training: offering feedback skills to partners ahead of the annual appraisal process, or interviewing skills for the graduate recruitment round or for partners involved in lateral hiring. This sort of skill development can be positioned as something that will help partners solve a problem they recognise: getting clear performance messages across; helping lawyers improve performance and progress; hiring the right talent. On a larger scale, as we will see in the case study below, if the desire is to shift the mindset of a significant proportion of the partnership, for example to be more ambitious or more collaborative, it is important to ensure that every element of a programme is clearly aligned to that aim. The pressure on time in particular means partners need to be really clear at every point in a programme why they are doing this, what is the purpose, how does it link to the real challenges they face in developing their practice, or in building and maintaining teams.

(c) Get senior sponsorship, with wide engagement

The best results are always seen when the managing partner or CEO not only

---

10 Brown, J, *The World Café: Shaping our Futures through Conversations that Matter*, (Berrett-Koehler, 2005).

supports but actively drives leadership development in a firm. This sponsorship means that developing partners to be leaders is embedded in strategy, and that the leader embodies in himself or herself the value of development and learning. Often the in-house teams responsible for learning and development have to operate without this sponsorship and there are many ways to do this, by engaging with individuals or groups of partners who have an interest in development and building incrementally from there. Working with partners in transition, newly promoted partners or new leaders can provide a starting point, which can grow in influence as more partners become engaged in the process. I have found however that there is a limit to this sort of growth, and a point comes after which unless the managing partner or CEO is fully engaged, the change process is halted or dissipates.

In addition, try to engage partners in the activity of designing and delivering skills and leadership development. Professionals learn most willingly from other professionals like themselves, so bring in senior partners to sense-check design and content, to front the programme, bring their experience to complement external and internal subject experts, and to lead discussion. The added benefit of this is that senior sponsors learn a huge amount about themselves and about their own leadership, because they are forced to reflect. It helps to select partner sponsors who are highly credible and successful in the business, especially if they are known to be tough sceptics.

(d) Space to think; conversations that matter[10]

Time is the one thing partners do not have enough of. Helping them learn and change involves creating a space for them to think afresh, and together, on questions that matter to them. Most often that means people generate the questions themselves, either individually or as a group; or you can devise relevant questions for discussion from the research conversations, if you made that part of your design process. Making it real in this way, and ensuring you design in some real action planning time and accountability helps people focus on what matters, and take action afterwards.

(e) Keep it practical

I have found it helps to keep a strong business focus even when working on personal development topics. Questions that are always at the forefront of lawyers' minds include, Why are we doing this? How will it help me build my practice and be successful? These concerns need to be met if partners are to engage with skills that may be outside their comfort zone or experience. Creating trust is essential for learning and we need to do this by recognising the real-life context of lawyers' working world. Introduce just enough theoretical frameworks to prompt thinking and to develop a common language, but make sure it is always clear how exactly they relate to legal practice. It needs to work for the sceptics. A mix of external or internal subject experts with experienced partners to lend credibility to the training faculty works well. Get lawyers working together on real-life problems early in the session. Nobody likes the idea of role play, but you need to get partners practising new behaviours or conversations.

(f) *Make it stick*

Making learning stick is all about what happens before and after the programme. Here are some ways to help partners develop the skills they have learnt and make them their own:

- *Pre-work:* Helping people get into a mindset to learn. Depending on the scale of the programme, this can be anything from sending a relevant article to read ahead of the programme, to offering 360 feedback, psychometric assessments and coaching to help partners identify the areas where they want to improve.
- *Real work:* Building in real opportunities to put learning into practice, and setting the expectation that partners will report back on progress. This can often best be done in a group setting. A small group of partners who have attended a workshop or programme can agree to meet to share experience and offer peer coaching (similar to action learning). Skills development is always most effective when connected with a real challenge – whether that's the career transition of a new partner, or a business challenge such as building a practice.
- *Reflection:* There is a range of techniques for helping partners to track their learning, such as journaling or blogging. Making a clear written commitment to what they intend to change or do differently helps to cement intention. Design a simple form of development plan for partners to refer to or discuss with their mentor or coach.
- *Coaching and mentoring:* For long-term sustainable change, high-quality coaching or mentoring is essential.
- *Maintaining networks:* Find ways to help partners who have learnt or developed together to stay in touch, either virtually or by reconvening as a group, or in pairs.

4.3 The working environment

However you design a skills development programme, it needs to be supported by the organisational culture. Cultural change is a topic that goes beyond the subject of this chapter, but we need to work realistically within the culture that we have, or commit to change it.

(a) *What do we reward?*

The organisational culture will strongly affect what can be achieved through skills development of partners. If you design a great programme but the partners believe that they are not recognised for demonstrating great leadership skills, it will be difficult to engage them, and cynicism will spread.

(b) *Peer and management support*

Partners, like anyone else, need to feel that what they have learnt will be supported by others in the workplace, and that they are not a lone voice. This means that partners in management roles need to be clearly aligned with the skills and attributes we are asking all of our partners to develop and demonstrate. The importance of management support is generally thought to be paramount in embedding learning and change, and yet in law firms the nature of partnership is such that there is little or no 'line management' link as we would commonly find in other sectors. This leaves the individual partner in a hard place when trying to change or improve their leadership skills. Peer support becomes more important, and ensuring that partners have a sense of others who understand and support the changes he or she is trying to make is key. This can be helped by building in support for networks or buddying.

5. Hogan Lovells: a continuing case study

This section is intended to show how some of these principles have worked in practice at global law firm Hogan Lovells. The firm has invested significant effort at the most senior levels in developing leadership capability distributed across the partnership. This is a continuing journey, with much learning along the way, and no doubt more to come. Law firms are unlike corporate entities in that any change has to be adopted 'partner by partner'. It is not possible just to roll out a change programme wholesale and expect it to stick. And developing partners as leaders is very much part of a cultural and mindset change.

In the six years since the creation of Hogan Lovells we have built a foundation of partner development intended to support the firm's vision and strategy. Where we started, and the route we took, was a reflection of the particular moment in time of the two merged firms. Every firm will have a different starting point, and it is important to make a detailed assessment of the situation of the particular firm before starting to design development programmes.

5.1 Where we started from

In May 2010, Washington-headquartered Hogan & Hartson, and London-headquartered Lovells combined to become the global firm Hogan Lovells. The two firms had very different histories of developing partners' leadership skills. One firm had a comprehensive but over-bureaucratic mentoring programme designed to ensure all lawyers had access to a partner mentor. The other had a strong suite of development programmes for new partners, but nothing to develop the leadership skills of partners as a whole. The agreed approach during and immediately after the merger was to take the best of each firm in terms of processes, functions and business services, and where possible to create a new 'best' for the new firm. This gave us a unique opportunity to start with a clean slate and design development programmes afresh, uniquely tailored for our new firm.

(a) Development for integration

We began with one of the most visible and sensitive processes in any firm: the advancement of lawyers to partnership, and the transition of new partners into their roles in a way that fosters success. It was important to ensure that we quickly developed a single process that worked for the whole firm, to reflect the 'one Hogan Lovells' ethos. It was obvious that by making this process and the development programmes that support it global, we would be making a strong contribution to the integration of the two firms, at the critical level of individual relationships. We designed three programmes to develop the skills of partners and aspiring partners: one about 18 months before potential promotion to partnership, one for new partners immediately after promotion, and a third about 18 months after promotion.

Four factors are key to the success of these programmes:

- Every programme is a global programme, bringing together people from across geographies and practices. This was an important factor in integration, and is always significant in creating strong networks which support collaboration and generate work. Culturally, it enables people to build trust and to develop a fuller understanding of the whole firm's capabilities. Within each programme, we design all the sessions to ensure maximum mixing of participants through various exercises, to increase these connections.
- Before we design each programme we try to speak with all of the participants or a cross-section of them, together with other stakeholders, to ensure we are designing a programme that reflects the felt reality of participants. This ensures a high level of engagement.
- We have a large number of experienced partners involved as sponsors, sounding boards and contributors to each programme. The visible support of senior partners is important for the credibility of the programme. It also amplifies the personal and business connections which are such an important side product of development programmes. Finally, it exposes a range of senior partners to development activities that are not otherwise available to them. Partners learn by working with the people development team, developing their own skills and knowledge along the way.
- We continually improve and update each programme. This means that as the firm evolves, the programmes are constantly evolving too to reflect changes in the business and ensure we are always designing solutions to the next problem.

(b) Top team leadership

In July 2014, a change of CEO brought a fresh focus on developing partners as leaders. A new, leaner, senior team was formed and spent time developing their own understanding and practice of leadership. Senior engagement in leadership development created a step change in the firm's approach to partners' leadership behaviours and skills. A clearly articulated vision, strategy and statement of leadership behaviours resulted. This has formed the bedrock for all subsequent development activities.

It was important that the leadership behaviours were a product of the management team itself, rather than an imposed generic leadership framework. They are framed in language that partners understand and can relate to, not in 'management speak'. This does not mean to say that the result is an arbitrary list. On the contrary, it resonates with many established models and frameworks of leadership attributes, but it was important that it was generated from within the firm and is therefore strongly held as a set of core values.

Since then we have gone on to develop a framework for the firm which incorporates both the leadership behaviours, and the activities for which partners are accountable ('What we do' and 'How we act').

(c) ***Distributed leadership***

Our next challenge was to create a cadre of partners who would become 'culture carriers', bringing these behaviours to life within the partnership, becoming role models for other partners, and inspiring and empowering their teams. With the active support and involvement of our CEO and other senior partners, we have developed a leadership programme for a selected group of experienced partners. The aim was to put around 10% of the partnership through this programme, focusing on partners personally selected by the CEO and the senior team as having the potential to create significant change through their leadership within each of their particular business contexts. As a result we are now working with a cohort of around 80 partners globally to continue to support their leadership efforts. All of the senior team, including the CEO, have attended the programme themselves, alongside other partners, creating an atmosphere of exchange and dialogue across generations of partners. Most recently, the whole cohort met for a day, ahead of our global partner conference, to deepen their skills, refresh their network, and prepare to take a leading role in the business of the conference.

The programme, called *Redefining Leadership*, focuses around two residential modules designed by Oxford Said Business School, working closely with our own people development team, and with the active sponsorship of the senior partner team. Participants each identify a real leadership challenge, centred on their practice, and select a senior mentor to act as 'thinking partner'. They are immersed in a range of leadership learning experiences which have proved transformational in many cases. The content focuses on deep learning for each partner about his or her own authentic leadership style, how to develop that, how to articulate it and how to step up as leaders within their own teams. They have individual coaching during and after the programme, with the benefit of 360-degree feedback and psychometrics. Content of the programme itself draws on the Oxford faculty and focuses on developing emotional intelligence, narrative leadership, and developing awareness of individual strengths and weaknesses in leadership style.

Partners are of course individuals and they take different elements of the programme to heart. These are just a few examples of how partners have taken the learning back to their teams and applied it:

- A partner in our Miami office has established Mindfulness workshops and a website for all employees in the office.
- One of our Denver partners engaged associates in his vision of what the value of providing feedback was and how it might benefit them. As a result, two of his associates have initiated workshops on this topic, empowering associates to seek and get quality feedback.
- A partner in our Paris office actively engages in mentoring female talent, publishing articles on gender diversity and speaking publicly on this issue.

(d) ***What we've learnt***

This is a major change programme and we are just at the beginning of our journey. In any firm, developing leadership skills to engage and retain talent cannot just be in the territory of the HR or learning team; it has to be owned by the partnership, and made real, one partner and one conversation at a time.

CEO Steve Immelt said:

Our way forward can only happen if we have distributed leadership – people across the business who understand the firm's direction and feel empowered to lead. This program is about giving people the tools and the real experience to step up as leaders. Attending the program I certainly learned some things about myself – what to keep and what to let go of, and what enables me to bring the best of myself to my role.

It has become clear to me that developing leadership for partners has three interlocking components, and these need to be skilfully balanced:

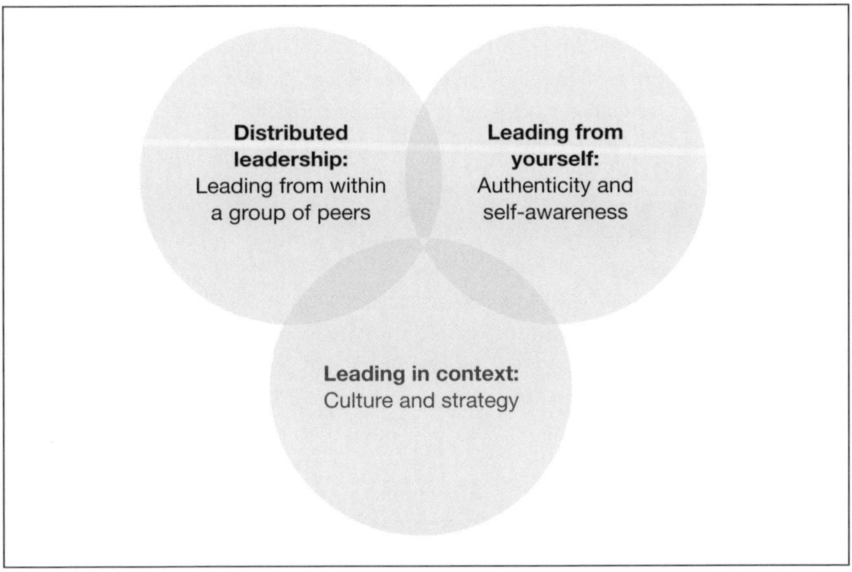

'Distributed leadership' in a law firm means stepping up into a lead role from within a group of peers and leading from within that group. This carries its own challenges. 'Leading from within yourself' means developing self-awareness and skill to lead others in a way that is authentic and therefore credible. 'Leading in context' means aligning to the firm's strategy and taking account of the individual firm's culture and context. Leadership skills in partners have to be developed in all three circles simultaneously.

6. Final thoughts

Leadership skills are not a technique. They are a way of being with other people. And the way you are with people matters to them, as we saw in the survey described at the beginning of this chapter. By paying attention to the quality of relationships, partners become enablers, not controllers. Experience of partners' most frequent default style of leadership is often of the pace-setting, lead by example, 'come with me' sort. This works well up to a point, inspiring people to work incredibly hard for long hours. But it does not produce the kind of leadership that transforms relationships and organisations. And real transformation is what is needed in law firms now and will be needed more urgently in the coming years of increasing globalisation, complexity, generational change and technological innovation. For me it has been an inspiring experience to work with talented and successful partners who really want to make this transformation, and who are prepared to risk trying new ways of being and behaving. The potential rewards, for firms and for individuals, are immense.

Coaching lawyers through change

Antonin Besse
Besse Executive Coaching and Training

My 22 years as a partner with a magic circle firm, and my experience as a coach, have taught me a fair bit about what works well and what does not work in law firms. I have noticed in particular how the power of coaching, especially around the subjects discussed in this chapter, can catalyse motivation and performance at the individual level and, where it is used systematically as a tool in recruiting, developing and retaining legal talent, can lead to real cultural and behavioural change in a firm.

1. Creating the environment for successful development

1.1 What characterises lawyers?

Lawyers enjoy autonomy to a greater degree than most other professions, and they are jealous of it. Autonomy is a great source of drive, creativity and empowerment, so the challenge for management in law firms is to nurture it while at the same time ensuring structure, method, collaboration and discipline. All this in a population which considers free agency, and being first among equals, to be an essential part of their identity.

1.2 Carrots, sticks and coaching

The downside to autonomy is that it can erect strong barriers to behavioural change, financial discipline and effective, joined-up teamwork across departments and offices. The main factors that incentivise lawyers to adopt behaviours which contribute to the greater good of the firm are leadership, trust, reward and threat. Every law firm will rely on a mix of these to keep the partnership cohesive and profitable. That being said, coaching is also an effective way of motivating and managing legal talent: it creates choice and autonomy, and channels that autonomy towards a purpose. It can also encourage and develop key energising behaviours.

1.3 Energising behaviours

Of the many behaviours and mindsets that can make law firms more attractive working environments as well as more effective businesses, I have suggested a 'top ten' below. Several firms I know have successfully brought about some of these in parts of the organisation. The challenge is to ensure that these become universal and integral to a firm's DNA and culture:

- listening and communicating;
- regular feedback to and from clients and colleagues;

- transparency and inclusiveness;
- planning, setting goals and visualising the future;
- walking a mile in another's shoes;
- cooperation and collegiality;
- autonomy and entrepreneurialism;
- accountability;
- management and leadership training;
- role modelling.

We will be looking at these topics in more detail in the context of coaching lawyers through change. First, let us examine what those changes look like.

2. Types of change in a lawyer's career

2.1 Types of change and their challenges

(a) *The future mindset*

As surely as death and taxes, a lawyer will face several seniority transitions throughout his or her career. A key ingredient in these transitions is forging a 'future mindset', that is, understanding and thinking oneself into the new role. Many lawyers assume that seniority transitions are just an extension of their existing roles, and the gradual, linear nature of many transitions will feed that illusion. So when asked how they see themselves a few years into the new role, most lawyers will describe the future in terms of what they do already. The role of a good coach is to help the client really understand, visualise and 'live' the new role so that he or she can mentally plan and grow into it proactively over a period of time. This is dealt with in more detail later in the chapter.

(b) *Changing practice areas and retooling*

As the markets evolve and law firms seek to meet strategic goals, every lawyer will almost inevitably be called upon to specialise in a different practice area or change their practice mix at least once, if not several times, in their career. The challenges here are acquiring new skills, a new track record and new clients. This can amount to a radical reinvention of one's professional identity. Many of the coaching issues here involve confidence, building internal and external support and profile raising. They also involve learning how to leverage existing skills, support and client networks to 'grow' into the new practice area. It is also partly about developing a growth mindset, and understanding how learning and experimentation can be a source of enthusiasm and motivation.

(c) *Moving offices*

The important issue here is often the cultural and environmental disruption that comes with moving offices within a firm. The assumption is often made that the culture, environment, values, ways of doing things and politics of another office will largely replicate that of the previous office, particularly in the case of moves from the head office to a regional office or a local office abroad. This is often a very basic misconception, and can lead to a misguided attempt to replicate (and even impose on others) the culture and methods of the previous office. More often than not, this will cause resentment on both sides (ie, on the part of the new arrival and colleagues in the host office), and lead to the new arrival becoming isolated. Coaching can help the client explore the new environment, understand his or her place in it (and particularly how others perceive them), build a local support network and act their way into their new role and practice.

(d) ***Career breaks***

Returns from career breaks can often generate doubts and internal conflicts about work–life balance, a feeling that one is not competing on a level playing field and issues around flexible working. Coaching for confidence, learning to sell oneself effectively, building a personal brand and role modelling are among the topics that come up most frequently in this context.

(e) ***Moving firms***

The major issues here are around understanding and adapting to the culture, values and methods of the new environment, building internal support and preserving and developing a book of business. For example, there is potentially a huge change in terms of cooperation, not to mention other areas, when moving from a lockstep to an 'eat what you kill' environment. This may not suit someone who values collegiality above all things, but may well suit those with a strong taste for autonomy, politics and an entrepreneurial drive. The converse is true as well: moving from a highly autonomous and entrepreneurial environment to a lockstep firm can cause cultural problems and behavioural clashes. Coaching can help clients explore, before making the decision to move, what their strengths, values and personal drivers are and whether the new environment will be a good fit for these. It will also enable clients to assess the impact that the move will have on work–life balance. The ability to weigh these factors effectively will often get lost in the sturm, drang and excitement of a potential move, not least its financial attractions. Post move, coaching can (as in the case of the move to a new office, discussed above) help clients explore the new environment, understand their place in it (and particularly how others perceive them), build a local support network and act their way into their new role and practice.

(f) ***Integrating new teams and mergers***

The main challenges of integrating laterally hired teams or integrating them post merger is fostering trust and collaboration, and avoiding tribalism. After the initial enthusiasm, resentment may build. This might be, for example, because of the perception that special deals have been done, or because of the new team's alien culture and methods, which may cut across conventions in the host firm. Political tensions and rivalries develop fast in those circumstances, and can undo the synergies and other benefits of the new hire or merger. Strong leadership and clear direction is essential in those circumstances, and team coaching can help considerably.

2.2 The stages in a lawyer's career

(a) *The four-dimensional lawyer*

First, I would like to propose my model for a lawyer's career development. The model has four dimensions:

- the Thinker (the black letter lawyer, analyser and creative solution-finder);
- the Doer (the solution implementer, deal doer, negotiator and contentious lawyer);
- the Developer (the business getter and relationship builder); and
- the Supporter (the people developer, leader and team builder).

How developed each of these dimensions are will, of course, vary according to natural ability. However, the environment and culture in which lawyers evolve play a big role in supporting development in these four dimensions. In addition, there are contemporary evolutions in attitudes that also affect things: for example, the expectations of Gen Y entering the profession today are changing. They aspire to become Doers and Developers earlier in their careers and do not necessarily aspire to partnership. Work–life balance and learning are their priorities.

The following discussion focuses on the typical career path of a lawyer in a large international firm, although it can be transposed to a large extent to other types of firm as well as in-house counsel.

(b) *The trainee and junior lawyer*

In terms of development goals, a good trainee and junior lawyer is expected to show more thinking and doing skills, but will also be expected to demonstrate the potential to become a Developer and Supporter.

Junior associates transitioning to senior associate status are often ignorant of, and unprepared for, the Developer and Supporter roles. Coaching can help considerably here. The key coachable skill is communicating effectively. Learning to listen, conduct critical conversations and client networking conversations, delegate well and take and give regular feedback are all key communication skills that underpin effective Developer and Supporter roles.

(c) *Senior associates and junior partners*

Another important characteristic of a lawyer's development into senior associateship and through to partnership is the ability to reach out, engage proactively with others both inside and outside the firm and think ahead, both strategically and tactically. A lawyer will start his or her career receiving instructions, and be expected to execute them well. Their world at this stage is a small one: it generally consists of their immediate colleagues, particularly the senior associate(s) and partner(s) who give them most of their work. These will form their professional sphere. Their contemporaries will be their principal support network. As a lawyer progresses in seniority, she or he will need to expand their world-view by learning to reach and out and develop direct client contacts as well as political and professional support networks within the firm beyond their immediate teams. The time horizon of their world-view will also need to broaden considerably: they will need to fix goals and visualise where they want to be and the role they want to play increasingly far ahead, and plan their actions accordingly by deciding the professional development actions that they will need to take, the external and internal brand that they will want to build, and the alliances that they will need to form to those ends. That will require understanding one's potential and place in the firm and in the market, how one is perceived by colleagues, the resources that one can leverage, and an ability and willingness to reach out to people, take control of one's career and make things happen. A law firm, with the degree of autonomy that it allows, is a great place for those things to happen. But often lawyers fail to grasp what they need to understand and do to make them happen. This is why good coaching is so essential. It can raise awareness about potential, widen horizons and facilitate goal setting, which are the key elements to progress.

(d) A word from the sponsor

An additional crucial element in the transition from senior associate to partner in particular (but also in the transition from fixed share or local partner to equity) is the need for a strong, politically connected sponsor to back the candidacy. Senior associates are often ignorant of this dimension. While a good coach should not tell, a discussion of support, network building and profile raising in preparation for the transition may well bring this issue to the table.

(e) Partnership, post honeymoon

As the junior partner settles into the new role, things can become lonely. The dynamics of support start to change, as the partner becomes his or her sponsor's competitor, and the need to develop independent client relationships becomes greater. In addition, the need to develop and nurture one's own team and raise one's profile in the market become stark realities. These are factors that those with ambition and a growth mindset find energising, but for some they may pose a challenge, particularly in terms of confidence. And as one progresses as a partner, it can become more difficult to talk openly to other partners for fear of exposing vulnerability. In those circumstances, the safe environment for open discussion offered by coaching can prove extremely valuable. Partners can also use coaching to decide what new or substitute support they can build to replace their sponsor, and formulate a plan, and the means to achieve it.

(f) Ten years a partner

Ten years in, things might be less lonely, but existential issues can spoil the fun. At this stage, questions around 'What next?' might arise, and there may be a need to renew one's energy by formulating a new plan and purpose. Overlaying all this, some may find themselves in the grip of the tensions of a mid-life crisis. All this can lead to drift, loss of confidence, and despondency. At this stage, the issues referred to earlier about not feeling able to open up to one's fellow partners for fear of admitting vulnerability come very much to the fore. Once again, the safe environment for discussion afforded by coaching, together with the opportunity of reassessing one's place in the partnership, and one's professional goals, make coaching invaluable for mid-career partners.

(g) *Leadership and management*

To misquote Shakespeare's *Twelfth Night*, in law firms some are born leaders, some achieve positions of management, and some have leadership and management thrust upon them. Lawyers are not natural managers, and many lack leadership skills. And yet the majority of law firms put partners into leadership and management positions without giving them any formal training. Those who assume those positions are often rainmakers with proven Doer and Developer skills, but less well developed Supporter skills. However this is changing as more firms offer their leaders and managers leadership training, coupled with coaching.

One of the issues with partner managers in law firms is that they are seen as firsts among equals, and sometimes afforded little respect for their management roles. In times of change or crisis they have to implement difficult decisions involving fellow partners and often take a lot of heavy flak from others who cannot get their way. It is not a job for the fainthearted.

One area where partners often fall down as leaders is clarity of strategy, transparency and communication. Lawyers, like most of us, want to know what plans our leaders have both for us and to make the team, department or firm great. Very often, partner managers are too preoccupied with how they are going to meet their targets or their own futures, to formulate, communicate and implement bold strategies. What ideas they do have are often poorly communicated, or not at all, with the result that trust drains away at both partner and associate level, as everyone feels rudderless and undervalued. In those circumstances, coaching can be extremely useful to help clarify goals and strategy, raise awareness about others' perceptions and needs, and encourage good communication and leadership behaviour.

The following examples illustrate both sides of this type of behaviour.

The first involves a practice head in a local office of a large firm. The profitability of the office had fallen considerably below the firm average and the practice in question was struggling to maintain market share. The practice leader was a poor communicator and mistrustful of others. If he had a vision and strategy, he never communicated it and failed to engage with anyone other than his protégés. Associate morale was low principally because of lack of regular feedback about performance and ignorance about strategy and goals. Enthusiasm and buy-in were non-existent. Apprehension and rumours about redundancies were rife. Associates would stay cloistered in their offices, behind closed doors. Several partners and associates left. When laterals were brought in with their teams, senior associates became resentful. This ultimately led to further defections. No leadership training or coaching was ever offered to the practice head or any members of his group.

The second example involves a specialist group practice head in a large firm which had suffered from personality clashes and attrition in the past. The firm recently introduced a leadership training and support programme for its group leaders. The practice head was offered coaching as part of the programme support and used it to work on leadership and communication skills. She developed clear goals for where she wanted to take the group in the following three years and a strategy for getting there. She formulated the goals and strategy (which, incidentally, involved plans to bring in a lateral hire) in consultation with the partners and the senior associates in her team, listening to and taking their thinking into account, and making it clear to all the associates that their efforts were integral to the group's success. As a result, her team became stakeholders in the group's future and she succeeded in creating real enthusiasm and buy-in for her vision. Moreover, thanks to the practice head's transparency and communication, the senior associates understood that bringing in a lateral was integral to the group's future financial and reputational success, and would therefore contribute to the business case for their partnership chances rather than blocking their career progression.

(h) *Pre-retirement*

Partnerships, particularly those operating in the United Kingdom as opposed to the United States or continental European models, tend to encourage retirement earlier than in other professions, the principal reason being to ensure that younger partners are afforded access to, and a fair share of, equity in their most productive years. This leaves a generation of partners in their mid-fifties contemplating what they are going to do next. This is unsettling for many who, having devoted several decades to the law, have very little idea of what to do next, or how to go about it. This can create an 'elephants' graveyard' of partners who are despondent or hang on to their positions and clients.

Pre-retirement coaching programmes, which some firms are adopting, help dissipate the fear surrounding the idea of loss of status and identity and support partners in starting to think beyond the anxiety of retirement itself to the possibilities that lie beyond. Formulating plans and beginning to road test them while still in work can help build confidence and enthusiasm about moving on. This will help ease client handovers and possibly accelerate retirement for those who are simply hanging on for fear of letting go, and also boost morale in teams whose leaders are retiring. That can only be good for firms, and retiring partners, alike.

Many of the techniques for successful pre-retirement coaching are common to most types of transition and are discussed in Section3 below. However, there are a number of considerations which are fairly specific to this situation. One of them is expectation management: senior retiring partners often have unrealistic expectations and aspirations about how their experience and former status will be perceived by the outside world. So if a coach can help the retiring client discover and develop a sense of what really matters to them, as well as patience, resilience and humility, that will help considerably. Other relevant topics in this context may revolve around the confidence to experiment, the ability to listen, learn, let go, visualise possibilities, develop a personal narrative or 'brand' and motivation. And there may well be discussions around priorities, status, identity, self-worth, family, financial issues, using existing support and business networks, building new ones and identifying the community that will replace the working environment that is being left behind.

3. Preparing a lawyer for successful change

In the third and final part of this chapter, we will look at how coaching can prepare lawyers for, and accompany them through, successful change. It is presented as a coaching plan with methods and tools that can be adapted to many of the issues which lawyers may face in this context. The plan, illustrated below in Figure 1, starts from the centre with self-discovery before moving out in concentric circles to an understanding of others and their perceptions, then an appreciation of the wider context and environment, and finally a shift into the future with the formulation of goals and plans for a successful transition.

Figure 1: Knowing yourself

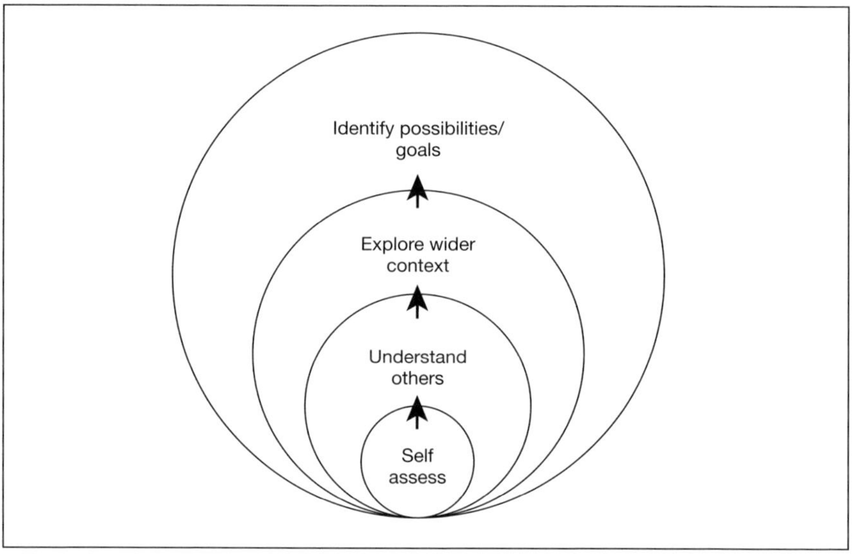

3.1 Visiting the oracle

In ancient Greece, those visiting Delphi in the hope of obtaining guidance on the future would be met by the maxim γνῶθι σεαυτόν (know thyself), inscribed in the forecourt of the Temple of Apollo. This maxim, like the pronouncements of the oracle, meant different things to different people. One interpretation might be that it pays to know yourself before looking for answers elsewhere, as many of those answers will come through self-awareness. One of coaching's primary aims is to raise self-awareness and as it does so it creates choice, which in turn builds confidence and autonomy. Those are the essential steps in embarking on any journey. So the first step in our coaching plan might be to turn to some self-awareness-raising tools which will help build a picture of how the client sees themselves, how they deal and engage with others and how others see and engage with them.

3.2 Self-assessment

Before starting a coaching assignment I will often ask the client to do some self-reflection 'homework'. It might sometimes be helpful to start with a strength survey. I've used Realise2 (www.cappeu.com/R2StrengthsProfiler), Gallup StrengthsFinder (https://www.gallupstrengthscenter.com/) and Via (https://www.viacharacter.org/www/Character-Strengths-Survey). I also ask the client to do the following:

- Ask colleagues, friends and family to describe them in a few words or to give them an example of when they saw them at their best.
- Write about their three proudest moments.
- Prepare a personal statement or sales pitch describing their key strengths (for the new role, for example) in about 200 words.

This preparation will enable the coaching client to 'hit the ground running' from the first coaching session. It is a particularly useful way of preparing for coaching around confidence, resilience and profile-building. These issues will often come up in transition coaching.

3.3 Anchors and drivers

A useful aspect of any self-assessment exercise in a change context is to build an understanding of the client's anchors and drivers. There are several tools available to explore these, including Schein's Career Anchors (https://www.careeranchorsonline.com/SCA/startPage.do). This aims to identify the one thing (among the eight Career Anchors distilled out of longitudinal research conducted by MIT Professor Edgar Schein with Ivy League graduates over 40 years) that you would not give up if you had to make a series of tough choices about your career. I also find David Rock's SCARF model helpful. This was developed out of neuroscience studies on social needs. SCARF stands for Status, Certainty, Autonomy, Relatedness and Fairness. These models can help raise a client's awareness about what really matters to them in a work context. It will help them to gain a perspective on the energising and energy-draining factors in their current environment, and the factors that will matter in any post-transition environment.

3.4 Readiness for change

An important self-awareness issue to be explored in any transition coaching is the client's readiness for change. Prochaska's Stages of Change model may be useful here. The model divides the change process into five stages. It is applicable to many types of change, including career transitions as well as habit or behavioural change. It is helpful for the client (and the coach) to understand that these stages exist and to identify the stage at which the client finds themselves. The client may then feel more comfortable if, for example, they feel any doubts about the change or do not yet consider themselves ready to move on. The stages are as follows:

- Pre-contemplation, in which the client may not have considered change. The coach can help raise awareness by asking questions around how things might improve, and the implications to the client of not changing.
- Contemplation, in which the client may have seen the need for change, but remains ambivalent about it. The coaching can help explore that ambivalence and possibly the reasons behind it.

- Preparation, in which the client has made the decision to change but is still exploring whether he or she wants the change and is still thinking about the way forward.
- Action, in which steps are being taken to make the change. Here the coaching can support the planning and goal-setting process and monitor results.
- Relapse to a previous stage, which may occur, in which case the coach can reassure the client that this is normal.
- Maintenance, in which the action towards change or changed behaviour is maintained for a sustained period.
- Termination, at which point the change has taken place or the modified behaviour has permanently taken hold.

3.5 Walking in another's shoes

(a) Understanding others

Having coached the client around the question, What do I know about myself?, the next stage in the coaching plan for supporting our lawyer client through change is to look at the question, How do I interact with people and my work environment? We will start with feedback and 360-degree reviews before looking at tools and techniques for exploring and demystifying interpersonal perceptions.

(b) Feedback and 360 reviews

I also find it helpful, before embarking on a coaching assignment involving personal development with a view to career progression, to conduct a bespoke feedback exercise by interviewing colleagues of the coaching client at various seniority levels. These interviews can be conducted in person or by phone, will generally last about 20 to 30 minutes, and will deal with three questions:

- What is X doing well?
- What might X do more of?
- What might X do less of?

I contract with the interviewee on confidentiality by stating that what I am told will not be fed back on an attributed basis, but will form the basis of an anonymised report which I will prepare using my own words, drawing on the results of the other interviews, and that the report will be delivered to the client and nobody else. I also contract with the client and the firm that neither the report, nor the conversations on which it is based, will be disclosed to the firm or other third parties without the client's consent. The report can be debriefed alongside the latest annual appraisals, recent 360-degree survey and/or assessment centre results if available, and the discussions from the three-way session with the line manager if relevant. Together these will form an excellent support to inform self-awareness coaching around strengths and development areas as perceived by the client, and also by others. Identifying blind spots (ie, differences between the client's and third-party perceptions), is also an essential product of this exercise.

(c) ***Taking it impersonally***

A potential difficulty with feedback and discussions of others' perceptions is that the feedback and perceptions can be taken personally. It is extremely helpful in this context to conduct a psychometric assessment exercise with the client. The benefits of this are particularly useful to illustrate and explain how differences in individual behaviour, preferences and needs contribute to very different perceptions that we all have of each other and of the world. This helps depersonalise sensitive feedback messages and helps clients understand that 'It's not me, it's the way others see things'.

(d) ***Perceptual positions***

One of several possible 'walking in another's shoes' exercises that can also help in transition coaching situations is where there are difficult interpersonal issues or awkward team dynamics. One such exercise is to have the client describe the issue, reactions and feelings from their perspective, then from the point of view of one or more other protagonists, and then from the point of view of a detached observer. This can do a lot to 'defang' a difficult interpersonal problem and help the client prepare for a critical conversation or carry a lighter load by reaching a different perspective.

(e) ***Looking through the Johari Window***

Among the many different tools to help with self-assessment and understanding how communication and feedback might be helpful, my favourite is the Johari Window (Figure 2), created by US psychologists Joseph Luft and Harrington Ingham.

Figure 2: The Johari Window

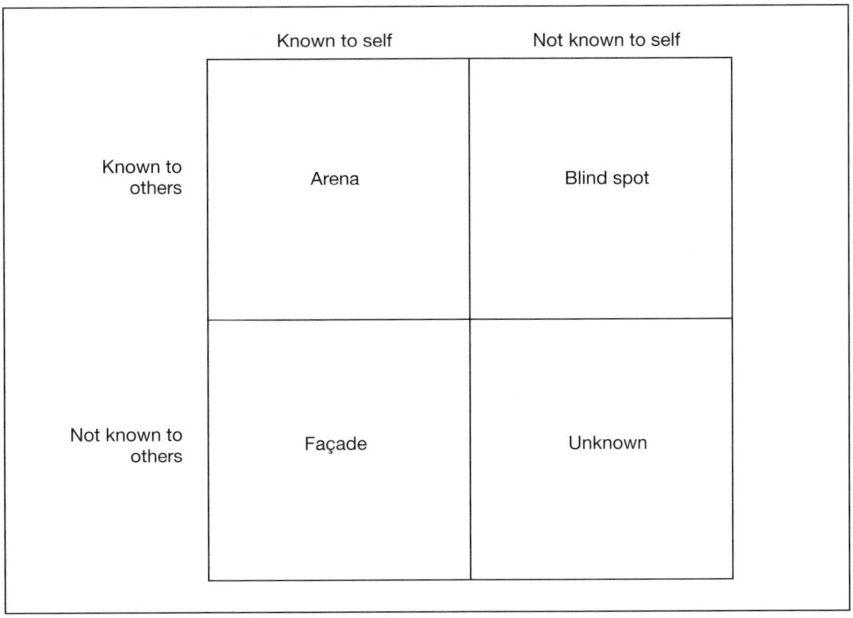

The client picks a number of adjectives to describe him- or herself, and then asks half a dozen or so friends, family and/or colleagues to provide a similar number of adjectives to describe the client. Adjectives chosen by both the client and others will go into the Arena. Adjectives chosen only by the client go into the Façade, which contains information known only to the client and not others. The client then has a choice as to whether to disclose that information to others. Adjectives which are chosen only by others belong to the Blind Spot, and provides information about others' perceptions of the client which may not be shared by the client. The aim of good communication and feedback is to increase the size of the Arena.

3.6 Mapping the environment

(a) *Becoming an environmentalist*

Transition coaching in any organisation is not properly done without the client acquiring a full understanding of context. The next stage in our coaching plan is therefore to help the client map the context. By 'context' I mean the day-to-day workplace environment, the interpersonal dynamics involving immediate colleagues (what I will call the local neighbourhood), but also broadening out to an understanding of the wider firm's culture, values, strategy, challenges, the political forces at play within the firm and the place of the firm in the market (what I will call the wider universe). In a transition from one role to another or one office or firm to another, that same mapping exercise should be conducted not only for the current environment, but for the future environment as well. The aim is to be able to answer the following questions:

- What aspects of my current local neighbourhood play to my strengths, values and fulfilment, and which aspects do not work for me?
- What does my support network look like today, and what will it be in the new role?
- What aspects of my future local neighbourhood will be positive or negative?
- How does the wider universe influence what I am doing today?
- How will the wider universe impact what I will be doing, my goals and what is expected of me in, say, one year and five years?
- How can I shape my new role in a way that works for me?
- How can I engage with my future environment (both at the local neighbourhood and wider universe level) to influence it in the way that will work for me?

(b) *Breaking it down*

Many of the answers will be evident from the earlier stages of the coaching plan, including the self-assessment and feedback. Those that are not will require the client to do some thinking, and reach out to their network (or even beyond it) to ask questions. The point here is to help the client think about the new role not simply as an extension of the existing one, but one in which the context will be vitally important. It is a small step then to appreciate that investigating that context and engaging with it early are vital components of transition planning. This is essentially about taking a wide view, taking initiative and control, and thinking politically.

(c) Keeping it up

Once in the new role, continuing self-assessment, feedback and communication to map the new local neighbourhood and wider universe are key. That will then inform the adjustments that the client could make to their behaviour, habits and support network to adapt better to the new environment and ensure a successful integration. The temptation is often instead to replicate previous behaviours and habits in the new environment, and hope for the best. As we have already seen, this is particularly true when entire teams relocate to new firms. The danger there is that the oil and water phenomenon – failure by the new team to reach out, communicate, adjust and mix – will lead to tribalism and mistrust and, ultimately, an unsuccessful transplant.

3.7 Knowing goals and managing expectations

(a) Where do you want to go?

Once the client has a good understanding of themselves, the environment, and their interaction with it, the next step is to fix goals, and commit to them in writing. Nobody gets into a cab and says 'Just drive!', except in the movies. This is not about committing rigidly to a plan. It is about developing the future mindset: planting flags, visualising the path ahead and discovering the self-motivation that comes with that process. Reality, as it plays out, will of course always be different: life is what happens when you make plans.

(b) Goal-oriented questions

Fixing goals comes in several flavours, ranging from writing a personal business plan with performance and business development targets for the following year to answering broader questions, for example:

- What would I like my work–life balance to look like in the next year and in three to five years (and perhaps beyond)?
- What do I want each of my four dimensions as a lawyer (Thinker, Doer, Developer, Supporter) to look like – section 2.2(a) above.
- What difference would I like to make in my new role?

(c) Great expectations

There is also another line of useful questions around communication and managing expectations, such as:

- What is expected of me, and do those expectations match my goals?
- What have I communicated to others about my goals and what I believe is expected of me?

These questions go hand in hand with the feedback and environmental mapping described earlier.

(d) Visualisation

Goal setting is not always an easy task, particularly for lawyers whose immediate task focus often relegates proper planning to a secondary role. Visualisation can be a helpful tool to get the ball rolling, the questions that I find helpful being:

- What will it look like to be in the new role (eg, as a newly promoted partner)?
- Can you describe how a typical day might unfold, from start to finish?
- What will you feel in your new role?
- What will your work–life balance look like?
- What will your important personal relationships look like, both outside and in work?
- What will success look and feel like?

3.8 Weighing up change

There are many helpful questions, methods and tools for weighing up a move or change. Some of these are described briefly below.

(a) Motivations

Where the move is voluntary, useful questions for the client might be:

- What are my real motivations for moving?
- Could I satisfy those motivations in my current role/firm, or only in the new role/firm?
- Could I change things to the way I want them here?

Figure 3: Swot analysis

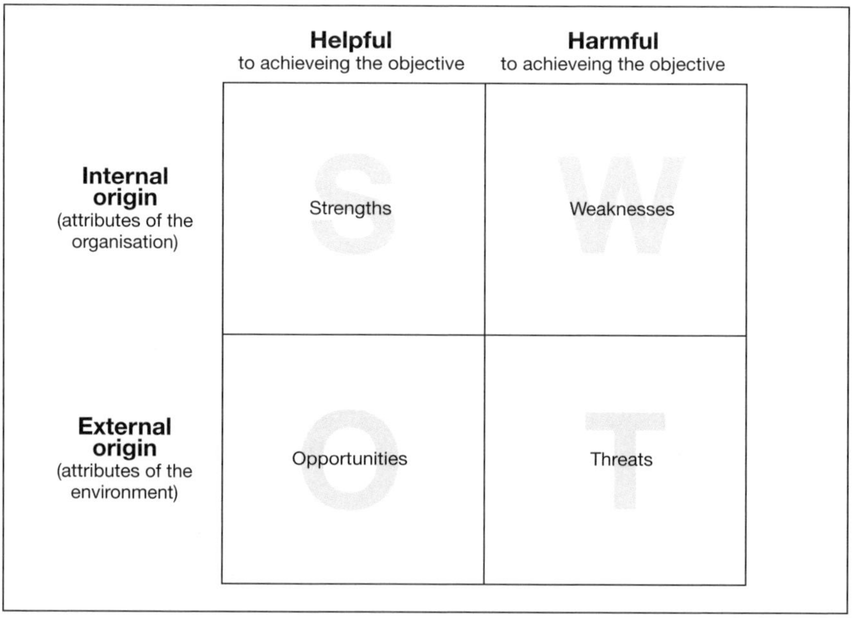

(b) SWOT analysis

It might be helpful to convert a simple pros and cons list into a SWOT (Strengths, Weaknesses, Opportunities and Threats) analysis. Strengths and Weaknesses are things which are innate to the client or which are within the client's control. Opportunities and Threats are things which may happen but which are outside the client's control. It may be easier to break the change down into headings or objectives, and do a SWOT per objective. For example, higher remuneration might be one objective, and professional development another. A SWOT grid is illustrated in Figure 3 above.

(c) ***Optionality***

In thinking things through before a move or change, the client might ask herself:

- What options am I gaining/can I gain here (long term and short term)?
- What options am I closing off?

Take as an example a fixed share partner looking to move firms to take up an offer of equity. That equity offer might be leveraged in the short term in negotiations to obtain equity at the current firm, which will widen the client's options. The move can also, in the medium/long term, make it easier for the client to move to another equity partnership elsewhere at a later date. On the other hand, moving to the new firm may narrow the client's lifestyle options in the short and medium term because of the energy and time that she will have to divert to building her new practice, although the move may increase those options in the long term because the remuneration may enable her to improve other things in her life.

(d) ***Nurturing vs draining analysis***

It may be useful to look at the move or change in terms of its energising or de-energising (or draining) effects. Questions here might be:

- What will be nurturing about the move (ie, what will energise me and play to my strengths, enjoyment or fulfilment?)
- Conversely, what will be draining or de-energising?

(e) ***Balance sheet***

This is a variant on a standard list of pros and cons. The client simply writes what he stands to gain (both tangible gains, such as remuneration, and intangible gains, such as happiness or fulfilment) on the assets side of the balance sheet, and what he stands to lose on the liabilities side. On the liabilities side the client should also include the extra time and energy that he will need to expend to make the move a success. Then (and this is the real difference from the standard pros and cons list) the client should ascribe a points value to each item and see where it gets him.

(f) ***Project management analysis***

This brings together some of the other analyses. The client might consider the following questions:

- What are my objectives in making the move?
- What is the scope of my new role going to be?
- What are the assumptions I am making about the move and are they realistic?
- What are the risks I am taking in making this move?

- What are the concrete things I need to do to make this a success?
- How do I define success?
- What is the time frame for success?
- Can I realistically achieve success in the time frame?

3.9 Motivation

Motivation is relevant to coaching lawyers through change for two main reasons. First, the motivation to make the transition is key to success. Secondly, the motivation to do the things necessary to bring about the change and to adopt and embed new behaviour is equally important. Edward L Deci and Richard Ryan's Self-Determination Theory is interesting in this context. It proposes a link between motivation and needs for autonomy, competence and relatedness. It also examines the distinction between intrinsic motivators (ie, motivators that come from within) and extrinsic motivators, which come from outside. It is worth noting one of Deci's findings that giving people unexpected positive feedback on a task increases their intrinsic motivation to do it, because that feedback was fulfilling people's need for competence: Deci, EL (1971), "Effects of externally mediated rewards on intrinsic motivation", *Journal of Personality and Social Psychology* 18: 105–115.

Daniel H Pink, in his 2011 book *Drive – The Surprising Truth About What Motivates Us*, proposes that in situations where people are fairly paid, intrinsic motivation is based on mastery (the drive to become competent), autonomy and purpose. This dovetails with my own experience that lawyers are often poor at visualising possibilities and formulating a vision of the future, When, through coaching or other support, they find the confidence and ability to do so, this turns out to be a powerful source of purpose and motivation.

3.10 Communication, feedback and critical conversations

Communication skills are crucial to successful client and people development, leadership and negotiation among other things. This has already been alluded to several times above. These skills are therefore essential to successful legal career development and change, and an essential coaching topic in the context of recruiting, developing and retaining legal talent.

(a) Communication

Perhaps because law firms are made up of autonomous, task and target-focused individuals, communication is not their strong point. In addition, lawyers are reluctant to share personal issues in troubled times because, quite simply, vulnerability is perceived as weakness. On the other hand, a law firm culture that encourages communication and feedback can bring huge benefits.

Lawyers who communicate well with colleagues at the start of and throughout a matter will create a sense of equality, partnership and buy-in, which in turn engenders trust and collegiality. What so often happens instead is that colleagues in other departments and offices are instructed at the last minute or well after the matter has got under way. This conveys lack of planning, lack of respect and a feeling that they are being treated as second class citizens.

Regular communication with clients, if only on cost reporting, will manage expectations and show transparency and good project management skills, thereby earning client trust. More often than not, lawyers will wait until the end of a matter to raise cost overruns with the client, which will inevitably raise hackles.

(b) *Feedback*

Feedback is usually something that happens once a year in the context of a somewhat bureaucratic annual appraisal process, possibly accompanied by a 360-degree exercise. It is rare for partners to give regular (eg, quarterly or monthly), feedback to associates, and even rarer that associates ask for it. It is rarer still for that feedback to be given by partners to each other. Downward feedback to trainees and junior associates is often poorly handled: a busy associate might prefer to rewrite a junior's work themselves than go through the time-consuming task of sitting down with the junior, working through the draft with constructive criticism, and getting them to redraft it in the knowledge that it may require a second or third round of review and constructive criticism before it can be sent to the partner or client. This disempowers and demotivates the junior, and deprives the senior of an opportunity to pass on valuable lessons.

Lack of proper feedback, either about their career direction or specific tasks, leaves lawyers, who are naturally under-confident overachievers, feeling unfulfilled and undervalued. This is an especially strident complaint by the millennial generation, who are more focused on work–life balance issues and whose sense of loyalty to employers is looser than that of previous generations. They value responsibility and they want to feel that people take an interest in them. Failure to do meet these needs will have an adverse effect on talent retention, and employer reputation can suffer instantly through social media.

Post-transaction reviews, both internal and with the client, are often ignored or botched because lawyers dread receiving criticism. And yet regular, honest feedback sessions with clients are critical to building client trust and loyalty.

(c) *Coaching, listening and critical conversations*

The key is introducing lawyers to the power of listening, and to the techniques for conducting critical conversations. Individuals will suffer a cost if they do not have critical conversations.

Good coaching is founded on listening, and a lawyer who has experienced it will understand the benefit of simply listening for understanding. They will also appreciate that listening for understanding is an aim in itself, whereas their natural instinct to conduct a solution-focused debate is not always the right approach. In an ideal world, every lawyer would be familiar with Nancy Kline's Listening Environment as described in her 2002 book *Time to Think: Listening to Ignite the Human Mind.*

(d) *Effective client conversations*

Walking a mile in the other person's shoes is a habit that lawyers can also usefully learn through coaching. One area where this is particularly obvious is business development. Lawyers will instinctively tell the client how good and how well suited they are to handling the client's business. Clients, on the other hand, would generally prefer to be asked knowledgeable questions about their business and the issues they face by an interested listener. Having lawyers conduct role plays in a coaching context to rehearse critical client conversations can be invaluable.

(e) ***Difficult conversations***

The 'difficult' feedback conversation is another area where coaching can be extremely helpful. In tense interpersonal relations, the tendency is to avoid a conversation. This will often stem from a fear of being criticised. The art here is to depersonalise the conversation by identifying the issue or the behaviour clearly, and describing the effect it has had on the speaker. This will avoid the other person feeling accused by shifting the focus to the effect of their actions on others. It is also helpful at the outset to agree that each party will have a set time – three minutes, say – to express themselves uninterrupted by the other, and then to switch over so that everyone feels that they are being afforded equal treatment and respect. At the conclusion of the conversation, each party should undertake action to improve matters, if only by agreeing a date to meet again to discuss progress.

The ability to conduct effective listening conversations in which both parties feel that their point of view is valued rather than feeling threatened is an easy skill to learn, and may lead to feedback becoming routine rather than something that has to happen once a year, or at the end of a matter, or to be avoided altogether. Armed with this skill, lawyers can transform their environment into one where trust, collegiality and accountability become the norm.

3.11 Confidence

(a) ***Confidence***

Coaching for change often involves coaching for confidence. The change itself may be a source of concern based on limiting beliefs, which in turn may hold the client back from doing the things which may be necessary to navigate transition successfully. Coaching will naturally lead to understanding of choices, and the autonomy that comes from appreciating the ability to exercise those choices. That in itself is a great source of self-confidence. This may speak particularly loudly to lawyers, given the large part that autonomy plays in their lives.

(b) ***Confidence and the art of networking and profile-building***

A perennial confidence-related issue in transition coaching is networking and profile-building. The ability to do both is a precondition to successful change partly for political reasons (building a strong, wide support network) and partly for business development purposes. This ability rests partly on the confidence to reach out, make and nurture contacts, and to advertise successes. What holds clients back most here is the perception that they are having to convince others that they are worthy of attention. This, with the attendant fear of rejection, is a powerful demotivator. Good coaching can replace this with the understanding that successful networking depends not so much on 'selling' oneself as showing others that you are interested in them. For that reason, the art of networking is largely asking others questions about themselves, which can be as simple as "What's on your mind right now?". That makes the initial approach much easier, as all you need is to find the excuse to have the conversation. Coaching will also help clients understand their own drivers and others' perceptions of their qualities, which will help them become comfortable with delivering a narrative about themselves that comes across as genuine and engaging.

Retaining women lawyers: the need for new perspectives

Ida Abbott
Ida Abbott Consulting

"Whether you can observe a thing or not depends on the theory which you use. It is the theory which decides what can be observed." Albert Einstein

Law firms want to keep women lawyers and see them succeed. They are starting to realise that their failure to retain and advance women is jeopardising their ability to compete and thrive in the modern marketplace. Research has shown that greater gender diversity has a statistically significant positive impact on both client satisfaction and law firms' financial performance.[1] In contrast, the lack of women in leadership prevents firms from meeting client expectations for gender-diverse teams and women leaders; it handicaps firms in the intense competition for top legal talent; it deprives them of women's professional strengths and perspectives; and the steady loss of highly experienced lawyers weakens profitability. Firms try to keep women by adopting various policies and programmes, but the results are usually disappointing because firms define the problem incorrectly. They base their actions on biased mindsets and incorrect assumptions about what women want and need, then offer programmatic solutions when what is required is a new law firm culture. For better outcomes in retention and advancement, law firms must reframe the way they view and address the problem.

Firms have created and perpetuated a culture based on a preference for masculine thinking and acting. This culture expects round-the-clock work availability, values aggressive competition and self-promotion, and measures success by compensation based on the most hours worked and the biggest book of business. They may offer some flexible alternatives (eg, reduced hour schedules) but stigmatise lawyers who use them. This 'ideal worker' model benefits employers at lawyers' expense. While some lawyers thrive in this culture, it has led to problems more serious than attrition, such as extremely high rates of depression and alcoholism.[2]

While women are more dissatisfied than men with firm culture, compensation and work environment,[3] resistance to the traditional model is growing among young lawyers of both sexes.[4] And since millennials (those born between 1980 and 1995)

1 Acritas Diversity Report, Acritas Research Ltd, 2016.
2 "Lawyers and Depression", Dave Nee Foundation; Mark Cohen, "Why Are Lawyers So Unpopular and Stressed?", Big Law Business, Bloomberg BNA, 30 September 2015.
3 Rachel Marx Bouffard, "Why Are Women Lawyers Unhappy?" Vault, 21 March 2013.
4 Claire Cain Miller, "The 24/7 Work Culture's Toll on Families and Gender Equality", The Upshot, *The New York Times*, 28 May 2015.

will make up nearly half of the workforce by 2025,[5] firms have to rethink their expectations, norms and values. Instead of trying to help women fit into the current culture, law firm culture will need to adapt to the changing labour force.[6] Resolving the issues that have long troubled women in law firms will create a workplace more appealing to men as well.

Creating a more balanced and inclusive culture is, of course, a complex, multi-faceted, multi-year undertaking, so law firms that want to build a culture where women will stay and succeed cannot delay. (See Appendix A for examples of transformative initiatives.) To begin, you have to redefine your operating premises. Lawyers know that the way you frame an issue dictates your analysis and conclusion. To find effective solutions, firms must reframe the issues:

- not 'gender diversity' but 'gender balance';
- not 'why do women leave?' but 'why should women stay?'
- not retaining women but engaging them;
- not a women's issue but a strategic business issue;
- not led by women alone but led by men and women together;
- not how do we 'fix' the women but how do we fix the firm.

By looking at the problems differently firms can better understand what they must do in order to keep and get the most from the great female lawyers who are otherwise walking out the door.

1. Move beyond gender diversity to gender balance

Instead of just trying to increase gender diversity, focus on achieving gender balance. Increasing gender diversity suggests raising numbers and percentages. Creating 'gender balance' involves building an inclusive culture where women are accepted for who they are as individuals; valued and fairly rewarded for all they contribute to the firm; can achieve their highest potential; and are equitably represented in the firm's power structure. Statistics about gender diversity are important measures but do not tell the full story about women's status. It has been said that 'diversity' is being invited to the party; 'inclusion' is being asked to dance. Women are invited into law firms and well represented at entry levels, but they leave because they are not made to feel included.

This shift of perspective acknowledges that the problem is not simply one of reversing female attrition; it is a matter of getting more women into firm leadership. In fact, industry-wide attrition rates are uncertain. Although some authorities state that women leave firms at twice the rate of men,[7] others show that the rate is about the same for men and women.[8] But with so few executive women, every woman's departure has significance. When women leave it reduces and discourages the pool of women who remain; if those women do not want to become partners or do not try because they think it would be futile, the firm's diversity figures remain low.

---

5 Christie Smith and Stephanie Turner, PhD, "The Radical Transformation of Diversity and Inclusion: The Millennial Influence", Deloitte University 2016.

6 Joseph Collins, "How to Hire a Millennial", Working Knowledge, *Harvard Business Review*, 8 April 2016.

7 Selena Rezvani, "Large Law Firms are Failing Women Lawyers", *The Washington Post*, 28 February 2014.

8 *2016 Update on Associate Attrition*, The NALP Foundation, 2016.

2. Why should women stay?

Firms have been assuming that women choose to leave them because they cannot cope with work–family conflicts, they lack ambition, or they are not tough enough to succeed in the firm. So firms adopt family-friendly policies and start women's initiatives, to which they proudly point as evidence of their support for women. Some of those policies and initiatives do indeed help women and enable some to stay at work longer than they otherwise would. Yet even after firms take those steps, women continue to leave. This reinforces firms' underlying and mistaken assumptions that the problem of high attrition is due to women's failings and inadequacies.

The problem persists because as important and valuable as they are, family-friendly policies and women's initiatives have not addressed the heart of the problem: inherent cultural, structural and institutional biases that favour men and disadvantage women. What if we look at the situation a different way?

Women begin their careers with the same ambitions as men.[9] Hired in numbers equal to men, they watch men advance faster and earn more than they do no matter how much, how well or how hard they work. Women with the intelligence, talent and drive to be partners, leaders and rainmakers do not enter the top ranks on a par with similarly qualified men. In Latin America, women are 49% of associates and only 20% of partners.[10] In the United Kingdom, women have been 60% of entry-level lawyers for 20 years but are only 19% of partners in the top 20 firms and 16% of the senior leaders at the top 50 firms.[11] In the United States, women have been entering law firms in about the same numbers as men for three decades, but are still less than 18% of equity partners and less than 4% of chairs, managing partners and executive management.[12] Women equity partners make 20% less than men equity partners, even when they bill the same hours and have comparable books of business.[13]

Law firms fancy themselves as meritocracies, but more than merit determines the outcomes of decisions about promotions, clients and pay, especially when those who define merit and make the decisions are overwhelmingly men. Instead of assuming that women leave because of babies and a lack of ambition, firms should be asking, 'Why would women stay when the odds are stacked against them?'

In today's highly mobile labour market, women – like men – do not hesitate to move when better opportunities are presented. Talented women lawyers have many work options and not just in the traditional places like established law firms. They can also choose from a rapidly growing number of 'alternative' legal service providers and innovative start-ups that offer interesting and challenging legal work, flexibility and autonomy, high compensation, and more chances for professional growth and advancement than they see in conventional law firms.

---

9 Robin J Ely, Pamela Stone and Colleen Ammerman, "Rethink What You 'Know' About High-Achieving Women", *Harvard Business Review*, 2014; Eileen Patten and Kim Parker, "A Gender Reversal on Career Aspirations", Pew Research Center, 19 April 2012.

10 Joachim Bamrud, "Latin America: The Challenges for Female Lawyers", Latinvex, 2 July 2014.

11 Natasha Bernal, "Where are the Women Law Firm Leaders?" *The Lawyer*, 9 March 2015.

12 Lauren Stiller Rikleen, *Report of the Ninth Annual National Survey on Retention and Promotion of Women in Law Firms*, National Association of Women Lawyers and NAWL Foundation, October, 2015.

13 *Ibid.*

In a sense, the burden of proof has shifted. In the past women had to argue the business case for themselves. Women tried to adapt to existing law firm cultures because they were trying to break into the legal profession and be taken seriously on the basis of their skills, ability and work ethic.

Today, the market is making the case for women: clients insisting on gender diversity, the costly exodus of female talent, and in some countries, regulations[14] requiring greater transparency about gender diversity. Now that women lawyers are prized and needed, it is law firms that must adapt. Firms that genuinely want to attract and keep women lawyers today must prove that the opportunities and work conditions they offer are better than what women can find in another workplace. Firms must look at themselves through women's eyes and make the business case that would persuade women to stay.

3. How can you engage women?

Instead of merely retaining women, firms should be trying to engage them. Engagement is a state of intellectual and emotional commitment, and it is a critical factor in how long people stay in their jobs. Engaged lawyers feel respected and valued; find their work interesting, challenging and meaningful; and believe they can achieve their highest potential in the firm. Engagement should not be confused with satisfaction. Satisfied lawyers may feel good about their job, the people and the firm, and do what is expected of them. When lawyers are fully engaged, they perform at the highest levels, identify with the firm and want to stay there even when there are opportunities to work elsewhere.

Many factors can generate engagement, so successful engagement efforts must be tailored to each lawyer, taking into account her motivators, development needs, personal circumstances at work and at home, and career goals. But some factors are universal. Lawyers want firms to help them acquire the legal and business skills they need to be excellent lawyers and provide opportunities for them to constantly develop and stretch their abilities. They want partners to take a personal interest in them, providing instruction, guidance and mentorship. And they want a workplace culture that is collaborative and inclusive, where leaders are supportive and women feel that they fit in and are appreciated for who they are and what they contribute.[15] While the desire for this kind of culture may sound naive or 'soft' to some law firm leaders, it is not. These conditions are necessary not just to engage women, but to engage young men as well.[16] A 2016 study by Deloitte and the Billie Jean King Leadership Initiative showed that 83% of millennials are actively engaged when they believe their organisation fosters an inclusive culture, compared to only 60% of millennials who are actively engaged when they believe their organisation does not.[17]

---

14 Kat Green, "BigLaw Gender Pay Gap Under Pressure With New EEOC Rule", Law360, 29 January 2016; Liz Bolshaw, "UK Law Firms Face Compulsory Diversity Reporting", *Financial Times*, Women at the Top Blog, 8 August 2011.

15 Corey Laplante and Katie Larkin-Wong, "Perspective: Millennials in Big Law – Let's Get to Work", Big Law Business, Bloomberg BNA, 4 April 2016.

16 Joseph Collins, "How to Hire a Millennial", Working Knowledge, *Harvard Business Review*, 8 April 2016.

17 Christie Smith and Stephanie Turner, PhD, "The Radical Transformation of Diversity and Inclusion: The Millennial Influence", Deloitte University 2016.

The importance of this difference translates into dollars and cents because organisations with high numbers of engaged employees have been shown to outperform others by more than 200%.[18]

In an inclusive culture, lawyers would be able to see enough diverse male and female role models that they can envision a future for themselves with the firm. This point is especially vital for women. Law firms have few prominent women rainmakers and leaders. Unlike the wide variety of men who are law firm partners, the scarcity of women partners, especially at the top, severely limits the role models available to women. Because women have had to be exceptional in order to become successful partners – more so than men – many women leaders and rainmakers are perceived as 'superwomen', and younger women may find them intimidating rather than inspiring. Young women become discouraged when they see few women leaders with whom they can identify and thus cannot envision themselves becoming partners at the firm.

To counteract this perception, women need to know that partnership, especially equity partnership, is both attainable and desirable. They need to be told clearly and honestly what it takes to succeed in the firm, how to do it, and what their chances are of making it. If they are on track, they want sufficient encouragement from supervisors, mentors and sponsors who believe they can make it, urge them to try and agree to support them. And they have to believe that their sacrifices and hard work to get to the top are worth it.

Pillsbury Winthrop Shaw Pittman LLP has benefited from this kind of culture. Pillsbury holds the distinction of being the first global law firm to elect a woman as its chair and it has had many other women serve as high-profile leaders. In the firm's Los Angeles office, where 30% of the equity partners are women, men and women partners personally support the career progress of women associates and junior partners. They routinely talk to the women associates they supervise about what it takes to become a partner and how to position themselves for partnership. They do more than just advise these women. They give them challenging and high-profile client responsibilities, often stepping back and letting the women take the lead. They teach women the business and economic aspects of practice. They invite women along to business development activities, introduce them to younger in-house counsel and encourage them to build those relationships. They push women out of their comfort zone and encourage them to reach ever higher. Partners do this one-on-one, not because of any programme but because such behaviour is part of their culture. As a result, women thrive.

4. Gender balance is a strategic business issue

Many firms treat gender balance as a 'women's issue'. It is not. Retaining half your talent pool is a strategic business and talent issue that goes to the core of the firm's ability to succeed in the marketplace. Instead of firms asking, What is wrong with women if they cannot make it to the top in our firm? they should be asking, 'What is wrong with this firm if talented women cannot make it to the top?'

18 *Ibid.*

Firms cannot afford to continue losing female talent. Women now represent more than 36% of all lawyers worldwide; in most countries women represent 30% to 50% of lawyers and the percentage is even higher in some countries.[19] As the proportion of women lawyers continues to grow, and the market for legal talent becomes ever more competitive, women will flock to firms where they can flourish, and the firms they leave will be at a severe competitive disadvantage.

Firms with gender-diverse senior teams are better able to address clients' expectations because clients increasingly expect firms to have such teams. Even more important, increasing numbers of those clients are women. Many of those women make hiring decisions and manage outside counsel, and they place far more value on 'feminine' attributes that the business world previously undervalued.[20] With an increasingly female client base, a dearth of women leaders and women-led teams deprives a company of perspectives needed to understand and serve women clients.

In addition, women's leadership strengths are especially suited for leadership in the modern marketplace.[21] As the business world changes, law firm leaders need to forge new kinds of working relationships with colleagues, employees, vendors, competitors and clients, more and more of whom will be women. Leaders will need to use behaviours and leadership styles that women tend to demonstrate more than men, such as emotional intelligence, team building, collaboration, empowering others, and participatory decision making.

Moreover, abundant research shows that more gender-diverse executive teams produce tangible business benefits, including better financial performance and organisational health, while the lack of gender diversity in leadership is very costly to the bottom line.[22] As stated in a recent study, a large and growing body of research is "delivering unassailable proof that accelerating women's advancement in the workplace and creating gender-balanced teams, boards and governments produce better outcomes and create prosperity".[23]

A law firm's growth, endurance and profitability depend on retaining and optimising the talents of all its lawyers, including women. It is simply a business imperative – and should be a top strategic priority – for firms to keep women lawyers and place them in leadership and decision-making roles where they can have the greatest impact.

Many firms rationalise that there are not enough 'qualified' women to fill those senior roles, or believe that women do not want those positions. But most firms could find plenty of women who are equally or more qualified than men if they used unbiased leadership criteria, groomed women for those roles (as some are starting to

19 Ethan Michelson, "Women in the Legal Profession, 1970–2010: A Study of the Global Supply of Lawyers", *Indiana Journal of Global Legal Studies*, Summer 2013, Table A6.

20 Cathy Benko and Bill Pelster, "How Women Decide", *Harvard Business Review*, September 2013.

21 Julia Sperling, Chiara Marcati, and Michael Rennie, "GCC Women in Leadership – From the First to the Norm", McKinsey Middle East, July 2014; Georg Vielmetter and Yvonne Sell, "Leadership is about to get more uncomfortable", HRR Blog, 1 July 2014; *Americans Crave a New Kind of Leader – And Women Are Ready to Deliver*, Pershing LLC, 2014.

22 Acritas Diversity Report, above; Beth Brooke-Marciniak, Uschi Schreiber, and Karyn Twaronite, "Women: Fast Forward. The Time for Gender Parity is Now", Ernst & Young 2016; The Catalyst Research Center For Equity In Business Leadership, Catalyst.

23 Brooke-Marciniak, *et al*, *ibid*.

do – see Appendix B), or simply had the will to act. One leader who took direct action is Greg Jordan, the former managing partner of the global law firm Reed Smith.

Reed Smith's executive committee is an elected group of representatives from every firm office. In 2000, the firm went through a series of global mergers. The firm amended its partnership agreement to add three seats to the executive committee, to be appointed by the managing partner, for the purpose of increasing 'balance'. At the time the intention was to enhance geographic balance and hasten firm-wide integration by adding representatives from newly merged offices. As geographic balance improved naturally during the integration process, Jordan began to appoint women to fill the three extra seats. Over time, women began to run for executive committee seats because it became 'normal' for women to be on the firm's top committee. Eventually more women were elected rather than appointed and women came to represent 28 to 33% of the executive committee.

5. Men must join women in leading gender balance initiatives

Once a firm acknowledges that the need for more women leaders is a critical business issue and makes it a strategic priority, it becomes less marginal and more urgent, and men can no longer avoid sharing ownership of it. In order to take advantage of the enormous benefits and opportunities that gender balance can offer, men, especially those in leadership, must ensure that the promises of greater gender balance are realised.

Until now, most initiatives to retain and advance women have been led solely by women. The work they have done has established a strong and necessary foundation: establishing internal women's networks for mutual support; building external business networks with women clients and community leaders; sponsoring business development and leadership training for women; and lobbying for family-friendly programmes and policies. Although these activities are vital, they keep women away from the men who control the firm and their male clients – the very people who hold the power, connections and support women need to get ahead.

The success of initiatives to achieve gender balance is more likely when leaders are visibly, actively involved.[24] Since most law firm leaders are men, meaningful change depends on men taking leading roles in the effort. To date, few men have stepped forward. The absence of men places extra burdens on women, especially women leaders who spend considerable non-billable time running these initiatives and being available to younger women as mentors and advisers.

It is unfair to expect women to bear the full responsibility for finding a solution for what is essentially a failure of male leadership. As long as men hold overwhelming control of firm management, clients and money, they control the keys to greater gender balance. Women alone cannot change the cultural norms, mindsets, and systems that govern law firm advancement, leadership and rewards. There are too few powerful women in most law firms to drive significant institutional changes without the support of men at the top, where it can make a difference. It

---

24 "A CEO's Guide to Gender Equality", *McKinsey Quarterly*, McKinsey & Company, November 2015; "Women in the Workplace 2015", LeanIn and McKinsey & Company, 2015.

will take committed men, working together with women, to create the conditions in which gender balance can be attained.

Women, too, must accept and welcome men into women's initiatives. In many firms women prefer women-only activities because they offer women a greater sense of camaraderie, safety and control. But by excluding men, women have deprived men of opportunities to learn from women, be mentored by women, and fully understand the challenges women face. This may have left potential male supporters untapped and possibly even alienated them.[25]

By educating each other but not men, women's initiatives have missed the chance to correct the mindsets, myths and unconscious biases that create barriers for women. Indeed, educating men is critical, since a high proportion of men deny that women face gender bias or other disadvantages at work.[26] Moreover, by being for women only these initiatives fail to assist men who challenge gender norms in ways that promote desirable cultural changes, such as fathers who face work–life conflicts or work reduced schedules.

In some ways excluding men has undermined the larger objective of creating a more inclusive culture. It has made it more difficult for men to develop sufficient trust, understanding and comfort to speak candidly with women, give them honest feedback and advice, and offer them mentorship and sponsorship. When men believe women want to do it without them, they do not appreciate what they can contribute or how they can best be of help.

One area where this is especially problematic is sponsorship. Sponsors are powerful partners who help propel a lawyer's career upward. They urge colleagues to make her a partner and raise her compensation; introduce her to clients and appoint her to high-impact committees; and do other things that boost a lawyer's chances of success. Research has shown that the reason more men than women get promoted is not because of any inherent differences between the sexes in ability, talent or drive, but because far more men than women enjoy the sponsorship of powerful leaders, the vast majority of whom are other men. This research also shows that when women do have senior-level sponsors, they get promoted at the same rate as men.[27] As an example, when the Women's Initiative Network of Reed Smith (WINRS) determined that the lack of powerful sponsors limited women's ability to move up, they identified senior women associates who were or should have been up for partnership and as a group, WINRS championed those women and advocated for their promotion. All the women they sponsored in the first year of the programme were elected to partnership and in each subsequent year, between 27% and 57% of women they sponsored were elevated.

It is well known that men prefer to sponsor other men rather than women for various reasons: unconscious gender bias; uncertainties about women's career

---

25 Jeanine Prime, Corinne A Moss-Racusin, Heather Foust-Cummings, "Engaging Men in Gender Initiatives", Catalyst 2009.

26 "A CEO's guide", above; "Women in the Workplace 2015", above; Sandrine Devillard, Sandra Sancier-Sultan, and Charlotte Werner, "Why Gender Diversity at the Top Remains a Challenge", *McKinsey Quarterly*, McKinsey & Company, April 2014.

27 Sylvia Ann Hewlett, (*Forget a Mentor) Find a Sponsor* (Harvard Business Review Press, 2013); Heather Foust-Cummings, Sarah Dinolfo and Jennifer Kohler, "Sponsoring Women to Success", Catalyst, 2011.

ambitions; worry that something they say or do may lead to misunderstandings or claims of impropriety; and concerns that an opposite-sex relationship may cause complications such as an affair or office gossip. These issues need to be discussed and addressed by men and women together. Men need to be made aware of the factors that may cause them to overlook or avoid women protégées in favour of men. These discussions need to take place in a setting where men and women feel safe discussing concerns they have about opposite-sex sponsor relationships, and are given tools and techniques to make opposite-sex sponsor–protégée relationships work.[28]

The time has come for a new version of women's initiatives – renamed 'gender balance initiatives' – that preserve the vital women-only events that are important to women, but which also promote greater interaction, trust-building and involvement by both men and women. A gender balance initiative would expect men to take visible roles in promoting gender balance and advocating for the cultural and institutional changes it requires. It would teach men and women how to talk about gender bias and work in tandem toward gender equality. If the objective is to create a more inclusive firm culture, then more needs to be done to help women and men build it together.

6. Fixing law firm culture: identifying and eliminating gender bias

The slow progress toward gender balance in law firms is caused principally by unconscious gender bias. Gender bias today is subtle, unspoken and unconscious, but it remains firmly embedded in "cultural assumptions and organisational structures, practices, and patterns of interaction that inadvertently benefit men while putting women at a disadvantage".[29]

Although it is unconscious and not deliberate, gender bias determines how people in the firm view, judge and treat each other, and in most firms they do so through a traditionally masculine lens. When leaders make judgements and decisions based on inaccurate and biased assumptions, they give men unfair advantages even though they may not realise it. One recent study, for example, found that politically conservative partners consider women as 'less promising', so they do not give women associates the same work opportunities and promotions they give men. This reduces the partnership chances of those women by 80%.[30] In order to reverse the unwanted attrition of women, firms need to take a close look inward and tackle the biases that permeate law firm culture and block women's ascent.

There is a large body of literature about the many forms of gender bias and how they unwittingly create barriers that subject women to higher standards and double binds; undermine women's confidence and ambition; exclude women from important networks; prevent them from getting profitable work, business, and promotions; and keep women undervalued, under-compensated, and under-utilised as leaders.[31] Women are viewed as less competent, ambitious and competitive than

---

28 Ida O Abbott, *Sponsoring Women: What Men Need to Know* (Attorney at Work, 2014).

29 Herminia Ibarra, Robin Ely and Deborah Kolb, "Women Rising: The Unseen Barriers", *Harvard Business Review*, September 2013.

30 Vivia Chen, "Bad News for Women with Republican Bosses", *The Careerist*, 8 April 2016.

31 Ibarra *et al*, above; Rachel Emma Silverman, "Gender Bias at Work Turns Up in Feedback", *Wall Street Journal*, 30 September 2015.

men; if they are mothers, they are considered less committed than both women without children and all men; and no matter how women behave, they are criticised. Like Goldilocks, women are too soft or too tough but rarely just right. If collaborative, compassionate and modest, they are either ignored or viewed as likeable but 'too feminine' to command respect. If they act with authority, decisiveness and strength, they are denigrated as 'unfeminine', arrogant and pushy.

Gender bias also harms men. Men who do not conform to expectations of masculine behaviour – by working part-time to care for their kids or being soft spoken and gentle rather than aggressive and tough – may be ridiculed or written off as 'not leadership material'.

Gender biases, and the stereotypes behind them, may be unconscious but they have a pernicious effect on women. Firms must aggressively root them out and eradicate them. Classes in gender bias are only a start; they raise awareness but do not get rid of the bias. The difficulty, as explained earlier, is that biases are 'hidden', based on unconscious mindsets, and therefore hard to find. And the challenge is compounded because these biases are embedded in law firm culture and institutional systems that affect how women are evaluated, promoted and rewarded. Firms can begin by taking a close look at systems and processes that affect women's work experience, assessments, promotions to partnership, business development, client referrals, leadership selection, and compensation.

6.1 Work allocation

The most critical element of professional development is work experience, yet few firms have formal systems for assigning and monitoring work. Instead, partners informally give work to associates. Without a system in place to track associates' work experience, partners who have less confidence in women or feel more comfortable working with men may give women less challenging work, less client contact, less visibility in the firm, and fewer opportunities to prove how good they are. This denies women many of the work experiences they need in order to learn and advance, and prevents them from establishing reputations for leadership and excellence. Mothers, especially those who work reduced hours, are at particular risk of receiving too little, too much or inferior work.

6.2 Evaluations

Performance standards should be explicit and performance assessments should be based on objective, observable, and measurable criteria. Otherwise, evaluations may harbour subtle biases that result in women receiving lower scores than their performance would justify, reducing their chances of becoming partners. In a study of associate evaluations at a Wall Street law firm, women received more positive narrative assessments (eg, 'excellent', 'stellar', 'terrific') than men, but only 6% of women – as opposed to 15% of men – were mentioned as potential partner material. What's more, women who received the same narrative comments as men about their technical competence and partnership material nonetheless received lower numerical ratings than men. Because the firm relied on numerical ratings for partnership consideration, men in the firm were three times more likely than women to be promoted to partnership even when women exhibited the same performance, competence and partnership potential.[32]

6.3 Partner promotions

In making partnership decisions, women are often held to stricter readiness standards. Decision makers may give men the benefit of the doubt based on their future potential, while judging women on their past performance. So if a man and a woman have made identical but not yet successful efforts to land a new client, they conclude the man 'just needs a little more time' while the woman 'hasn't shown she can do it'. If they both do land a client, the man may be congratulated for his skill while the woman may be seen as 'lucky'. Moreover, during partnership selection discussions fewer women than men have powerful sponsors to advocate for them and challenge these biases.

6.4 Business development

Women partners are frequently left out of client pitches, social events with clients, and other business development activities. Women are often overlooked or excluded from pertinent business promotions, presentations and client activities even when they have pre-existing relationships with a client or are leading experts in the field being discussed. Whether unconscious or deliberate, the effect is the same: women are deprived of opportunities to originate or share in new client business.

6.5 Client referrals

Partners acquire clients internally in two ways: when rainmakers have new business to distribute and when partners retire and ask lawyers to take over responsibility for their clients. Male rainmakers (who are the vast majority) often assume that 'since the client likes me, the best partner to handle the work or take over my client is someone like me'. Even when they know women partners who would be excellent candidates they overlook them, so women are left out of the running and men get the business. This keeps women from receiving or inheriting significant client relationships.

6.6 Leadership selection

When selecting people for leadership positions, most law firms do little formal planning to identify and prepare the people best qualified for them. The lack of leadership criteria and succession planning hurts women's chances for being selected. Unlike men, women are not automatically perceived as leaders, are not as well connected in the firm power structure, and do not have influential sponsors grooming and advocating for them. Formal succession planning using objective selection criteria has been shown to reduce favouritism and promote equal advancement opportunities for women – but few firms do it. When the firm develops and uses leadership competencies to guide the process of identifying qualified

---

32 Monica Biernat, M J Tocci and Joan C Williams, "The Language of Performance Evaluations: Gender-Based Shifts in Content and Consistency of Judgment", *Social Psychological and Personality Science*, published online 18 July 2011.

candidates, women are more likely to be included in the list. Similarly, when decision makers are given specific characteristics to look for and a directive to consider women, they necessarily take notice of a wider pool of candidates, which increases women's chances of being selected.

6.7 Compensation

Women partners (equity and non-equity together) are paid 32% less than their male peers, an average difference of $250,000.[33] Research has repeatedly concluded that compensation disparities between men and women partners in law firms cannot be explained by performance, productivity, or any factors other than biased practices.[34] One study found that the presence of three or more women on compensation committees significantly narrows the pay gap, but few firm compensation committees have that many women members.[35] In the absence of clear, fair and consistently applied criteria, compensation committees may make biased assumptions about the commitment, achievements and potential of women (especially mothers), and use decision factors that favour men and undervalue the contributions of women to the success and economic wellbeing of the firm.

7. Accountability

Before a firm decides on a course of action and sets goals for increasing gender balance, it needs to collect and analyse basic data about retention and attrition rates and patterns, and about lawyers' experiences and perceptions. Likewise, it needs data about current policies and practices, how often they are used, and their impact on lawyers' status and career progress. For example, more than 90% of law firms have policies permitting part-time work, but less than 6% of lawyers actually use them because they fear it will jeopardise their careers.[36]

Having an accurate picture of the firm's lawyers and the policies that impact gender balance enables the firm to identify its gender disparities, areas of strength, and points of vulnerability and weakness. You can look for disparities between men and women in such areas as exposure to valuable work experience and client contact; representation in leadership, management, governance, and important committees; business development opportunities; compensation, rainmaking, and credit for business origination; election to equity partnership; and hiring and integration of lateral associates and partners. If you find that such disparities exist, you can investigate why and find ways to correct the situation by examining the existing governance and reward structures, leadership and compensation decision-making processes, and personal behaviours and practices of lawyers in the firm.

---

33 Julie Triedman, "A Few Good Women", *The American Lawyer*, 28 May 2015. (Note that the gender disparity cited in footnote 12 relates only to equity partners, while the figure here compares pay for all partners.)

34 Natasha Innocenti, "Show Me the Money", Major, Lindsey & Africa, 12 September 2014; Dr Silvia Hodges Silverstein, "White Paper: Gender Study", Sky Analytics, March 2014; Lauren Stiller Rikleen, *Closing the Gap*, (American Bar Association, 2013).

35 Rikleen, *Report of the Ninth Annual National Survey*, above.

36 Deborah Rhode, "Law is the Least Diverse Profession in the Nation. And Lawyers aren't Doing Enough to Change That", *The Washington Post*, 27 May 2015.

Don't assume you know about what women experience, perceive or feel about the firm. Ask them. Compare the data by seniority levels and across offices, practice groups, departments and industry teams. Ask qualitative questions too, about all aspects of life and experience at the firm. Collect the same information from men and compare their responses to women's. To provide just a few examples:

- How do they feel about the way they are treated in the firm?
- Do they believe the firm is meritocratic?
- Do they believe they experience gender bias?
- Do they have role models they admire in the firm?
- Do they receive the work experience and opportunities they want?
- Do they have mentors and sponsors who are invested in their career success?
- How many internal client referrals do they receive?
- How engaged are they? How long do they plan to stay?
- Where do they go/what do they do when they leave your firm?

Your data analysis provides a baseline. It should give you a clear picture of the firm's unique gender disparities and allow you to develop data-driven strategies tailored to these findings. Once you understand women's experiences and perceptions, and know when, where and why women leave, you will have a better sense of where intervention and change are needed. For example, if you determine that women are receiving inferior work assignments, insufficient client contact, or lesser bonuses, you can put systems in place to ensure that work assignments and client opportunities are fairly distributed, and decisions about compensation are made using unbiased criteria.

As you develop and implement strategies for change, it is essential to set targets and priorities. Specific targets are important to keep everyone focused and establish clear measures of success. Firms that set gender balance goals are more likely to make progress than those without them. Setting priorities is important so that energies are directed properly and for greatest impact.

The team in charge of the overall initiative should be diverse, with prominent male leaders in the forefront who are respected by colleagues and accept a stake in the outcome. They should track developments closely to ensure that plans are being well executed and making the desired progress. Monitoring implementation allows them to see what's working, what isn't, and what needs to be dropped, added or tweaked. It allows them to assess the effectiveness of the initiative over time. And it enables them to recognise patterns and trends and respond quickly.

Critical to this process is tying actions to consequences, so that everyone is held accountable for the success of their efforts. Accountability is crucial in order to maintain momentum and achieve both short- and long-term objectives. Leaders at every level and in every office and practice area should have plans for their constituents tied to the overall plan, and report to the firm regularly on their progress and results.

One example of how firms can build accountability into an initiative is by setting clear expectations for partners and holding partners to them. For example, one AmLaw50 firm has developed diversity and inclusion competencies that deal with education, behaviour change and visible leadership. Each of these three foundational competencies is explained in detail, along with examples of associated behaviours, skills and action items. All partners in leadership roles create their own 'diversity and inclusion action plans' that set out what they will learn and do to improve and apply these competencies. The personal goals they set are tied to critical firm business goals, and their plans incorporate specific action steps that move them toward their goals.

8. Conclusion

Women – and men – will stay longer and perform better in law firms where the culture is inclusive and lawyers believe they can have fulfilling legal careers without sacrificing their personal lives or authenticity. Firms with the foresight and determination to create a better workplace will have a significant competitive advantage. The time to start is now.

Appendix

A Transformative women's initiatives

Many women's initiatives (WI) offer programmes for women at all levels of seniority and across generations, such as educational and social networking events, mentoring circles, book groups, and training in business development and other skills. The most effective WIs do more than sponsor programmes and events. They seek to transform firm culture through consistent, strategic efforts that include changing systems and behaviours; driving policies that deal with everything from parental leave to pathways to leadership; reaching out to men in various ways; and drawing attention to women as leaders.

As an example, Baker, Donelson, Bearman, Caldwell & Berkowitz, PC expanded and reinvigorated its WI in 2013. Its objective is to create an inclusive culture where women lawyers thrive, and that objective is explicitly tied to the strategic and economic priorities of the firm. The WI is working toward this goal in many ways. For example, recognising the pivotal role partners and decision makers play in this process, the WI sponsors a 360-degree review process for firm leaders that evaluates them on factors like their respect for diversity, support for all group members' growth and development, and whether they treat everyone equitably. The WI is also writing new job descriptions for managing partners and practice group leaders with an emphasis on diversity and succession planning.

Men are actively involved in the WI, which operates through committees. Influential male partners chair or co-chair some of those committees. The firm's chair and CEO, a man, serves on the women's initiative advisory committee, which is comprised of prominent male and female leaders from throughout the firm. A detailed annual plan enumerates goals for each committee, and each aspect of the annual plan is monitored, measured and reported. In addition, the chair of the WI is allotted time at management committee meetings to keep the firm's top leaders informed about progress and to provide them with tools and resources to support women's advancement.

Baker Donelson's WI is producing positive results. In each of the years 2014 to 2016, 42% to 62% of the lawyers elevated to partner have been women, and women now make up 33% of both the firm's board of directors and practice group leaders.

B Initiatives that identify and groom women leaders

Some firms conduct intensive leadership and business development programmes that identify and groom high-potential women lawyers. In most of these programmes, women are nominated by their practice groups, submit written applications and go through interviews. The women who are selected participate in a number of developmental activities and are given access to firm leaders and career-supporting resources, such as:

- educational programmes on topics like business development, client communication, leadership skills, gender dynamics, personal branding, and law firm economics;
- meetings with senior partners, firm leaders and executive-level committees;
- sessions with executive, business development, and other types of coaches;
- discussion opportunities with women partners and exposure to a variety of role models;
- reunions with alumnae of the programme.

Here are three examples of firms that prepare women for leadership:

(1) Norton Rose Fulbright's Career Strategies Programme (CSP), launched in 2010, was intended to raise women's confidence in pursuing partnership and show managers how to encourage women toward that goal. The CSP is designed to help women become successful partners, understand their value to the business, and demonstrate the firm's commitment to retaining their expertise. It also educates supervisors on how to discuss, manage and promote the career progress of the women they supervise.

Norton Rose Fulbright has 3,800 lawyers in 50+ offices around the world. The initial goal of the CSP was to raise the number of women partners in its offices in Europe, the Middle East and Asia from 16% to 21% in three years – and they met that goal. In fact, they now have 25% women partners, with a new target of 30% by 2020. Results of the CSP have been impressive in other ways as well:

- Attrition for CSP alumnae is 7% lower than overall female attrition.
- In 2012/2013, CSP graduates financially outperformed other women partners by 53.6% and male colleagues by 36.5%.
- 20% of CSP alumnae have been promoted to partner, 80% of whom were promoted within two years of attending CSP.

In light of the programme's success, the CSP has been expanded to Australia, Canada and the United States.

(2) Holland & Knight LLP was the first law firm to create a leadership development programme for women when it started 'Rising Star' in 2003. The goals of this year-

long programme for five annual participants are to help prepare women for leadership opportunities, elevate their profiles within the legal profession and community, and increase their success in business development. Since its inception, 65 women have graduated from the Rising Star programme. Among those graduates, 19 were promoted to non-equity partner, 10 have become equity partners, and many have assumed major leadership roles.

(3) Perkins Coie LLP also targets women with the potential and desire for leadership but uses a different approach. The firm considers committees to be training grounds for firm leaders because they provide the chance to learn, practise and demonstrate leadership ability, and over time, to step into increasingly important committees and more significant roles. The firm encourages women, including junior associates, to apply for committees. The managing partner makes committee appointments after consulting the committee chair and the chief diversity officer (CDO), among others, to discuss the skills, ambitions, needs and readiness of each candidate. Through this selection process, more women apply, receive appointments, gain experience, confidence and visibility, and move up through the ranks. Over the last seven years, women have comprised one-fifth to two-thirds of each new partner class.

In-house careers

Cecilia Poullain
Natixis Asset Management

In the competitive market for legal talent, in-house legal departments are able to offer a wide variety of legal positions suited to different personalities and skill sets. Generally, the working hours are regular. There are a whole host of other advantages, including providing the satisfaction of understanding and participating in the development of the company's business and the growth of strong relationships with internal clients.

In preparing this chapter, I have had the privilege of meeting with six other professionals. Let me introduce them to you.

Both Nathalie and Laurent have always worked in-house in French institutions. Nathalie started her career in a bank, worked for two asset managers for a number of years and now manages a team of seven lawyers. Her team works on capital markets master agreements and structured funds, and includes two people concentrating on lobbying on capital market issues. Laurent has always worked in project finance. He has never changed jobs, but the organisation he works for has changed around him. He now works for an asset manager and manages one other professional.

Sarah worked for over 10 years in international US and English law firms. She very reluctantly agreed to a secondment in a real estate asset manager, afraid that she would get terribly bored. As it turned out, she loved working in-house so much that she left the law firm and joined the asset manager permanently. She is now their legal counsel and manages a team of 20 people.

Guillaume worked for a large French firm then an international firm for seven years. In order to better understand his banking clients, he moved in-house, intending to stay for three years. Three years turned into 20, but he has recently moved back into a law firm and says "I have never been so happy."

Francesca, an Italian lawyer, worked for two major US firms in France and a large Australian firm in Sydney. She also worked in a supra-national organisation in France. She now has her own practice.

Sophie works in human resources in an asset manager. She is particularly interested in how to work with the individuals that make up an organisation in order to improve efficiency.

As for me, I graduated in Australia, before spending a year with a major law firm in London. For personal reasons, I moved to the North East of England where I worked for a community law centre, before moving back to Sydney to take up a position in one of the big four Australian law firms. In 1996, I moved to France, where I have worked in a French bank, a US law firm and a French asset manager. I no longer work as a lawyer, but as a structurer in the fixed income department of an asset manager. Twenty years later, I am still living and working in France.

The observations I make below are therefore from the perspective of major law firms and financial institutions, with a strong French flavour. It may be that my observations do not apply in smaller firms, in different industries and in different jurisdictions.

1. Salary

The most obvious way of attracting talent is pay. While the best-paid legal talent is to be found in the big international firms, companies are able to offer a wide range of positions with the associated wide range of salaries.

For the majority of in-house lawyers, and certainly those at the bottom end of the scale, salaries do tend to start relatively low and to evolve slowly.

However, top professionals, especially in financial institutions, can earn extremely well. A significant part of their salary package can include stock options and annual bonuses. Bonuses are less common in firms, and certainly less systematic. And salaries are stable, compared to earnings. According to Sophie, because of the wave of new regulations that apply to the finance industry, it is currently extremely difficult to recruit internal lawyers at salaries that are consistent with those of the existing team, and her company is consistently forced to pay salaries at the top end of the range.

2. Prestige

It is generally considered more prestigious to be an external lawyer than to work in-house. This is certainly the case in France, where the exams to become an *avocet* are extremely competitive. Of course, prestige matters more to some people than to others.

Unlike an external lawyer, an internal lawyer is not a fee earner but part of the support staff. As such, they are a cost to the business rather than a profit centre and do not have the same social status within the organisation as a solicitor in a firm. Lawyers moving in-house from a firm can sometimes find this change in status difficult, and may not always fully appreciate it before the move.

That said, in the finance industry, where regulation has multiplied following the 2008 crisis, the trend is to consider lawyers as an integral part of the business, rather than as a brake. They tend to be more involved in projects, and at an earlier stage. This increases their ability to influence business decisions and the development of the company generally.

3. Manageable hours

If higher salaries and status are available in firms, can in-house legal departments compete by offering shorter and more predictable working hours? The response, generally, is a resounding 'yes'.

There are few jobs where people work as hard as in the top international firms. It is the only job where people work for days at a time with no or very little sleep, and are in the office for 16, 17 or 18 hours a day for months or years at a time. It is the only job where people routinely cancel dinners and weekends because of work. Francesca complained that she had cancelled not a few, but hundreds of dinners. Amazingly, she only discovered what some of the shops in her street sold when she left the law firm; she had never been at home when they were open before. I personally found the most difficult thing about law firm hours was the unpredictability: after a quiet week, I absolutely hated having to cancel my plans for the weekend and go into the office on an urgent matter. However, we are all different in this respect; some of my colleagues thrived on the unpredictability.

Although many in-house lawyers work hard, they are able to manage their time better. Lawyers with less high-powered positions tend to have very regular working hours. Those with more responsibility, such as Laurent and Sarah, work long hours, and Guillaume worked 18-hour days when he was in-house. However, they all agreed that the work-flow was relatively regular. This is for the following reasons:

- Their 'clients' work for the same organisation. They have no choice: they have to get sign-off from their legal department (although in at least one French bank, internal clients can choose between using the legal department and briefing out). An internal lawyer is able to say 'you'll just have to wait'. If the pressure is too great on a particular lawyer, questions of priority can be determined by the business people or by the head of the legal department. For an external lawyer, this is not an option: he or she has to pretend that every client is their only client.
- In-house lawyers have a fallback: for urgent or major matters, it is often possible to brief out. For external counsel, the only fallbacks are lunch at the desk, late nights and weekends in the office.
- Because they work closely with the business people, they are better able to predict the work-flow.
- There is no time-recording or billing. When I was working in a firm, unless I was working on a big matter, I found I needed to work 10 or 11 hours a day in order to bill six or seven, and I believe my experience is fairly typical. The time-recording system certainly increases the pressure on external lawyers to work long hours.
- There are simply lower expectations of long hours. A colleague moved from a law firm to a bank and stunned her new work-mates by doing an 'all-nighter' the very first week.

The attitude of young lawyers in firms seems to be changing as regards their working conditions. Before, they were willing to work all hours of the day and night in the hope of one day making partner. A number of current partners, astounded, have told Laurent that young lawyers now refuse to work late if they have made other plans. Is this because starting salaries are low and partnership seems unattainable? Is it a more fundamental change in the work ethic? Or is it because they are more able to resist the social pressure to work long hours?

Sophie commented that couples often have the same types of qualifications: lawyers are married to engineers, or to consultants, or to accountants, or to other lawyers. When children arrive, something has to give, and more often than not it is the woman's career rather than the man's. This works in favour of companies, who can generally offer more regular working hours, compatible with childcare. As a result, there tend to be a lot of women working in in-house legal departments. However, this also means that women are choosing to take on less challenging roles, at least when the children are young. This becomes a problem later on, both for the women and for their employer. For women, it makes it difficult to catch up with their male colleagues and to fully realise their professional potential. For companies, it makes it difficult to find enough qualified women for senior management positions. Some people may consider that this is not a particular problem for the company. However, it is becoming widely accepted that organisations benefit from having more women at all levels of management. This is not because women are better managers per se, but because a more diversified management structure makes decisions that are appropriate for a more diversified clientele. To put it more simply, women managers make decisions that appeal to women clients.

The working day for internal and external lawyers is very different. In France, lawyers generally start late – coming in at 10.30am is relatively normal. They often take long lunches and then work late into the night. One of the tax partners in the firm I worked for in Paris regularly came into the office at midday or later and worked through until 4am the next morning. In firms, perhaps the time-recording system encourages people to be seen to be staying late, in addition to the actual hours on the time sheet. There can also be a fairly unhealthy 'superhero' mentality, pushing people to work very long hours without sleep. I do wonder how lawyers functioning on very little sleep manage to think clearly about complex legal problems. As a client, I am not sure I want to be paying top dollar for a lawyer who has not slept all night!

Lawyers in companies generally work more regular hours. In my company, for example, a normal day for most professionals starts at 9am and finishes between 6.30 and 7pm.

4. Stress levels

Can in-house legal departments offer less stressful jobs than firms?

The question in itself is interesting. If there was no stress in a job, there would be no challenge, it would be extraordinarily boring and there would be no opportunities to learn. When people are asked about the work experiences they enjoyed the most, they almost always think of times when they had a challenge which they were not sure they could meet.[1] This has certainly been my experience. Interestingly, recent studies show that our physical reaction to stress depends on our attitude.[2] If we approach a stressful situation with a positive attitude, as an opportunity to learn and grow, our physiological response to the situation is quite different.

Stress on lawyers in top firms can be immense and unrelenting. They are expected to work fast and accurately on sometimes very complex problems for long

---

1 Maurice Thévénet, "*L'enjeu de l'engagement au travail*", TED Talks, 30 October 2014.
2 Kelly McGonigal, "How to make stress your friend", TED Talks, September 2013.

periods of time. They regularly deal directly with demanding clients who expect them to have the answers at their fingertips, who are paying big money and who can and do change firms at a moment's notice. In addition, if the lawyer makes a mistake, the firm may be legally liable. In Australia, all my lawyer friends had the number of the firm's insurer stuck to their telephone.

Although working in-house has its challenges, it is rare to find this level of stress on in-house lawyers, mainly because they are not dealing with external clients. In other words, it is much easier and quicker to lose a client than to lose a job.

In France, as in many other jurisdictions, there is an additional pressure on external lawyers. Generally, they are not salaried but *profession libérale* – or independent professionals. If their contract is terminated, they have no right to any unemployment benefits whatsoever. In a country which puts so much emphasis on workers' rights, and indeed, in any country, this situation is anachronistic and plain unfair. Obviously, in-house lawyers benefit from the same legal protections as any other salaried employee.

In large companies or organisations, there can be a multitude of different people from different departments working on a particular matter. This can make decision-making slow and make it difficult and frustrating to move projects forward; but it does mean that in this type of organisation, the pace of work is slower, the individual has more time to analyse and respond to problems and to discuss issues with a variety of other professionals. In comparison, the structure of a law firm is relatively simple: there are the partners, the other lawyers and the client. In firms, most matters are urgent and need to be dealt with immediately. As a result, information moves quickly between the client, the partner and the solicitor working on a file. For the lawyers, this means taking in and dealing with large amounts of information in a short period of time, which can be demanding and stressful.

5. A wide choice of careers

In the legal departments of many companies, there are generally a number of different opportunities with different levels of responsibility. In the finance industry, for those lawyers who wish to remain relatively unexposed, there are a host of less demanding positions. Of course, the work can be relatively repetitive, but this suits some people. Nathalie, for example, has people in her team who are likely to evolve very little. They are less ambitious than others, and are not able or willing to deal with overbearing or aggressive business people. She allocates files accordingly.

But there are also challenging positions for more motivated lawyers. People who have moved in-house from a law firm, such as Sarah, almost always have more high-powered roles, but these roles can also be filled by lawyers who have worked their way up. In my company, for example, the head of the legal department has never worked in a firm.

In addition, companies are able to offer opportunities to in-house lawyers outside the legal department. If I take my own career as an example, when I was working on collateralised debt obligations (a type of structured credit product) in the legal department, I was asked to move to the front office in order to structure these products. My role has evolved, and I now structure debt funds. Although I continue to use my legal skills, I have also developed my financial, marketing and project management skills.

That said, the pyramid structure can make it difficult for companies to offer sufficient opportunities to talented young lawyers. In a big company or group, although positions can be available in different legal departments or subsidiaries, there is often only one head of department. If that person is unlikely to move, an ambitious young lawyer will be forced to change departments or companies in order to evolve. When he was managing a legal department, Guillaume's objective was to move lawyers around regularly in the first 10 years of their career, potentially overseas (with the risk that they would not come back ...) so that they would have more opportunities later on. This also had the benefit of maintaining their interest and making them more well-rounded professionals.

If it is not managed carefully, the lack of opportunity for younger lawyers can create frustration and tension, especially if the head of department is feeling pressure from his or her subordinates.

In order to address the pyramid problem, certain companies try to develop two different career paths –one for managers and another for experts. The idea is to allow lawyers who are not interested in management, or not cut out for it, to progress. In my experience, the solutions found are not yet totally satisfactory, as the management route is still perceived as the better way to get on.

6. A broad skill set

Being an internal lawyer requires a broad range of skills. In-house lawyers deal with all the business that it is not appropriate to brief out, and in this have a similar role to external counsel. For example, in his project finance transactions, Laurent drafts all the corporate documentation himself. In Nathalie's team, most of the negotiations are conducted in-house, as her team are experienced negotiators and it would be far too costly to brief out. There is a team of 20 people in my company who draft all the fund prospectuses and mandates.

However, the role of an in-house lawyer is in many ways very different. He or she has to determine what to brief out, to manage the process of selecting external counsel, perhaps via a tender offer, and to negotiate fees. Once counsel has been appointed, the internal lawyer then has to act as an interpreter between the business people and external counsel. This involves explaining the position of external counsel to the business people, and understanding the concerns and priorities of the business people and explaining them to external counsel. The in-house lawyer is also responsible for managing the relationship with external counsel and keeping costs under control.

External counsel tend to see legal risk everywhere they turn, and to raise every possible issue. To a certain extent, this is their role – and they may be liable if they fail to do so. The internal lawyer's role is to challenge them and to make a determination about the real extent of the risk. It is difficult for other people in the organisation to play this role. In Laurent's words, "the business people don't have the know-how to put a brake on the lawyers." The internal lawyer is not required to have answers to all the legal questions that are raised; his or her role is to identify and frame them for outside counsel.

Because in-house lawyers are by definition specialised in a particular industry, they often become expert in the regulatory environment that applies to that industry and have hands-on experience of how it works in practice. They can be involved in external legal working groups or lobbying for the industry, giving them opportunities to follow and understand the detail of regulatory changes. They not only come to understand the regulatory environment, but they also acquire an in-depth knowledge of the actual industry.

Business people can turn to experienced in-house lawyers for advice and leadership on issues that are wider than legal issues. Laurent is regularly consulted on how to run negotiations on business points, for example. This adds to the interest of the job.

One of the advantages of not being a fee earner is that the in-house lawyer's services are never marketed or sold. Firms sell their legal expertise; companies sell their services or products. External counsel can spend a lot of time on client development and are permanently worried about where the next file is coming from, which is not the case for in-house lawyers.

7. An effective learning process

All three in-house lawyers I spoke to emphasised that they loved the contact with other types of professionals. Because internal lawyers work for the client, they have the luxury of spending a lot of time with business people. This not only makes their job more interesting, it also helps them to understand the business, to understand how legal issues apply in the real world and to act as intermediary with outside counsel, as discussed above. They are able to acquire a feel for the business as a whole and to understand how their work contributes to its growth. Not only do they feel useful, but working in a team also helps them to care more about their work. In Sarah's view, external lawyers are paid too much too soon, which makes it too expensive for them to attend lengthy meetings with the business people. They are therefore deprived of the learning opportunities that in-house counsel have.

I personally found it very frustrating working in a firm after having worked in a bank, because urgent matters would come through the door, be dealt with and disappear. There was no continuity in relation to a particular file. Working in-house allows lawyers to follow and understand how the business is evolving, make suggestions and improve the process. This can be more interesting than treating isolated files or enquiries.

In-house lawyers not only learn from their colleagues on the business side. They also learn from the variety of external counsel they work with. In addition, if they are doing cross-border work, they are required to understand the laws of different jurisdictions. It can be very interesting to compare how different legal systems deal with the same problem.

There is, however, a risk that internal lawyers become too highly specialised and end up doing the same sort of work over and over again, especially in larger structures. They can also end up doing so much paperwork that they lose sight of the law. In my experience, perhaps because they are not writing legal opinions and advice and because there is so much routine work, in-house lawyers can neglect to keep up to date with legislative changes and important court decisions.

In this sort of structure, it is important to ensure that lawyers are regularly challenged. As Nathalie put it, "I have to make sure I give my team enough to eat and drink." They can also be challenged by regularly moving into different practice areas.

8. Corporate culture

It is very difficult to make generalisations about corporate culture. Atmosphere is highly subjective and will vary from organisation to organisation, from department to department, from day to day and from individual to individual. Each year, my company asks its employees to respond to a questionnaire about the working environment. One year, I was responsible for interviewing the people in my department to see what ideas they had for improvement. I was struck by the extent to which their responses were influenced by each person's values, and the huge range of perceptions among a small, relatively uniform group of people.

That said, I will risk making some generalisations and share some of the experiences of the people I interviewed.

For external counsel, clients come and go. If a lawyer and a client no longer see eye to eye, there are always other clients. However, for an internal lawyer, the 'client' is its employer. The lawyers and business people work together day after day, month after month, year after year, particularly in smaller organisations. This can create very strong, long-term working relationships. These relationships are key to retaining talent. To put it another way, if people are working with their friends, they will find it much harder to leave.

For in-house lawyers, this teamwork can pose challenges. Lawyers and business people can, and should, on occasion disagree. The lawyers must be able to say 'no' when their business colleagues want to make a decision that would put the company at risk. It can be difficult for the lawyer to take a stand when the relationships with the business people are too close. Sarah's approach is to focus on major risks; because she lets minor points go, the business people listen to her when she does raise an issue.

Guillaume was fed up with the many different layers of management and the politics of working in-house. He went back to a law firm as a partner, and prefers the simplicity of the structure and relationships. Francesca had a different experience: she found that lawyers in the firms she worked for, and particularly those at senior associate level, could be very competitive, with very little empathy between them.

I would like to finish with an example of how employers can improve the corporate culture. In recent years, at my present employer, there has been an initiative to improve the working environment. Seven years ago, top management started a 'Sustainable Development' programme. There are now five Sustainable Development groups, one of which is 'Conviviality'; another deals with the work–life balance and the career progression of women; and a third which promotes the integration of people with disabilities. The other two groups deal with environmental issues and support for a local homeless people's shelter. More than 20% of the workforce has volunteered to participate in these groups at one time or another. In addition, a formal working group run by the human resources department works on improving the atmosphere. There are also regular lunchtime conferences on all sorts of topics that can be related to work, but generally are not.

These initiatives have made a significant difference to the atmosphere of the company. They have created links between employees and brought together people who are concerned about the same issues. They have also added a positive new dimension to the company's corporate identity.

These initiatives are one of the reasons I enjoy working for my company. They have given me the opportunity to meet other people with the same values and interests, and I find it reassuring to know that my employer has the same values as I do.

It would be fantastic if all employers, whether companies or law firms, had the same sort of social commitment – apart from the fact that it is good for developing cohesion among employees, commitment to the employer and a great marketing tool.

9. Conclusion

Half a day a week, Nathalie teaches law at one of the French universities. She does this for a number of reasons, one of which is to talk to students about the variety of legal careers available in-house. She finds that they are often not aware of what sorts of positions are available or of how interesting the work can be. I personally have found that working in-house has taken my career in directions I could never have anticipated.

Recruiting and retaining talent in first-generation law firms

Anna Grishchenkova
KIAP Attorneys at Law

1. First-generation law firms

To paraphrase the famous quote from Leo Tolstoy, 'Successful first-generation law firms are all alike; every struggling first-generation law firm struggles in its own way.'

What are first-generation law firms in the first place? A typical answer would be 'it depends'. It depends on the age, size, specialisation and mission (if any) of the firm. What do we imagine, when we hear the term 'first-generation law firm'? If the firm is new, we probably imagine happy young faces, bright colours, enthusiasm, the taste and effect of champagne – an upbeat mood, euphoria: 'we can do it!'

As time passes, the taste of champagne is replaced by that of whisky or cognac – solid and firm, but not so much fun. Faces become more serious and colours become darker – more official. Light and bright clothes are changed for tweed and wool – more impressive and professional.

We can imagine the life cycle of first-generation law firms as changes in the seasons – spring, summer, autumn, winter and ... spring again.

Approaches to recruiting and retaining talent also change during this time. Firms in each 'season' have their own concerns and struggles.

1.1 Spring

Beginning in spring, founding partners are inspired by the idea behind their firm. The main struggle at the beginning is to survive and to find enough work, and then to create something different from their previous (negative) experience. Enthusiasm is high and the future is unpredictable.

Usually, at this stage there is no specific strategy for recruiting and retaining talent; partners gather people from their previous teams. Depending on the firm's strategy and the amount of work, the firm can focus more on recruiting rainmakers or 'working hands'. However, either form of recruitment is difficult, because it is necessary to persuade people to believe in a new firm. A lot depends on personal trust in the founding partners and in their ability to succeed.

1.2 Summer

In summer, everything becomes slightly easier. If a firm survives – which only a few manage to do – it becomes known in the market. At this point it is very important clearly to formulate specific features of the firm and to make it 'an ideal employer' for the right people. This focus on 'the right people' is usually overlooked. All too often, firms lack a clear vision as to which people are needed and their long-term strategy for recruiting such people.

Young people will often be drawn to a firm that has achieved general recognition. However, frequently such people are not the 'right people' for the particular firm. One of the reasons is a current trend (at least in Russia and CIS countries)[1] that only 1 to 2% of undergraduates from top universities are ready to undertake the relevant work and all law firms are in competition for talented individuals.

Identifying and entering into competition for young talent will involve the following:

- lectures in major universities;
- special events promoting law firms in universities;
- internships for young lawyers;
- having a presence in professional associations and conferences;
- participation (or coaching teams) in moot courts;
- using young colleagues in the firm as a source of information about potential candidates;
- using social networks (both as a way to publish information about the firm and as a way to observe other lawyers and their behaviour).

It is possible to argue that there is an inverse relationship between the remuneration a firm offers its lawyers and the creativity needed to recruit and retain them. The more you pay your people, the less creative you need to be and vice versa. If you cannot pay high salaries, you need to be really creative. Relatively young firms are usually unable to pay high salaries and must create other advantages for their people. In these circumstances it becomes necessary to rely on motivation, social activities, corporate events, principles of work–life balance and support for working mothers.

However, the idea of providing work–life balance and flexible working hours, the possibility of working 'offshore', and a Google-style office environment are becoming increasingly appealing. How do you compete when everybody claims that they provide work–life balance?[2] What other factors can help to attract talent?

The best firms really think about these issues; but some only think that they think. The closer it is to autumn, the more firms think that they succeed the way they are, and the more difficult it becomes to change ongoing attitudes and strategies.

1.3 Autumn

Firms in the autumn of their existence usually lose the enthusiasm of their early years. Partners are older and new people may have their own vision of their career within the firm and ideal strategies for retaining talent.

In some firms, the way to a partnership is clear and transparent; in some it is less so. This may have a major impact on morale among a firm's lawyers. People may

---

1 Statistics are based on interviews and discussions with different lawyers and HR specialists in Russia and CIS countries.

2 Another question to consider is how many law firms can honestly say that they have flexible arrangements that work well? Probably not very many.

start to look for other job opportunities at shorter intervals. Better firms will be courageous enough to learn the reasons for this and even to make changes within the firm.

Firms can aim to:

- replace short-term thinking and cherry-picking by a long-term strategy in recruiting and retaining the right people (including in some cases waiving later hiring of senior staff and fostering young talent to partner level instead);
- implement systems of mentoring and training (and reward those lawyers who actively engage in these activities);
- implement motivation systems taking into account not only billing, but other types of contribution, as well as flexible working hours;
- create transparent and effective partnership systems;
- create a healthy working atmosphere of trust and support.

1.4 Winter

Winter is coming. First-generation firms look more like other firms which have existed over several generations. One of the differences is that first-generation firms are usually founded by strong leaders and rainmakers. Thus, when founding partners start to think about retirement they may discover that people in their firm look like them, but lack strong leadership qualities. This is because they were chosen not for their leadership skills, but for their high-quality technical work for clients of the founding partner.

This is a crucial point in the life of the firm; spring can return if founding partners share their legacy with young people. Alternatively, spring can start elsewhere with young people from the firm starting their own firm.

Of course it may be wrong to generalise, but in some ways almost all first-generation firms use a cherry-picking strategy in recruiting talent. Where this is the case, the founding partners and their colleagues will not have a particular strategy for recruiting and retaining talent. They do not have a long-term strategy like the big international law firms, but rather choose people based on the firm's current needs (ie, young assistants, or senior colleagues, or partners with teams (if the firm has an aggressive strategy)).

Tactics for finding talent can be different. However, regardless of what tool is used, the people selected will often be very much like their employers. As with the saying that 'the apple never falls far from the tree', people in first-generation law firms tend to be similar to the founding partners.

Often, but not always. The smartest law firms know that diversity is an asset. This should be a vision and a powerful tool for creating a lively and successful firm. When talented people are recruited, another goal must be to retain them.

2. Creative approaches to recruiting and retaining talent

Rates of remuneration are obviously a key issue in the process of recruiting and retaining talent. However, as noted above, first-generation law firms often have limited financial resources and therefore need to put other types of motivation in place.

For example, after a number of years' service lawyers often feel exhausted, bored, overwhelmed by routine, or sometimes even disenchanted by the legal profession. This is especially so for generation Y lawyers.[3] Motivation is key for such people.

For example, taking account of this trend, KIAP decided to make legal work more entertaining and creative, more interesting and playful, without diminishing the quality of the work. We try to use modern ways of providing traditional legal services. This includes using visual aids (eg, infographics, Prezi, videos) in presentations and even in applications to the court, where appropriate, using social networks and different platforms for exchanging ideas, and creating special apps to assist in day-to-day work. This kind of approach can be very appealing not only for young lawyers, but also for senior lawyers in more traditional and conservative law firms.

One of my favourite examples of creativity is a technique used by German law firm RAUE which has to compete with international law firms for its lawyers. Among other things, this firm specialises in art law. Its founder is a famous art collector in Germany and friend to various famous artists. The firm offers its newly hired lawyers an opportunity to choose any art object from the collection and to put it in their office. For example, one partner with whom I spoke chose a work by Andy Warhol and put it in his office. I think that the possibility of working in a place surrounded by beauty and art is a really appealing form of motivation.

Another way to motivate your people is to show them that they are valued and appreciated not only for their billable activities, but also for their personal interests. There are different ways of doing this. Some law firms support their lawyers in their interest in non-traditional areas of law. For example, one Russian law firm supports the participation of its lawyers in different competitions relating to space law.

Other firms encourage their lawyers to participate in something meaningful – something 'bigger than themselves'. One example would be charity sports activities for lawyers, such as a marathon for Russian lawyers called the Legal Run, or charity sky diving, offered by UK law firm Peters&Peters. All money collected from such events is usually sent to charities to help children or old people. On one hand, such activities are entertaining and enjoyable; on the other hand they help lawyers to feel that they are doing something meaningful. We know that one of the principles of Maslow's hierarchy of needs is that people at higher stages of this pyramid need self-esteem and self-actualisation. Self-esteem can depend largely on helping other people. I believe that lawyers need this self-esteem and feeling of fairness and equity even more than other people, as far as these elements are fundamental to the law itself. Firms who genuinely support and share these ideas are very appealing employers.

These examples are of course just parts of the bigger picture. To become really successful in attracting and keeping talent, it is necessary to have a comprehensive and consistent approach.

---

3 It should be noted that in a business which is reliant on the ability of your people to communicate with clients, it is crucial to take into account the psychology of your people, and understand and accept differences between generations and personality types. These issues are dealt with elsewhere in this book. However, it is important to stress that acknowledging differences between generations and personalities is one of the main challenges for first-generation firms.

2.1 Emotional intelligence in recruiting and retaining talent

In a business that depends on your people communicating with clients, it is crucial to take into account the psychology of your people. Much has been said about different generations, and this is dealt with in other chapters of this book. But it is also important to be aware of other differences between individuals irrespective of their age, sex or nationality.

There are many different personality types including sanguine, choleric, melancholic, phlegmatic, extrovert and introverted. For example, the Meyer-Briggs model distinguishes 16 different personalities, arising out of the following pairs:

- introversion or extroversion;
- intuition or sensing;
- thinking or feeling;
- judging or perceiving.

Dr Adizes posits different groups of people, based on a combination of four major roles:

- integrator;
- entrepreneur;
- administrator;
- producer.

Another typology, which can be useful, describes personalities in accordance with their basic interests.[4] These can be divided very roughly into three main groups:

- a focus on relationships between people;
- a focus on action, practicality;
- a focus on data, logic, and intellectual challenge.

Before we go further, it should be emphasised that this division does not mean that people from a particular 'relationship' group will not like intellectual challenge or do not take action. The division reflects general preferences.

(a) Focus on relationships between people

People from this group focus on relationships with other people. They need attention and appreciation from other people. They think a lot about what other people think about them and place great stress on such opinions. They try to gain the attention and affection of other people by different means.

Helpers: Such people

- try to help everyone and to be valued;
- try to guess what other people (clients, colleagues, employers) need, and they try to meet these needs;

---

4 Ginger Lapid-Bogda PhD. *Bringing Out the Best in Yourself at Work; and Bringing Out the Best in Everyone You Coach* (McGraw-Hill, 2004, 2009).

- are good at reading the emotional states of other people, which makes them compassionate and caring;
- feel good when people thank them for their job;
- need appreciation and gratitude from other people in order to carry out their role well;
- can be depressed when they feel under-appreciated and undervalued.

Such skills are very important in relationships with clients and colleagues. However, some tasks which do not have a direct connection with the client and which do not create the possibility for obtaining feedback can be more difficult for a helper (eg, writing a complex legal memo or dealing with abstract issues). With such people, constant positive feedback is crucial.

Achievers: These people

- try to win the attention of other people by achieving goals and appearing to be successful and confident;
- feel good when other people praise them for their victories and achievements and see them as valuable;
- want to be the best, even if this is sometimes at the expense of others;
- find it difficult to participate in team projects with 'weaker' colleagues who can lessen their chances of victory, or to handle weak court cases.

The achiever can be very efficient and successful. However, other people will sometimes feel insecure around achievers and not trust them, and this can create an unhealthy atmosphere in the team. In addition, because achievers avoid failure, they can limit their involvement in situations where this might occur and/or reframe failures as 'learning opportunities'.

Creators: These people

- win the attention of other people by creating deep and unique relationships;
- want to be seen as different and special in some way;
- create new ideas, different approaches to a problem and so on;
- want to be motivated and inspired by the work they are doing;
- prefer strong feelings and emotions.

Creators are good at creating new ideas and inspiring other people, but can sometimes be regarded as moody or even dramatic. For creators, standard routine tasks with no connection to feelings, people or creativity can be a disaster.

(b) Focus on reality and practicality

People in this group think about other people, but their primary focus is on practicality, survival, power and pragmatism. They try to use their abilities and resources to influence the world around them, but to remain independent.

Bosses: People in this category

- like to keep situations under their control;
- want important things to happen;
- take charge and assume responsibility easily;
- are quick to anger, because they see anger as an energy that helps to solve problems;
- respect power and confidence in other people and dislike lack of confidence in other people;
- can be seen as rude, intimidating and tough.

Bosses like to manage the big picture, charting the direction of work and providing oversight so that it goes well. At the same time, they intensely dislike micromanaging and being involved in the detail of work. Bosses are efficient and energetic and are valuable in huge complex projects; but sometimes other people can be afraid of them.

Energetics: People in this category

- try to influence the world with their optimistic approach;
- pursue enjoyment and excitement;
- are full of new ideas;
- involve people in projects and communicate readily and easily;
- can find it difficult consistently to manage several projects to their completion.

The energetic is great at devising new ideas, motivating and relaxing people. At the same time, she likes being busy, juggling different issues and multitasking. This may mean that she finds it difficult to assess real possibilities to accomplish everything in the time available. In addition, the energetic intensely dislikes anything that puts restraints on her time and freedom.

Mediators: People in this group

- seek harmony and positive mutual regard;
- dislike conflict, tension and ill will;
- like details that assist in understanding the overall structure;
- like routine tasks which help them to feel secure;
- dislike being forced to do anything.

Mediators are good at helping to recognise and respect differences between people and differing opinions, and mitigating conflicts. At the same time, mediators can be passively aggressive with regard to uncomfortable tasks that they do not wish to undertake. This may mean that they say yes to taking on tasks whilst meaning no, and then try to avoid bringing them to completion.

(c) Focus on data, logic, and intellectual challenge

People from this group focus less on people and their feelings, but more on principles, rules, information and intellectual challenge. They constantly look for some 'objective' guidelines to follow.

Perfectionists: People in this group

- constantly pursue perfection in themselves and in others;
- are structured and self-controlled;
- like rules and clear structures and procedures;
- try to control everything they say as well as monitoring others;
- find it difficult to achieve a state of relaxation and enjoyment and are very self-critical.

The perfectionist can be an ideal lawyer. However, because she constantly looks for perfection in the fulfilment of her role, she finds it difficult to delegate ('I cannot trust other people to do a task to the same standard'). She wants to be recognised as right and perfect and respected. It can be a struggle to achieve the level of quality that she strives for.

Geniuses: This group

- consistently upgrade their education and their level of knowledge in their subject areas;
- want to be seen as professional;
- go deep into details, because they always think that their skills and knowledge are not enough;
- can be reserved and may find it difficult to communicate with other people;
- prefer working in isolation rather than thriving in a people environment.

A genius will be extremely knowledgeable about her subject. She will try to maintain minimal involvement with other people, because she is afraid that communication may be a waste of time and would rather spend time adding to her knowledge or receiving additional education. People may feel uncomfortable with her, because she may be prone to intellectual arrogance.

Sceptics: People in this group

- constantly anticipate worst-case scenarios so that they feel prepared in case something goes wrong;
- doubt everything and ask numerous questions;
- are dubious about simple solutions to complex problems;
- challenge ideas and people when they feel concerned;
- are loyal to people, teams and organisations because this helps them to feel more secure.

Sceptics are indispensable in crisis-management and assessment of risks, but they can be too hesitant in decision making and can sometimes irritate other people with their negative outlook.

2.2 The benefits of understanding personality types

Understanding different personality types among your people can help to

- achieve more effective communication;
- provide better feedback to others;
- prevent conflicts or resolve conflicts more easily;
- create more effective teams;
- achieve a better understanding of the strengths and weaknesses of the team.

(a) Examples of improved communication

The boss and the sceptic: A boss who likes to have everything under control can be very frustrated by the doubts and concerns of the sceptic and may appear to be rude or direct in communication. In its turn, this form of direct approach may unsettle the sceptic. In such cases, the boss should remember that having doubts is not a sign of lack of confidence, but is rather a state of mind. The fact that the sceptic may wish to probe a number of different possible outcomes of a given situation may reflect their desire to understand not just the big picture, but also small details. Equally, it is important for the sceptic to understand that the tough behaviour of the boss will usually be directed towards the problem, not the person.

The perfectionist and the creator: The perfectionist can be personally distant and relate to staff through rules. The creator may see this attitude as emotionally inappropriate, as a way of making rules more important than people. Creators need special treatment, and if they do not get it they can simply dismiss the rules. To stay involved, creators need personal recognition from an acknowledged authority. Understanding and discussing differences in attitudes can help to show the perfectionist that there is more to work relationships than following orders, as well as demonstrating that the perfectionist does not intend to undervalue the creator.

The perfectionist and the energetic: The perfectionist thinks in terms of right and wrong and relies on logic to implement a plan, while the energetic requires a flexible structure that is open to new technology and ideas. Perfectionists cannot always follow multi-optional thoughts of the energetic, while the energetic may feel limited by a logical, linear approach. The perfectionist may assume that the energetic is unreliable or will try to minimise the level of supervision. One solution may be to try not to focus on procedures, set reasonable deadlines and evaluate results only.

(b) Examples of providing feedback

As noted above, the genius will try to avoid unnecessary communication, having a preference for privacy and the possibility of working alone. If you need to ask his opinion on the subject or give him feedback on a matter, it is better to notify him about the matter in advance. Let him choose the time for a discussion and allow him time to prepare. Where this is the case, the genius may demonstrate professionalism and show a surprising eagerness to help.

(c) *Examples of solving potential conflicts*

Achievers working together: Difficulties may arise when achievers feel that they have to outperform each other. They thrive in a competitive environment, but if the merit system pits them against each other, they can become adversarial. Achievers work hard for bonuses and promotions, not so much because they are motivated by material benefits, but more because their psychological wellbeing is based on winning. Achievers always examine new job opportunities and may even secretly accumulate clients and contracts. It helps to give achievers their own domain to shape and direct and to encourage them to exchange information by modelling the efficiency of cooperation and by attaching status to a group win or a team effort.

The achiever and the sceptic: The manager-achiever must respect their employee's input. Achievers usually jump on good ideas without paying due attention to other people's contributions. If the sceptic invests in a project and does not achieve due recognition, then this will undermine their trust in the achiever and the sceptic will start to create worst-case-scenarios. Therefore, it is important for achievers to remember to acknowledge the contributions of the sceptic. Such acknowledgement will help to win trust and long-term loyalty from the sceptic.

The achiever and the boss: The boss may be direct and confrontational. Achievers can be like chameleons and change their behaviour so as to be liked. As adversaries they struggle for power. Achievers can see bosses as bullies, and bosses sometimes see achievers as insincere people. If the achiever feels valued, the partnership will grow. Achievers want tangible rewards for effort, and it helps to respect that inclination rather than try to control. It helps to establish guidelines relating to salary and status. Achievers respond to the opportunities within a system. They want a ladder to climb, and their ambitions can be channelled through that structure.

The creator and the genius: Creators overreact to lack of attention, especially if the genius strives for privacy and to communicate via intermediaries and memos. The attention-seeking tactics of the creator run the risk of irritating the genius. A balance can be found by a show of interest from each side. Creators seek personal recognition, and geniuses look for organisational efficiency without the burden of a personal presence. The employee-creator must move from an emotional position and the manager-genius from a primarily logical position. It helps when the genius encourages discussion and when the creator offers objective solutions that rely on structure.

The boss and the genius: The manager-genius is very often minimally present. Potential conflict may arise when boss-employee tries to fill the power vacuum created by the manager's absence. On her return, the genius sees the boss-employee as insubordinate, and staff feel caught up in a power play. The situation improves when the genius acts openly. A confident manager can transmit certainty to others, and once the facts are out, a boss-employee may no longer feel the need to control.

Ideally, to keep talent within the firm, it is necessary to take account of basic individual needs in relation to care, appreciation, support, trust, structure and so on. This is not an easy task and it demands a lot of energy and attention. However, it helps to establish within a law firm an environment that is sensitive to the needs of all different people.

3. Key attributes of a law firm in attracting and keeping talent[5]

(a) An atmosphere of respect

A key question is the extent to which people in the firm show respect in relationships with each other from the back office and couriers to the partners. It is crucial to have both personal and professional respect, because having one without the other can create an unhealthy and unstable environment.

Is your firm really honest, structured, disciplined and consistent? For example, a lot of firms declare that they want their lawyers not only to earn money, but also to participate in other non-monetary activities, such as business development. However, this message will be undermined if the firm offers only financial rewards for outstanding performance. Lawyers will quickly recognise the inconsistency of such a programme of reward and this will lead to disappointment and demoralisation.

(b) An atmosphere of caring for others

Another key question is how well those in your firm show care and support in their relationships with each other. Do people involved in decision making simply stick to rules, structures and guidelines, or do they also acknowledge the feelings of other people?

(c) Mutual respect

Do people in your firm show that they value one another? How well do you use the particular attributes (eg, communication skills, technical knowledge or leadership qualities) of your people? Can you minimise internal competition and use your own talents to foster the talents of other colleagues?

For example, in some firms there is a serious problem in communication between senior and junior lawyers and a problem with constant feedback (not only negative, but also positive). People want to feel valued; they want to know that they are doing a good job and meeting or even exceeding expectations. Let your people know that they contribute to the success of the firm; this can be a great motivation.

(d) Willingness to enter into deeper interactions and relationships

How well do you create deeper relationship with others? Do you have your own rituals, mutually enriching discussions and grow together? A potential problem with lawyers is that most of them are good talkers, but they may not be good listeners. To retain talent, you should aim to be a good listener with the ability to enter into a deeper interaction.

---

5 Special thanks to Marina Kaldina, who first formulated these principles for me.

(e) Encouraging the pursuit of knowledge

How often do you learn something new? How well do you encourage the pursuit of knowledge in your team? Do you try to understand and know each other better?

(f) Atmosphere of trust and support

One of the most discouraging things for employees is lack of trust in the firm caused by favouritism, partners not fulfilling the same standards as lawyers, failure to give credit to members of the team and not listening to people's concerns.

How well do you create a loyal and supportive atmosphere? Do your colleagues trust you and each other?

(g) Enthusiasm and enjoyment

Lawyers increasingly want more than just money and professional recognition from their work; they want to be intellectually and emotionally involved, and feel inspired and happy. How well do you create an atmosphere of joy, spontaneity, playfulness and enthusiasm?

(h) Sense of practicality

Ultimately, each law firm is a business and practicality is therefore essential. Every firm has good times and bad. An ability to assess a situation realistically and communicate concerns is crucial. How well do you create an atmosphere of practicality and a readiness to address inevitable difficulties?

(i) Understanding and accepting differences between people

Sometimes law firms only pay lip service to notions of diversity and respect for different opinions. Frequently, however, many firms struggle to deal with different personalities and approaches in a respectful and constructive way.

Therefore, last but not the least: Do you and your team understand and accept differences between one another? Do you feel comfortable with each other?

To summarise the above discussion, experience shows that first-generation firms frequently work with limited finances. They therefore need to be very creative and use non-monetary types of motivation in recruiting and retaining talent. In these circumstances, it is important to take into account the different needs of lawyers, as well as differences in their personalities. However, some values such as trust, support, care, receptiveness to exchange of ideas, transparency, enthusiasm and practicality are universal. A firm which genuinely nurtures these values is more likely to be successful in recruiting and retaining people.

I would like to thank partners Andrew Korelskiy and Mikhail Uspenskiy for discussions in helping to write this chapter.

Managing underperformance

Patrick J McKenna
McKenna Associates Inc

---

1. Introduction

Whenever I have had the opportunity to quiz any group of partners as to what is most important to each of them personally and what would need to be present for them to stay with the firm in which they are currently practising, what I hear most often is a variation on the following theme:

What any firm would need to do to retain my loyalty includes:

- *providing an environment where I am able to learn and grow my skills;*
- *where I am able to work on exciting client matters;*
- *with people who really care about each other;*
- *in a group that is going somewhere and establishing a recognised presence in the marketplace; and*
- *where I get personal recognition for what I contribute.*

In other words, if you dig deeper, what you will usually hear is professionals who actually value having some standards of performance, where disruptive behaviour and underperformance is confronted early, and where everyone contributes to building a shared culture in which high achievers are valued. What that then means is that one of the more difficult issues that any firm leader, practice leader or responsible professional will be faced with, is when you have to confront and possibly remove someone on your team who is no longer pulling their weight.

When you are faced with this challenge (and you definitely will be at some time in your career) you need to understand that the consequences of taking decisive action are rarely as dire as they might seem to you at first glance. Nevertheless, there are numerous reasons why intelligent and capable professionals will go to great lengths to avoid taking any action. In reality, not taking action is the same as announcing that you will continue accepting unacceptable performance.

Therefore, you need to recognise each of the following as traps:

1.1 The temptation to give the situation a bit more time

Situations in which sufficient data demonstrates that a particular professional is no longer doing the job are not always easy to accept. Some leaders are inclined to hold back, waiting for even more information that a colleague is not performing in the role. Yet other leaders have a high need to be loved, admired and respected by everyone within their group. This is an important part of their personal make-up and what attracted them to take on the position of being a leader in the first place. This need makes it particularly hard for them to deal with conflict of any kind and the thought of having to confront a colleague and peer is an especially painful situation.

I worked with the managing partner of one firm who had put off dealing with an underperforming senior partner for over a year, continually rationalising (mostly to himself) how this guy was slowly coming around. You have to ask yourself: What are you seeing that makes you think that things are really going to get better without some intervention? What are the specific signs that this individual is making progress?

1.2 Fear of how the professional involved will be impacted

If you are like some leaders, you will find it natural to be concerned about how the impact of someone being told that they are underperforming is going to be accepted. You are well aware that you are dealing with a professional where this may be seen as the first major failure they have experienced in their career. The shock of that failure, combined with any possible peer embarrassment, may be a crushing blow. There is an internal tension and huge reluctance to confront such people.

Yet at some point you do have to ask yourself how long you, and the team afflicted, can reasonably be expected to continue to tolerate underperformance or disruptive behaviour. And in many cases, we are talking about situations where decisions taken or avoided can have measurable economic consequences.

1.3 Concern for how confronting the underperformer will be viewed by others

There is also a profound fear that having to confront underperformance is not only likely to provoke embarrassment on the part of the professional involved, but will also potentially stimulate other partners to be concerned about their own personal worth.

You need to realise that even if the situation ultimately results in the departure of a firm partner, or even a couple of departures within a relatively short period of time, it is not going to destabilise the entire partnership. As you put in place a carefully developed remedial plan for addressing the underperformance, your fellow partners will soon realise that you are transmitting a powerful signal about how the firm is enforcing standards and about the level of performance that is required of all lawyers.

1.4 Your sense of personal failure

It is not unusual for an experienced leader to entertain some feeling of having personally failed at preventing the underperformance. It may be very natural for you to harbour remorse at not knowing how to turn this individual around or fix the situation. You believe that if you had only given this lawyer more guidance, clearer direction, or spent more time in providing personal coaching, none of this would have happened.

Your self-imposed guilt ignores a couple of considerations. In almost every case I have observed, the partner knows full well that they are not performing in accordance with required standards, or at the level at which they had performed in the past. The truth is that you can only do so much. For you to personally think that you can help make every professional a 'star', is simply not realistic.

1.5 You cannot delegate the responsibility to take action

One of the benefits of being a leader is that you can delegate some of the more mundane or distasteful tasks to others. But, unfortunately this is not one of them. The unavoidable fact is that some responsibilities cannot be delegated, and dealing with performance issues is one of the key tasks of any effective leader.

That said, before one takes corrective action it is essential to identify where the problem lies and whether there is any rational way to fix things. Very often we just rush into assumptions about why people are underperforming.

Assuming that your strong preference is to provide the underperformer with coaching and remediation to help them succeed, then diagnosis is the starting point. The diagnosis may point to areas where your coaching might be highly productive – having this individual develop a meaningful plan to get back on track, and then together thinking through how that plan might best be implemented.

2. Consider why he or she is underperforming

A common mistake in dealing with underperformance is rushing to talk to the underperformer without pausing to consider why he or she is underperforming. At a recent workshop session a group of practice leaders, department heads and managing partners were asked to list the common reasons why their colleagues may underperform.

Here is their list:

- trouble at home or other personal problems (divorce, alcoholism, depression, etc);
- 'burnout' – no longer finding the work interesting or challenging;
- fear of failure in trying something new and reaching for career progress;
- quality-of-life choices – lack of desire to contribute more energy or time to the practice;
- externally driven reasons such as the recent loss of a client or a downturn in their chosen sector;
- failure to keep up in their field – being less in demand;
- struggling because of poor time management or other inefficiencies;
- lack of knowledge about what they should be doing to succeed;
- being poorly managed;
- insecurity due to things such as firm merger discussions, and withdrawing into their shell, pending resolution of unresolved firm issues.

As you review this list, you can add any other possible causes that you think are missing, and then ask yourself: which of these reasons are the most common in your world?

This particular collection of leaders selected burnout, loss of enthusiasm, quality-of-life choices, personal/family issues, and externally driven market changes as the major reasons for underperformance in their groups.

One of our participants added:

It all ties together. The work is so demanding, and it is so hard on you, that the result is that you ultimately say, 'I just don't like to do this anymore'. That can also spill over into personal and family issues, and it can also make you say you really want a different quality of life.

The reason people are not performing is rarely because they do not know what to do; nor is it that they do not want to do it. The incentives to do it are probably there. If they are not doing what they should, it is probably due to something deeply personal in their lives. The only way to find out what it is, and to deal with it, is to talk about it.

You are now faced with two critical questions. Does you diagnosis indicate that this professional's performance shortcomings lie in a coachable area? Secondly, what results can be expected from you (or someone) coaching this individual and over what period of time – is the result worth the investment of professional time and effort to get there?

Those are very tough questions. Over the years I have counselled a number of firm and practice leaders on how they might deal with the challenge of either coaching or removing an underproductive professional. I never underestimate the complexity or the intense emotional investment involved in making a decision to take action.

3. Be careful how you approach the discussion

Meanwhile, I have witnessed this same scenario play itself out, time after time, and we never seem to learn.

Imagine the following: the practice leader has their attention drawn to the fact that one of our respected partners is underperforming. This leader knew that the particular partner was underperforming; it did not come as a shock. But they were content to let the situation drift without resolution, rather than have to confront the ugly reality of the circumstances. But today we have the situation, the statistics, the facts thrust before us and now something must be done.

This devoted leader, unaccustomed to having to deal with an interpersonal situation of this nature, makes a case for simply leaving the underperforming partner alone and instead sending this individual a message via the annual compensation review. The rationale is that by cutting this person's compensation they will quickly come to the realisation that they had 'better raise their game and get with the programme'.

Given that we are dealing with rational people the leader's argument reaches sympathetic ears and after some months, the compensation adjustment is finally executed. No effort is ever made properly to explain the compensation adjustment or to inquire as to why this partner's performance has declined. Has work dried up in their area of practice? Are they experiencing personal problems, or perhaps afflicted with burnout? Are problems at home creating a distraction? All potentially temporary in nature and capable of being remedied. But no one bothers to ask, 'what's going on here?'

LESSON 1: in an earlier era of lockstep compensation, if a partner was underperforming, it was quickly detected and resulted in someone discreetly visiting the individual to offer assistance to get him or her back on track. Today, when that happens, management simply abdicates their job under the guise of adjusting the individual' s compensation and sending them a message.

Now our underperformer has had their annual compensation adjusted downward. But after some months, there is still no change in performance. Did this underperforming partner really know that their performance had declined and was below expectations? Absolutely! I have never seen an instance where the relevant individual was ignorant to the realities of their situation. Did this underperforming partner know what they should do to get their performance back on track? Not likely. And, certainly, nobody has bothered to ask thus far.

Well, this situation continues to fester for a protracted period of time, sometimes for years (unfortunately) until someone in a leadership position finally (hopefully), decides that maybe they should talk to this partner. So a one-on-one meeting is scheduled.

Now, because this situation has been allowed to drag on for a prolonged period of time, it can be far more difficult for our underperforming partner to take the kind of remedial action that might have delivered results, had the discussion happened when the underperformance was first detected.

LESSON 2: difficult personnel or performance issues never get better over time.

Nevertheless, our persistent leader sits down with the underperformer and points out the issue and asks the partner 'what's going on here?' The partner now recognises that they are facing a time of reckoning, and at some point will enquire of the leader (guaranteed!) the most natural question, 'what do you think I should do to get my performance back on track?'

Our naive leader, in an attempt to be of help and offer some genuine guidance, now outlines a number of alternatives that this underperformer might want to think about doing. The partner picks one of the alternatives, the leader is delighted to see that action is being taken, and everyone goes back to their office to let the situation percolate ... for another six months, or year.

A year goes by, the performance has not improved and another meeting is scheduled. Our frustrated leader asks the underperforming partner what happened. The partner responds, 'I did exactly what you suggested, but it didn't seem to work for me.'

(Interpretation: 'It was your idea Practice Leader and now it is your problem, not mine. I tried what you wanted me to do ... but it didn't work.')

LESSON 3: who really owns this problem, or – who's got the monkey?

This reminds me of an article written in the Harvard Business Review many years ago, in which the author asked his readers, every time one of their people had a problem, issue or challenge to deal with, to imagine that problem as a monkey sitting on their shoulder. His message was that the next words out of your mouth will quickly determine who owns that monkey!

In other words while you may, as a practice leader, want to be of help to your partner and indeed that is your highest value activity, by taking ownership of your partner's problem you have actually hindered their development.

4. What to do

Step one: Practice how you are going to handle this discussion.
At some point you need to try doing a dry run on how you will actually explain to your colleague why it is necessary for them to step up their performance. It often helps to sit down and write out the specific reasons you would give. The resulting insight can be powerful. "When I looked at this list", one leader confided to me, "I could not believe I had closed my eyes to this situation for this period of time."

Take some time and have a trusted colleague work with you in allowing you to practice (role play) how your discussion with this individual might unfold. Very often practising how you are going to handle the interaction helps you think through all of the different ways in which this individual may react to your message and how you then need to respond. Whenever I have done this with a firm leader, there has invariably been a sense of surprise at how 'right' the discussion feels. In other words, this is a discussion that needs to happen.

Step two: Confront the underperformance problem.
Have a one-to-one discussion with the individual to identify the underperformance. Ask first. Start responding later. Do not let the situation fester. Your leadership task is to figure out for each professional, as an individual, which reasons for underperformance exist. You must accomplish that before you can both work together to formulate any appropriate corrective action plan. For example, there is no point in talking about the meaningfulness of your group's work if the problem is family trouble.

You must have a discussion and try to find out what's going on. Say something like:

I don't want to get things wrong here, but I get the sense that you're not fully engaged with your work like you used to be. You don't seem to be showing the normal levels of enthusiasm you have shown in the past. Something is going on. I would love to help you if I can.

It is important to remember that the goal is to convey a genuine concern – 'How can I help you?' – while leaving the responsibility for improvement with the individuals themselves: 'Is there anything I can do?'

Deal with this situation now. It will be far harder to deal with a few months down the road and far more difficult to resolve in a satisfactory manner.

Step three: Listen persuasively and express confidence.
Listening persuasively is the ability to ask questions to help your colleague come to his or her own conclusions. Ask lots of questions, seek to understand what is going on, and help your partner think through their various options. The key question you need to pose is: 'So what do you think you need to do to resolve this issue?'

Reassure your colleague of your confidence in them. This is important to the individual's dignity and self-esteem. We all want to feel like we have someone on the sidelines pulling for us.

Jennifer, I know there are times when work dries up a little for all of us. You're a competent professional, so I know you can turn this around.

The proper role of an effective leader, when dealing with thorny performance issues, is to serve as coach, catalyst, and cheerleader. The coach cannot win if the team loses. You have a vested interest in the individual performance of each and every member of your group.

Step four: Invite your colleague to identify a sequential plan of action.
Do not volunteer your ideas as to what you think your partner needs to do. Rather enquire of this professional, what specifically they are going to do, and by what dates, to turn around their situation.

I need you to understand that this performance is not acceptable to the partnership. You need to take responsibility for coming up with a remedial plan of action to get your performance back on track. I'll be here to help you in any way I can, but this needs to be your plan. You need to own this situation.

And if they do not know what they should do?

In that case, I think you might want to give this situation some considered thought, perhaps confer with some trusted colleagues. I'll let you take some time to do that and let's get back together at the same time next week. And when we get back together, I want your detailed outline of what specific action you are planning to take, together with some review dates whereby we can meet to see how things are progressing.

Invite them to think about the people within (or outside) the firm with whom they might wish to confer to get some ideas. But leave the ownership for developing a remedial course of action with the professional affected.

As mentioned earlier, in most instances you may have a number of constructive ideas that you believe, if acted upon, would help resolve the situation. However, you need to allow your colleague to come up with their remedial ideas first. It is important to remember that the underperformance issue and whatever action must be taken are the responsibility of that individual. If you shape their remedial action plan for them, you allow them the convenient excuse that this was not really their plan, it was yours.

Step five: Offer your assistance by scheduling frequent follow-up meetings.
Help your colleague by determining with them what they are expecting to do and accomplish, by what dates. It might be useful at this stage to take notes, put your mutual understanding in writing and ensure that your colleague gets a copy following the meeting. Set frequent follow-up sessions (eg, at least every second month), to check on their progress.

Step six: Encourage them to maintain their focus and help celebrate small successes.
Acknowledge any achievement, no matter how small, during your follow-up meetings, as soon as possible following that achievement. Your role is to 'praise achievements back to acceptable levels of performance'.

5. Dealing with the uncoachable

There are times when your diagnosis may reveal a more pervasive problem – for example, this particular individual is just not prepared to invest any of their non-billable time in building their skills to make themselves more valuable to clients, or to proactively engage in serious business development efforts. Sometimes your choice is clear – the individual's fundamental performance may simply be uncoachable and more extreme action might, therefore, be warranted.

Think about whether you have ever encountered someone who seemed to be a lost cause.

How do you detect a lost cause? Posing that question to a group of leaders recently, together we developed a list. A lost cause is some professional who:

- blames others or uncontrollable circumstances for their unacceptable performance or behaviour;
- rarely executes on those promises made to the group;
- is usually defensive and never accepts personal responsibility;
- is constantly disruptive, uncommunicative or disrespects colleagues;
- is combative and creates conflict and tension within the team;
- may ask for others' opinions but regularly rejects those views when given;
- acts as though he or she were a victim.

Here are just a couple of indicators that may signal when you are dealing with one of these people.

- They think everyone else is the problem. Some time back I worked with a particular leader who was concerned about morale, following two high-profile departures. He led a successful firm, but feedback indicated that he had favourites. When I reported this feedback, he completely surprised me. He said he agreed with the charge and thought he was right to do so. He did not think he had a problem. This successful professional has no interest in changing. If he has no desire to change, you are wasting your time!
- Then there is the underperformer who is pursuing the wrong strategy for her practice. If this individual is insistent upon and already going in the wrong direction, all you are going to do with your coaching is help her get there faster. It is hard to help people who do not think they have a problem.

Good luck with the perpetual pessimist. You cannot change the behaviour of unhappy people so that they become happy; you can only fix behaviour that is making people around them unhappy.

Many characteristics define someone unwilling to become a better version of themselves. They may be individuals who are looking for a list of answers – seeking the secret sauce to a recipe for success. They may only want to share their views and do not feel the need to listen to other people's experiences or ideas. They may get defensive when you offer a suggestion or an opinion. Some of the most intelligent professionals are unwilling to be coached. Unfortunately, it is difficult to get inside someone's head, so when dealing with someone you sense is uncoachable – depending on the severity of the situation – here are a few final options to consider:

- *Attempt to discern the cause.* Making a positive change can be difficult, and there may be understandable reasons why your colleague might resist trying new things or accepting your coaching. You are often dealing with very talented and successful professionals, which further feeds their belief that they do not need to change because what they have been doing has been working. Talk to the individual about what dynamics might be leading to their ongoing resistance. Those factors could include a deep-seated fear of failure, a pessimistic outlook that nothing can ever change – or even a fear of success.

- *Play a strong managerial role.* Rather than continuing to try to coach this individual, tell the person what you, as the practice leader, expect of them. Some professionals need external pressure and expectations to succeed.
- *Talk about gains and consequences.* Be frank. Sometimes, the most we can hope for is clarity – clarity as to what the consequences are if the performance or behaviour is not improved. 'What happens if you don't achieve the performance standards that the firm wants you to achieve?' All the while we are trying to create some intrinsic motivation.

An important lesson I have learned: know when to stop. It is exceedingly difficult to coach attitude, work ethic, honesty or intelligence. Perhaps this individual was an incorrect hire to begin with; perhaps they were promoted to partnership well before they demonstrated the appropriate skill set; perhaps they simply do not want to do the heavy lifting that is required. These are situations you are unlikely ever to win.

So, if all else fails, you may have to ask your colleague to leave the firm. In that event ...

6. Carefully manage communications

After any initial shock, give your colleague sufficient time to think and ask them to consider how they want to work with you to manage the communications surrounding their departure from the firm or changing their partnership status.

This situation should not cause undue embarrassment or harm to a professional's reputation, or be perceived to limit their future opportunities. Keep in mind that in the absence of reasonable information we can all gravitate to creating our own stories – sometimes involving dark conspiracies and shadow motives – eventually reaching our own misguided conclusions as to what really happened. You do not need that kind of scenario to unfold on your watch.

There are always reasons to put off the decision to take decisive action. A number of leaders have admitted to me that, in hindsight, they came up with all kinds of rationalisations to postpone a painful decision that they just knew was inevitable. In the end, all they succeeded in doing was hurting their team and limiting its possible progress in a highly competitive marketplace.

No leader will tell you that this is the easy part of the job. It isn't!

Working with legal search consultants

Guillaume Pican
Page Executive

1. Recruiting top legal talent

1.1 Building a consistent employee brand

Creating the right employee brand (employee value proposition (EVP)) for your firm is of vital importance in attracting and recruiting the people you need. What does your firm effectively deliver for your 'employees'?

This kind of issue is not limited just to human resources directors from the biggest companies or law firms – it is not just large firms that have to build an EVP.

The key words in a successful value proposition are: 'clear', 'consistent' and 'long term'.

(a) Clear

Your strategy for hiring the best lawyers needs a clear message about who you are and what your purpose is as a law firm. This does not have to be long; it just needs to be a clear expression of your firm's values.

(b) Consistent

You need to think about the consistency of the message. Does the message show the reality of the firm? Is your message in line with your core values? Is it aligned with your lawyers' perceptions of the firm?

(c) Long term

The reality of your message must be sustainable in the mid/long term to create trusting relationships between you and your associates.

Once you have established a consistent employer proposition for your firm, you are ready to work with a legal search consultant, as your message will now be clear and capable of achieving the best results in the market.

The process of building an EVP requires an investment of time in order to formlate your hiring strategy. However, this is an opportunity to develop a good team spirit by involving everyone and allowing people to express their feelings about the right values for the organisation. Depending on the size of the firm, the process can be carried out over a coffee, or by sending out an employee survey.

1.2 Choosing the best legal consultant

Having designed an EVP the question will then be, Which recruitment agency will be best at projecting your core values and competencies within the firm?

The legal search firm and, of course, the consultant will provide your firm's first contact with the candidate. The search firm must be fully in line and 'consistent' with your key value proposition (ie, who you are and what kind of image you wish to project).

This is not a question of size. It does not follow that, because your law firm is an international firm with offices in 20 countries, you need the same type of recruitment agency with several offices around the globe. In my experience, the main criteria relating to legal search firms are as follows:

Know-how

- the consultant's experience in your field;
- the candidate's network of legal search firms;
- references in the same field;
- the consultant's process for selecting candidates.

Soft skills

- the consultant's conduct;
- energy and passion;
- fit with your firm: trust, mutual respect, etc.

1.3 Know-how

As potential partners or clients of a legal search firm, you are looking for experience in order to get the best results as quickly as possible. Most legal search consultants work with many clients in a number of areas and sometimes in the same kind of practice – just as you do not work with just one client in a single area!

The objective of the legal search consultant is to create a consistent portfolio of clients across a number of practices, values and ways of doing business. The consultant's portfolio should include boutique law firms as well as major firms in order to provide several options to their network of candidates

As we note above, to run a search it is crucial that the consultant has a thorough grasp of your business, so as to have a full understanding of your needs. However, you must also control any potential 'off limit'[1] he might have with your main competitors in order to be sure of finding the right target in your environment. The key to success is, of course, to be as dedicated as possible in a sector, but if possible with the minimum of 'off limit' in your practice.

1.4 Soft skills

If you have to choose between two very good legal search firms, I would suggest picking the most generous and humble one. As in every recruitment assignment, it is difficult to predict the ability of your consultant to reach their target. It can take a few days or perhaps a few months. The consultant must be generous because they must enjoy meeting people, must ask questions, be curious and think outside the box. They must be resilient because they will have to follow you despite the potential

---

1 'Off limit': code of deontology not to recruit within current clients' companies (within a time limit which is usually set at a couple of years after the last recruitment in the firm). Boundaries also apply to candidates placed in the law firm: the recruitment consultant would never hire a candidate in a firm if he had previously placed him in the firm.

difficulties they will face. To assess the consultant's humility, I would suggest you ask about their last failure. If the consultant is honest they will talk about it and will explain how they resolved the particular issue. The most important issue is not the initial failure, but how the consultant went about finding a solution.

The market is changing fast in recruitment as in all other activities. The best recruiters are simply the most passionate!

1.5 The best network of candidates

The legal market is small and has its own rules and its own ways of reaching candidates. Legal search consultants build sustainable and strong networks to make introductions as quick and efficient as possible. More than in any other market, the ability of your legal search consultant to build a strong and reliable network of candidates is a key success factor. The challenge of your legal search consultant is, as far as possible, to build his/her network of candidates to suit your needs. To expand his network, a consultant will be in touch every day with approximately 10 candidates. Every week, the consultant will interview around 10 to 15 candidates (by phone, face-to-face interviews etc). The purpose of these interviews is to have a general discussion without specific job opportunities in mind in order to develop a better insight into the candidates' skills and willingness to find another role.

After defining the target in conjunction with you – the practice, the law firm, the company – the legal search consultant will draw up a list of names to aim for. Various options are possible to obtain access to the candidate:

- The consultant's own database, the website of the law firm, alumni websites, company or lawyer websites, etc. This is the most straightforward route.
- Professional networks (and this is why legal search consultants need very good networks), peer-to-peer networks. (Call your own network to reach the right person.)
- The consultant may choose to call the company or the law firm to reach the candidate, or have a drink with people in the target law firm to ask people directly. Almost anything is possible.

1.6 A good marketing and social network

Digitalisation has drastically changed the way to target potential candidates. Twenty years ago, the most important way to attract candidates was to post a press ad in the relevant newspaper. Every newspaper had dedicated pages each week to advertise the best positions in the legal market. The power of the information was mainly in the paper and every portfolio of candidates and clients was created this way. It was also the time of written letters ...

From around 2000, the newspapers faced competition from a new way to share information: Internet 2.0. The first internet job website also appeared at this time. At this point a number of commentators predicted the end of headhunting, based on the theory that everything would become faster and easier. In part they were wrong; but as regards the ability to work faster, and in terms of easier access to information (law firm websites, job sites, candidate databases etc) they were right. At this point the market started to become multichannel (ie, both physical and digital).

Over the last 10 years, the digital environment has drastically expanded with a growing professional network on the web. Moreover, the number of connections between people is constantly increasing.

One key factor in choosing your law firm is to assess its ability to use all these tools simultaneously and consistently. Some of the same tools were used 20 years ago (eg, university alumni meetings, dinner with classmates and so on), but many professional networks and internet-based marketplaces are new.

Nowadays, the number of business cards the legal consultant hands out is not their only network. That network will include their Twitter followers and relevant connections on LinkedIn and it will also reflect their ability to create insights in their area of expertise as a legal search consultant.

Is your recruiter involved in the following: law event organisation or sponsorship; market surveys; articles (press and also internet, blogs, etc); published books; or lecturing in a university or business school?

This is a good indicator for clients. These kinds of activities provide good insights about the market and should help to assess the best legal search team. You are, of course, buying into a network; but you are also relying on the ability of your consultant to disseminate your firm's values.

1.7 The best approach

What type of approach is best for hiring your future lawyer?

This really depends on your feelings about the right way to assess the candidate. Most recruitment search firms will propose the following process: face-to-face interviews, previous employment/salary slips, relevant diplomas and references checks.

Every week a legal search consultant will typically meet between 10 and 15 candidates. You may think this sounds a lot and that it is akin to an industrial way of working, but it is not. The consultant's job is to meet people. The reality is that a search consultant needs to be up to date on the market and the best way to follow the market is to know the environment.

There are various ways of conducting interviews (eg, by phone, face to face, or by video conference). There are many different methods, depending on the recruiter's experience and preferences. However, the goals are always the same: to understand if the candidate fits the role (skills), but also if they have the right behaviours.

During the interview, a consultant assesses the candidate in a number of ways:

- Strengths in relation to the position. We want to understand the types of organisation they have worked in, and on what types of projects. The idea is to understand the candidate's real experience in the field.
- Potential weaknesses.
- Willingness to change.
- The reason why the candidate made certain choices in their career path (eg, Why did they move from firm A to firm B? Why did they choose a particular area of law?)
- The candidate's analysis of their own career and their perspectives on the future.
- The candidate's general behaviour.

What conclusions can be drawn from a legal consultant interview? There are three potential options:

- There are currently no opportunities: the consultant draws up a summary about the candidate in order to build his/her network and to be able to locate them easily for a future assignment.
- The job matches: in this case, the consultant will debrief you about the candidate. They will send a report covering the following items: skills, main expertise, education and professional background, behaviour, recruitment assessment results and personal feedback.
- Candidate matches with your firm, but there is no role immediately available in the firm: the consultant sends the resumé directly to you with the agreement of the candidate. This proactive way of work can be very efficient, as the availability of specific talent may create an opportunity for a firm.

Part of the legal consultant's time is devoted to meeting their clients (current or prospective) to garner new information and new assignments and also to be an influencer in the market. A key part of each week's work will be to stay in touch with the wider market.

2. From the search for the right skills to the search for the right behaviour

Most legal education systems currently base their training courses on strong theoretical knowledge, with many hours needed to learn different parts of the law. In any education system, it is of course necessary to start by learning the basics and then to develop independent critical faculties at a later stage. There is no doubt that a solid educational background is important to develop the best options for a future professional career.

Nevertheless, the model in law firms is not just to look for the right educational background but also to find the right behaviour for the firm, and to find professionals who are in agreement with its culture and values. In nearly all jurisdictions, education systems do not address the soft skills needed for future lawyers to practice law. It is important to recruit people not just with the right skills, but most importantly with the right competencies and behaviours. This applies particularly to skills relating to:

- client service;
- entrepreneurship.

These two terms need some explanation. In Europe, we hear more and more about the 'entrepreneurship mindset'; you either have it or you don't. In reality, this is not true. In the past, we did not learn about it because we did not need it most of the time within law firms. In recent decades, growth in Europe and the increased need for more specialised/expert legal advice has created natural growth in the legal sector. Previously, it was possible to join a firm and grow within it year after year. Some of your colleagues were hired in-house. There was also an increasing chance that you would become a partner (ie, with a growing market and natural turnover).

The market is now much tougher. It is highly competitive and the in-house market is less dynamic than before. Moreover, clients have an extensive choice of law firms, so they will not necessarily initiate contact with you. The main consequence of this is that lawyers need to become more entrepreneurial.

All business schools teach how to run a business, how to improve your behaviour, how to become a good negotiator etc. These features are clearly lacking in the legal education system. The market is moving fast and all the partners I meet are looking for the same type of lawyers. I call them CEMO lawyers:

Client centred/**E**ntrepreneurs/**M**ulti-tasking/**O**pen-minded

Today, the challenge is not to have access to a database of candidates, but to pick the right lawyer with the right behaviour. The ability of a legal search firm to understand the difference is a key factor to success in your recruitment.

3. Building a strong relationship of trust between the client and the legal search partner

Let me finally share with you what I believe (based on personal experience) to be the most important factor in achieving results with your legal search consultant: build a strong relationship with them based on trust.

Having explained above the role of the legal search consultant, I hope you now understand that their job is not just a matter of sending CVs to your mailbox. This, might work occasionally, but not in the long run – and not if you want to receive expert advice about your market and get the best out of your search firm.

Another secret: if your legal search consultant enjoys working with you and your firm and has real respect for you, then they will do everything necessary to get the job done and find the best candidates on the market, whatever it takes.

This is the story of professional life. You are the client; the search consultant is the supplier. If you were a carmaker you would want to get the best raw materials. You would aim to establish a long, trusting and sustainable relationship with your automotive supplier.

To achieve success, it is important to spend as long as necessary at the beginning of an assignment to discuss the search. This is not limited to a discussion of responsibilities, the profile of the candidate, your team. Every law firm is now looking for the same type of profile – CEMO lawyers. You are not alone!

Unfortunately, all too often, I begin an assignment from some law firm without any brief other than three lines in my inbox, with the well-known CEMO profile. Don't forget you are not the only firm on the market. Think about your added value. If you want to reach the best candidates on the market to achieve your own goal, you have to spend time with your supplier. Of course there are constraints on your time, but you should aim to create the time you need to introduce yourself and your vision. This a key strategy for your firm and you will not harm your client relationships by investing your time in this way. The good news is that your supplier will be more dedicated to your cause and that is a good start.

When meeting with your legal search firm, you have to spend time talking about yourself (ie, your firm and yourself): why you are so special; why your strategy is the best on the market; your insight; your specific area of expertise. Talk about yourself, your firm and your values. Of course, people ultimately join a project, but at the end of a recruitment process they choose first:

- a partner/manager;
- a team;
- a project; and, of course,
- remuneration.

Your job as client is not over after this introduction. This is just the beginning. The tough part starts here.

First, you need to devote time to this search assignment:

- Prepare yourself to conduct a good interview. The candidate must prepare to make a good impression – and so should you. Making a good impression in an interview is a two-way process. The candidate will have a lot of questions about your context, your strategy, and, of course you and your firm. You must be prepared. It is important before each session to prepare yourself and your partner about the way to conduct the interview. Who will meet the candidate in the first round? What type of presentation will we make? The idea is not, of course, to have a process that is as rigid as that of a multinational company such as General Electric, but it is to avoid any weakness in the interview process. In the legal market, your CEMO is rare and you will have just one chance to get them on board. The better prepared you are, the more likely it is you will succeed.
- It seems obvious, but you need to dedicate time to interview a candidate. A question for you: if your legal search consultant sends you a CEMO, when do you set up the interview?

Answer 1: as soon as possible. Answer 2: in the next few weeks.

The right answer is as soon as possible. You must be as proactive as possible. In recruitment processes, time is money and your efficiency will be much appreciated on the market. Don't forget that your competitor could be more proactive than you in making an offer to the candidate.

At each stage of the process and for each candidate you will meet in interview, make sure you provide feedback. This is a key point in the process. The market is small and your employee brand is really important in making a difference in the market. All the candidates have taken time to meet you. They deserve feedback, whether positive or negative.

The last stage is also important in attempting to find the best candidate on the market. This stage relates to the best timing to make an offer to the candidate. In order to judge this, it is important to have a clear view on your firm's compensation and benefit policies. The idea is that you should know exactly what it is possible to offer and what it is not. Your search consultant can help to give you a good understanding of market rates. Some of them release interesting salary surveys. These can be a good means of giving you an accurate overview of the market. Don't forget that the candidate's first impressions will be key. If your offer is very low relative to the candidate's expectations, you will reduce your chances of hiring them. The market for candidates is highly competitive and you will not be alone in your interest.

A full recruitment process in your firm need not take more than three weeks (and this includes making the offer). It is always better to be the firm in the lead.

4. Onboarding

Even after the candidate has accepted the offer, the recruitment process is not yet over. It is important to prepare the onboarding of your new lawyer.

Work closely with your legal search consultant to ensure that the candidate is fully motivated. Most search firms will contact candidates on a regular basis before onboarding, and during the first few months in a new firm. It is important to avoid any potential communication failures. Your search consultant could let you know about any doubt, or any questions that that arise out of the regular contact.

On your side, work with your human resources department to establish the best way to integrate your joiner. The better prepared the onboarding process, the better will be the efficiency of your joiner in the firm. During the first weeks, you should organise meetings with all the partners and teams in the firm in order to develop a good understanding of the overall business. The joiner's ability to talk about their new firm will be dramatically improved and they will have an increased sense of belonging to your firm. In the early months you should create the time to hold regular meetings with the new recruit to discuss their work, and also to answer any potential questions.

During this notice period, your legal search consultant will call you to make the interface between you and your new recruit. You may think that building this type of partnership with your recruitment agency is a waste of time, but in my experience, it is the best way to make sure that you hire the best people for your law firm.

5. Conclusion

Today, the search firm you work with is your first employee brand contact on the market and you have to think about the footprint you want to leave on the market. We all know that recruitment of the best talent in your sector is one of the critical factors in achieving success. There is no guarantee that working in the ways outlined above will provide success, but I can guarantee that you will drastically improve your chances of reaching the best candidates in your market.

Case study: designing and implementing a new people strategy

Alessandro Portolano
Chiomenti
Gerard J Tanja
Venturis Consulting Group

---

1. Introduction: revising HR policies at large law firms and the case of Chiomenti's recruitment strategy

People's strategies in large law firms touch on a number of potential areas of intervention: recruitment, induction, coaching, management and so on.

Designing and implementing new people strategies in large law firms (national and international) are, in essence, major transformative and strategic change processes addressing and affecting the DNA, culture and key processes of the firm. It takes courage, leadership commitment and perseverance to execute such programmes and remain focused during their development and implementation. This is particularly true for law firms operating in 'traditional' professional cultures and strong organisational cultures.

From a more general perspective, a revision of the recruitment strategy within the context of a comprehensive people strategy can be, for large independent firms, a crucial factor in seeking to remain competitive and profitable, ensure succession planning, maintain market position (national and international) and win the 'war for talent' in the increasingly complex and competitive legal market.

Changes of the type described may require an incremental, step-by-step approach, including to 'test and pilot' every individual element of the new strategy, before introduction. This approach may be appropriate in order to organise commitment and trust among the partnership group, where proposed new practices and policies are innovative in relation to existing policies and practices and it is felt that partners need time to digest, comprehend and get used to all the changes and are provided with sufficient time to oversee the consequences of the introduction of the respective initiatives proposed and developed. In a complex and often highly fluid situation, engagement, trust and the involvement of its key partners may be required.

In section 2, this chapter sets out a specific case: the revision of the recruitment strategy at Chiomenti, one of the leading, independent firms in Italy with several overseas offices. The remaining sections then address possible additional changes that leading law firms may consider to complement their recruitment strategy.

2. Designing and executing a new recruitment strategy: the case of Chiomenti

At Chiomenti the leadership of the firm recognised that, given the rapidly changing demands of clients, trends in the legal market and developments in the (employment) market and subsequent changes for the internal business model, the firm had to address its current people strategy and to rethink several of its existing HR policies. Its policies and practices for the selection of candidates had served the firm well in past years and had contributed to its success in the market. However, in the light of significant market changes and likely future developments, the firm felt that a different approach might be appropriate.

The main goal of the exercise was further to strengthen the ability of the firm to select and recruit the right talent for the firm.

Chiomenti formulated two immediate objectives with its new recruitment strategy:

- It wanted to increase the efficiency and effectiveness of its recruitment process by streamlining its intake and improve the monitoring of applications among lateral recruits at graduate and more senior levels.
- It was determined further to increase the quality of the recruitment process by improving and adding new selection instruments/tools.

The recruitment process which was ultimately adopted comprises six steps. Every step builds upon the outcomes of the previous phase.

The process starts with a structured analysis of CVs. The CV is passed on to the professional charged with the (structured) interviews. A candidate will be interviewed by more than one professional. This ensures that senior associates are involved in the process, in addition to partners. Those who pass the interview phase then go on to a practical test/evaluation of their motivational drivers. Candidates are tested on technical knowledge, problem-solving, advisory and communication skills and team orientation. Experience has shown that key to the success of such tests is that they should be tailored to the profile of the candidate. If you are interested in a candidate because he or she spent several years at a competing firm working on insurance regulatory matters, it is pointless to test his or her knowledge of pure banking regulatory matters.

At the same time the candidate has to pass an English law examination, unless they have studied in English-speaking countries (eg, LL.M. graduates), or have advanced knowledge of other key languages (German, French etc).

For those who stand out, the firm makes use of several, tailor-made psychometric testing tools with a specific emphasis on the motivational drivers of the candidate, his or her perceived strengths and weaknesses and specific areas for development. Both the firm and the candidate receive a comprehensive report which shows the outcome of the test. Incidentally, it is worth mentioning that the Talent Motivation Assessment methodology may provide input for future talent developmental actions and performance management initiatives.

During the final phase of the process all information and recruitment data is collected, combined and discussed by the responsible partners and a final hiring decision is made.

Schematically, the process is as follows:

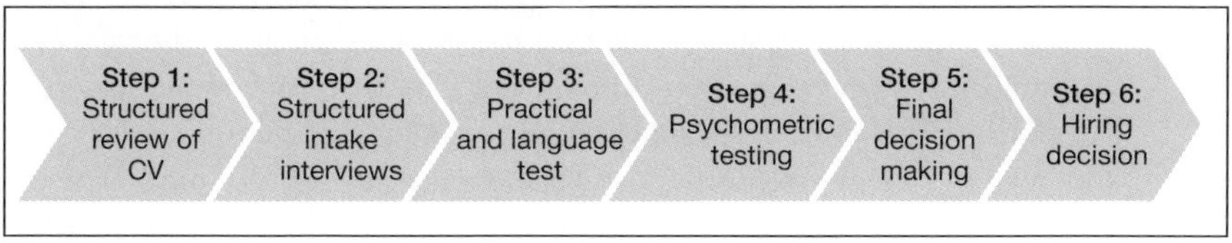

Step 1: Structured review of CV

Review applicants' educational history and motivation (study results; time line; legal expertise and extra-curricular activities with specific focus on language skills, study abroad and other additional criteria, like quality and structure of application/cv.

Step 2: Structured intake interviews

- Structured interviews with partners
- Presence/involvement of a senior associate during interview phase

Step 3: Practical and language test

- Chiomenti-specific testing, focusing on technical knowledge, problem-solving, advisory and communication skills and team orientation

Step 4: Psychometric testing

- Online capability and intelligence test
- Chiomenti-specific testing, focusing on motivational drivers of candidate, the values and required competencies/skills using the online Chiomenti HR portal for graduate and lateral hire candidates (Talent Motivation Assessment methodology)
- Reporting to partners and candidate involved in recruitment process

Step 5: Final decision making

- Collection and combining of all recruitment data
- Discussion of available reports and data by involved partners to prepare hiring decisions and validation

Step 6: Hiring decision

- Hiring decision by responsible partners

3. Blended induction, mentoring, training and development frameworks

As mentioned, the recruitment strategy must be considered as only a part of a more comprehensive people's strategy.

As a logical corollary to a recruitment strategy, firms should consider developing an integrated (professional and personal) training and development framework. Such a framework might, of course, take various shapes and forms. For example, it might comprise:

- induction programmes for lateral hires and graduate recruits;

- mentoring and coaching programmes for new recruits;
- skills and technical training programmes for junior and senior associates.

Of course, such programmes should not exist in a vacuum and should be fully integrated and aligned with the competency model of the firm and its goal-setting and review system (see section 4). The modalities for the organisation of such programmes may vary and may combine existing practice area training programmes provided in-house and the involvement of external providers.

Induction programmes, by contrast, are primarily delivered by internal resources and typically require strong involvement by the firm's leadership. They could focus on topics such as the history and strategy of the firm, the composition of its client portfolio, type of engagements and strategic key account initiatives, project management and law firm economics (eg, the RULES programme: Realisation, Utilisation, Leverage, Expenses (cost structure of law firms) and Speed of recovery and collection).

4. Putting it all together: the goal-setting and review process for fee earners

Typically, the final element of a state of the art talent development and performance management framework will be the goal-setting and review process. For most firms and their partners, this is often perceived as a time-consuming, intensive, once-a-year, mandatory exercise in which, in a relatively limited time frame, all associates are evaluated and their performance assessed on the basis of predetermined forms, criteria and formats.

Any revision of the review process for fee earners requires the prior collection of views of all the constituencies involved in the key elements of a proposed new approach, taking into account the main objectives of such a process:

- The selected approach/system must be practical and pragmatic and not be perceived by partners as bureaucratic: it must be 'meaningful'.
- The goal-setting and review system must result in productive and effective feedback and provide for regular, high-impact interventions/discussions to maximise performance feedback to fee earners.
- The review process must be ongoing, with clear goal setting for associates (financial and non-financial). It must also be transparent.
- The process must be fully integrated with the mentoring programme and aligned with the career and personal development perspectives and goals of the fee earners.
- The process must be simple, non-bureaucratic and easy to administer; partners and associates must feel 'engaged' and 'involved' and the goal-setting and review process must be viewed as a common responsibility.

5. Conclusion

The initiative to upgrade, professionalise and reconsider the HR strategy of large law firms is a truly transformative change process. At Venturis we have identified five stages in a transformative change process:

- clear and transparent goal and objective setting – to determine what we want to achieve and when are we successful (not yet implemented at Chiomenti Studio Legale);
- an objective assessment of the firm's (current) organisational design capabilities;
- designing and communicating transformation actions and initiatives;
- effectiveness, speed and quality of the execution process; and
- initiatives that need to be developed to be able to sustain the changes.

Alumni and the value of creating strong networks

Mahmood Lone
Allen & Overy LLP
Boyan Wells
Retired Allen & Overy partner

1. The value of alumni

Law firms are very largely 'people businesses' whose success or failure is dependent, first, on the quality of the people within that firm and, secondly, on the depth of that firm's relationships – most importantly with its clients, but also with other professional bodies (including its competitors) and the wider business world. Alumni programmes, if properly developed, can play a significant role in helping a firm recruit and retain those people vital to its success, and then maintain relationships with those people when they move on.

It is true to say that in the 20th century, alumni programmes, for law firms at least, did not exist. In such times, the most an alumnus could hope for was a drinks reunion once a year and, possibly, a copy of the firm's annual newsletter or brochure in the post. However, in the 21st century, alumni programmes have evolved dramatically as law firms – and businesses more widely – realise that alumni are a powerful network of people who can add real value to an organisation.

All firms strive to recruit the best people, as it is they who can offer the best service and enable the firm to achieve maximum success. Firms invest heavily in their recruitment programmes and in training and developing recruits; in turn, the recruits invest considerable time and energy in developing the business. Together, this investment gives a firm its best chance to become or remain successful. This model has not changed substantially over the last 35 years (the longest period for which our older co-chair can vouch). So why the emergence of alumni programmes as an essential part of maintaining that success?

In large part, this is a result of the traditional career path within law firms evolving – very significantly in the last 15 to 20 years. Modern communication, in particular, has made the task of working in an international law firm tougher and more stressful. Lawyers can expect to be on call 24/7. This is not for everybody. Added to this, the flexible nature of today's global economy and the differing priorities and objectives for new generations mean that people change jobs – careers even – far more than in the past.

Another factor is the material growth in size and global scale of some law firms. A&O, for example, has opened 25 offices in 16 new countries since 2000. As firms grow, and as people change careers far more often, so a firm's alumni population grows. Alumni programmes have, therefore, evolved to help firms maintain relationships with this group of highly capable people. Far from being a collection of disparate individuals around the world, alumni are becoming an extension of the business – a network of skilled professionals with whom there is an ongoing benefit to be derived from maintaining a strong relationship and sense of goodwill, both for the alumni and for the firm.

Fundamentally, this means offering ways for alumni to stay connected with each other and with the firm. But as McKinsey & Co – with one of the most well-respected alumni programmes in the world – has shown, there is even more organisations can and should do to support and value their alumni. The more organisations invest, the greater the potential of the network.

'Invest' does not mean simply spending more and more money. An established alumni programme can be maintained by a relatively small team of dedicated staff. What can be harder, we suggest, is to persuade senior staff, particularly partners and directors, of the potential value of alumni programmes, and to ensure that career transitions are supported and dealt with openly and honestly. For some, this can require a change in mindset and a desire to invest time in acting accordingly. Measuring and articulating the 'value' of an alumni programme is important in helping to get buy-in from those senior staff – but, as we discuss below, how to measure this 'value' is a conundrum that has been around as long as the alumni programme itself.

The most successful alumni programmes now make a commitment that their people will be supported in their career even after they have moved on from an organisation. It is an extension of the employment 'agreement' which acknowledges that the benefit and investment, for both the employee and firm, does not need to end when someone leaves. People are most businesses' best asset – this is certainly true for law firms. In a successful firm, given the high quality of the people and the investment made in them, most will go on to succeed wherever they end up. Therefore, by building a strong alumni network and maintaining positive relationships, your best assets need never be entirely lost.

2. Building a strong alumni network

The driving force for any successful alumni programme must be to build a sense of goodwill and loyalty so that your people feel supported when they are with you and valued after they have left.

The key points to consider when setting up an alumni programme are: who do you want to target and what can you offer them? The best starting point is your existing employees. They are the easiest group with whom to communicate and all are potential alumni. Some law firm alumni programmes are only open to lawyers; others apply certain criteria for membership (length of service or employment record). A&O takes an all-welcome approach – even students and graduates on vacation schemes are encouraged to join, as well as all staff and partners. A&O's alumni programme started 11 years ago and now has over 9,000 members (nearly 7,000 alumni and 2,000 current staff) in 70 countries. To a large extent, the strength and appeal of the network are in its size and reach.

Your people, past and present, are the most obvious draw for alumni: the chance to reconnect with former friends and colleagues, particularly for those who might have lost touch with the firm. Most alumni networks are based around a programme of opportunities to connect, through social events (class reunions, an annual global alumni reunion, local office events) and targeted business seminars – A&O's client alumni, for example, are invited to attend the firm's global client seminar programme.

As the network grows, offering more ways to build relationships and keep people connected is important. For an established alumni programme with a sizeable membership, a dedicated website is essential, not only as a platform for registering alumni, but also as a hub for events, news, interviews and thought-leadership articles from across the network. A&O's alumni website and annual Alumni Yearbook (launched in 2006) feature many interviews and profiles on alumni, and so offer a good promotional opportunity for alumni to reach 9,000 professionals around the world, particularly for those who have started their own businesses. Social media has also become an effective tool for helping to keep people connected and to build relationships, particularly as the network becomes more international. A&O's alumni programme has a presence on LinkedIn, Facebook, Twitter and Instagram. It allows us to make contact with alumni who are not yet registered on the programme and who we have not otherwise been able to trace. We share all content from the alumni website through social media and also use Facebook, Twitter and Instagram, in particular, to engage in a more personal way with alumni, sharing event photos and articles of interest generated outside of A&O.

Generating a sense of goodwill and keeping people connected must always be the cornerstone of building a strong alumni programme, but once the network grows in size and scale so too does its potential value for both the firm and the alumni.

3. Employability for life

Increasingly, the more forward-looking alumni programmes focus on providing career support, guidance and opportunities for alumni long after they have left the organisation. It is an acknowledgement that alumni are still part of an extended network, and a commitment that, if an alumnus works hard and succeeds in his or her time with an organisation, support will continue to be provided for his or her career once a decision is made to leave.

This is really an extension of the employment 'agreement' – the commitment that starts as soon as a person joins. Like other top law firms, we invest significantly in trying to recruit the best people. To make our recruitment offer as attractive as possible, we strive to offer them the highest quality training, the opportunity to work on exciting and challenging work (in an increasingly flexible way) and the support to realise their full potential.

Given the cost of recruitment and training, every successful firm will want to keep its staff for a minimum period to make the investment worthwhile. That has rarely meant keeping someone forever, but retention is increasingly hard today when we operate in a very different job market compared even to 10 years ago. Gone are the days of joining a firm as a trainee and staying for 25 years – it is simply a fact of life that associates now only stay for an average of four years. People are far more mobile and have access to careers in almost any part of the world. A big law firm is often seen by new recruits not as the end game but as the starting point.

There is an acceptance, therefore, that of equal importance to retention is to focus on people's career transitions and to build a culture of trust and support so that people can discuss their future, whether at the firm or not. There are so many different career paths available for lawyers and professional support staff alike that it is not just a case of putting in the hours and climbing up the ladder. Partnership is one goal, of course, but only a very small proportion of people will make partner these days and it is not necessarily what all lawyers want anyway. Therefore, the focus on managing people's careers and supporting their decisions for the future has had to improve.

Not only should firms create an environment where people feel able to discuss their future careers openly, they should set people up with the skills, experience and support required to pursue their career outside the firm. This is the approach McKinsey & Co takes. As an organisation, it is known for developing its people and, when it is time to move on (whether through the 'up-or-out' model or natural career progression), helping to place them in key roles in industry. The alumni retain strong relationships with the firm and refer work back throughout their careers. They are seen not so much as 'leavers', but as an extension of the business itself. The Boston Consulting Group even refers to its leavers as 'graduates'.

It might sound counter-productive to arm your people with the skills to succeed in another organisation – possibly even with a competitor. But the important point, possibly ignored in the past, is that when people leave they do not disappear. Many will end up as clients – in fact about half of all lawyers who leave A&O, and a third of all alumni in general, end up at client organisations. Surveys conducted with A&O alumni show that many who leave will recommend the organisation as a good place to work and some will end up returning to work for A&O again one day (in the past two years alone, over 200 alumni have returned to A&O). Even those who move to competitors should not be ignored – they can still refer work or recommend the firm to be on the other side of a deal, and who knows where they will move on to next? The crucial point is that a person who has worked for a firm has, in the large majority of cases, worked very hard and added to the success of that firm. If the person decides to leave, he or she deserves the respect and acknowledgement of the contribution made, and the support and assistance to move on – whether to a client, competitor or elsewhere. The person has made a decision to leave – respect the decision and recognise a new member of your alumni programme.

This, again, is the extension of the employment agreement – or 'employability for life' approach – and it is how 'people businesses' create the strongest relationships and networks for the benefit of both the alumni and the business.

This approach or mindset also extends to alumni. There are lots of ways an alumni programme can provide support for its members once they have left an organisation. On a practical level, there is the offer of office space for those who have gone on to be self-employed, as well as extending employee benefits such as discount schemes and referral incentives to alumni.

One important new initiative A&O also launched is its mentoring programme in which alumni and current partners and staff both mentor and are mentored by each other on career development and work-related issues. The mentoring scheme has proved extremely successful, with over 40 mentor pairings of lawyers and support staff already in place globally, and another 10 under way. One of the pairings has recently resulted in an alum (a former associate) being mentored by a current A&O counsel and returning to work for A&O's flexible resourcing business, Peerpoint. The mentoring programme assists in the development of both our past and present staff and provides an opportunity to link current and ex-members of staff on a worldwide basis.

Another practical area of support is offering a careers centre in which alumni can search for jobs at the firm, as well as post vacancies in their own organisations. Those looking for new career paths can post profiles and CVs in the careers centre for other alumni to view. It is also helpful to introduce exiting employees to alumni contacts at the organisation they are moving to – if it is a bank, large corporate or even another law firm in a large city, chances are the firm has alumni there. It also encourages current staff to touch base with recent leavers to see how they are getting on in their new role or in retirement.

4. Added benefits for alumni

It is useful to consider what else can be offered that is valuable to alumni. Busy people need a reason to get involved. Think: who are your alumni? Where are they in the world? What can we provide that is interesting, relevant and perhaps offers opportunities they might not find elsewhere?

This does not need to focus only on an individual's professional needs. One of the most valuable benefits to grow out of A&O's alumni programme has been the involvement alumni have had in the firm's global charity partnerships. During A&O's partnership with child rights organisation AfriKids (from 2012 to 2014), several alumni asked to join A&O staff on the AfriKids Experience Challenge – a week-long fundraising trip spent living and working with families on the poverty line in rural Ghana. One of A&O's former partners in Hong Kong, Catherine Husted, who took part in the Experience Challenge, went on to raise nearly £60,000 for AfriKids and very successfully mobilised existing A&O staff in Asia to support the two-year partnership, which broke all fundraising records for the firm. Catherine became so involved with A&O's charity partnerships that she has since come back to work with the firm in Hong Kong to support our current charity partner, Amref Health Africa, as well as A&O's wider charitable work in the region.

The ability to engage alumni with the firm's charitable and *pro bono* work has built very powerful relationships with the alumni involved and offers people something they might not easily find elsewhere, as well as the chance to reconnect with old friends. So has A&O's music programme, the brainchild of retired senior partner Guy Beringer and retired partner Don McGown. It started out as a small singing group of partners back in 2006 and has grown into a full orchestra and choir who have staged performances in the United Kingdom of *The Magic Flute* at Glyndebourne, *Carmen* at Sadler's Wells and *Oklahoma!* at Holland Park Opera House. Dozens of singers and musicians from A&O past and present have come from around the world to take part, with the performances even reviewed in the UK media. In many cases, the musicians told us they had ceased playing years before when careers got in the way of practising and playing. So to have the opportunity to pick up their instrument or start singing again has provided a unique opportunity for those involved.

Interestingly, these sorts of ideas and opportunities often start to be generated by the network itself once it reaches a certain critical mass – people with common interests usually have a way of finding each other. So these opportunities need not be part of the plan at the outset. Instead, the focus should be on starting small and concentrating your efforts on the biggest offices and those where there are already engaged alumni – in other words, where you have the greatest chance of success.

5. Measuring the benefits

Setting up and maintaining an alumni programme does take time and money. It is also a never-ending project: for example, bringing on new initiatives, engaging new offices and working more closely with the firm's HR team. An often-asked question, therefore, is what does an alumni programme really add to the business?

6. Client relationships and referrals

In an ideal world, it would be possible to put a financial figure on the tangible benefits of an alumni programme. Stating the obvious, we do not live in an ideal world. However, a good place to start is looking at the positions your alumni hold with key clients. A large amount of time, money and energy is spent by every firm in trying to protect and strengthen its key client relationships. The essence of any good client relationship is the personal interaction between those people in a firm acting for a client and those people in the client organisation. With alumni working for a client, the firm should be knocking on an open door. Alumni know first-hand the quality of a firm's services and of their former colleagues individually; in most cases they also retain a sense of loyalty for their old firm and particularly the people in it. It is highly common for a member of staff to leave a firm, join a client and work directly with the team or department he or she left. Maintaining a good relationship with that person should be a simple and enjoyable exercise, as well as crucial to the firm's overall client relationship.

To illustrate the importance of alumni within client organisations, we currently count 765 alumni contacts at our top clients globally. Of those alumni, we know that 275 referred work directly to us in 2015. This figure needs to be treated very carefully as, although the instruction may indeed have come from an alumnus, as a preferred law firm of that client, we may well have got the instruction anyway. The key point, though, is that an alumni programme can help significantly in building strong client relationships, which are crucial in today's increasingly competitive market. That in itself is a tangible benefit, even if it cannot be measured precisely in financial terms.

Equally relevant to the number of instructions or amount of billings that come from alumni is the quality of the relationships we maintain with them. In 2014, A&O conducted a global alumni engagement survey with current members of the network and found that 89% of respondents would refer us to potential clients as a good firm to instruct. That is a very high figure, but one that needs to be sustained. Once a former employee has been with an in-house legal team for a few years, alongside other lawyers with alumni affiliations elsewhere, relationships with individuals at his or her former firm can easily wane. This is why the quality of the alumni relationship and the 'employability for life' approach is so important – there is continued interest and value to be gained from maintaining the relationship for both the alumnus and the firm.

The other side of the coin, of course, is the potential work that can be lost if a former employee leaves the firm unhappy, joins a major client and actively works to stop his or her old firm from being instructed. If calculating billings from alumni is hard, quantifying how much you lose through disgruntled alumni at key clients is even harder – but we know it happens. It is impossible to ensure that every individual who leaves a business does so on good terms, but experience shows that even people who have left on difficult terms still have positive associations with their peers and feel proud of the work they have done. There are several success stories of disengaged lawyers who, a short time after leaving A&O, have joined the alumni network and rebuilt relationships with people.

7. Alumni returning to the firm – 'boomerangs'

Returning employees are another significant benefit. In 2014 we started to track the number of alumni who had returned to A&O and were surprised to find it was as high as over 200 people in two years. When we asked our alumni as part of the global survey, 31% said they saw themselves returning to work at A&O one day.

Clearly, this is the upside to the trend of greater mobility in the workplace – more people are leaving jobs than ever before, but more people, it seems, are also returning. That is, of course, if they have left on good terms and continue to feel a pull back to the organisation – something a strong alumni programme can help to deliver.

There are many examples of lawyers and support staff returning to A&O around the world. One that stands out is the launch of our Johannesburg office in 2014, in which three people returned to the firm to launch the new office: Jason van der Poel, a partner and projects lawyer, had previously worked for A&O in Amsterdam before moving back to South Africa in 2005; Allen Lueta, a director and also a projects lawyer, had worked for A&O in London and Paris before returning to Johannesburg in 2009; and Jane Waters, COO of the office, had been A&O's head of HR for the Banking practice in London before relocating to South Africa in 2003 (a good example of why alumni programmes should include professional support staff as well as lawyers).

The key to successfully launching in Johannesburg, as with so many new offices, was finding the right team. Therefore, to be able to find people with local market knowledge and experience, who already understood the firm's culture and had proved successful at A&O (and were extremely enthusiastic at being able to rejoin the firm in their home country), was immensely valuable and has contributed in large part to the success of A&O's operations in South Africa.

8. Talent pool

Having a strong global alumni network also provided a pool to recruit from when A&O set up Peerpoint, its flexible resourcing business, in 2013. Peerpoint was launched to provide greater flexibility in A&O's business model, to respond to both clients' changing needs and the differing career aspirations of lawyers. It is a network of experienced, top-tier lawyers who work as consultants on contract with A&O teams and with clients directly. It allows A&O to augment its workforce in periods of high demand or when there is a need for particular specialist skills, while offering Peerpoint lawyers greater control over when, where and how they work.

When Peerpoint launched, A&O's alumni network provided the perfect target group quickly to fill the initial base of 20 to 30 lawyers. When the business expanded to open a regional base in Asia Pacific in 2015, an A&O alumnus, Tony Corcoran, came on board as managing director. Peerpoint has now grown to hold over 120 lawyers on its panel with nearly 50% A&O alumni.

Maintaining a relationship with women who have left the firm and with whom, therefore, contact might otherwise be lost, is another important benefit of an alumni programme. The challenges for law firms (and businesses more generally) in retaining women at mid and senior levels are well documented. This is a real drain for law firms and significantly narrows the pool from which we can promote people to senior positions, including the partnership. Trying to retain women is an issue on which most firms are working. But many women who do have a career break will seek to return to work at some point in the future. Thus, by maintaining relationships and actively supporting women back to work through mentoring and other initiatives, their skills and experience are at least not lost for good. In fact, Peerpoint has provided the means for a number of women to return to A&O, as it offers the control to maintain a career at the top of the legal profession while at the same time focusing on other commitments.

In recruitment terms, returning employees are a clear benefit. It costs a lot to recruit, train and develop an individual – with the recruitment cost rising significantly the more senior the role is. So to rehire a person in whom the business has invested and who has already proved successful can be a very effective recruitment strategy.

9. Talent referrals

The next best way to recruit – after rehiring former employees – is through referrals. It is a more efficient way to find talented people, particularly when you consider how high the cost is of advertising a role and paying recruitment agents' fees. In our 2014 survey, 79% of alumni said they would recommend A&O as a good place to work. So within a strong alumni network you have hundreds – maybe thousands – of people who are, in turn, connected to many more thousands around the world. It provides a very useful source of high-calibre potential recruits, with easy communication channels for recruitment teams (eg, through a global alumni careers centre). Most large law firms offer a financial incentive to existing staff for referring a person who goes on to be successfully placed in a role. By extending to alumni the same financial incentive for referring people, it is easy to turn those 79% of alumni into active referrers of talent.

It is possible to measure this benefit if applications for jobs have come through your central website, careers portal or graduate recruitment site – a standard online application form can ask: 'Where did you hear about the role or about the firm in general?' But applications come from other places too, which are harder to track, so quantifying the total value of alumni referrals is tricky. It is something that HR teams are working to develop a better picture of, but incentivising your alumni network – thousands of people who feel positive about your organisation – to be a source of talent referrals is certainly of benefit to a business.

10. Gateway to a network of business professionals

On top of the very clear value a strong, engaged alumni network brings through a well-managed and developed programme – the client relationships, boomerang recruits and talent referrals – there is also a wider benefit in having access to a unique network of professionals around the world. No other organisation can replicate your alumni network, and no other business can access it in its entirety. For A&O, that is a direct communication channel to nearly 7,000 alumni in 70 countries, some of whom are the most successful and powerful people in their field. Whether they are potential clients or not, having a communication channel to these people is very valuable. They can be used as a sounding board for new products, gaining market insights, testing business tactics or even gauging the market's view of your organisation after major news announcements. For business development teams, your alumni are an engaged audience with whom to raise the profile of specific partners, practice areas and new offices.

The network also provides an excellent source of speakers for events, roundtables and training seminars, and A&O has made use of alumni to broaden the reach of surveys and research, and to tap into views and insights for publications and news pieces. While a third of our alumni end up at client organisations, the others pursue an incredibly diverse range of careers. In recent Alumni Yearbooks, for example, we have featured people who have gone on to co-found Tough Mudder Inc, one of the world's toughest endurance events; direct the charity mother2mother, helping HIV+ mothers and babies in Africa; and launch the international restaurant chain Aqua. They certainly make a fascinating and valuable network of people with whom to maintain a relationship.

11. Facing up to the challenges

One of the challenges of running an effective alumni programme – one that delivers all of the benefits we talk about above – is operating across, in A&O's case, the 31 countries in which we have an office. Not only are there many different cultures and business practices, but we have also been in some parts of the world for a relatively short amount of time. Integrating new offices and people within global initiatives takes time and consideration. In many ways this mirrors the challenge faced by any fast-growing international firm in maintaining a common ethos and culture. There is a careful balance to be struck between managing and offering support from a central team, and not appearing to 'dictate' to offices around the world what they should be doing. One of the ways we have tried to strike this balance is by establishing an alumni advisory board, on which sits a senior representative from as many offices as possible, along with several alumni. That way, initiatives can be discussed and decisions reached with input from across the international network. Underpinning that, the central alumni team work hard to be flexible and supportive and encourage any alumni initiatives that offices want to run.

Despite the clear benefits of having a strong alumni network, it is still not necessarily an easy 'sell' within a partnership where firms face an increasingly competitive market and pressure on costs. Setting up and managing a successful alumni programme takes investment and resources, and it continues to be difficult to demonstrate in hard terms the return on investment. But there are ways to measure the benefits. Putting in place mechanisms to track the number of returning employees, for example, is fairly straightforward (and produces a surprisingly large number for A&O). So too is capturing the number of alumni among key clients.

Another approach to demonstrating the value of the network is to record whether a piece of work has been referred by an alumnus at a client organisation, and thereby automate the task of calculating billings from alumni. These figures need to be treated with caution as it is hard to attribute winning business to one individual within a large client organisation (particularly when the firm is a member of, say, a global panel). But it is certainly useful to have some indication of the value of work alumni can refer.

Another useful tool to gain buy-in is showing how engaged alumni are and how positively that reflects on the business. In the global alumni survey of 2014, we were able to report back to the firm that:

- 87% of alumni felt a general sense of goodwill towards the firm;
- 89% would recommend us to clients as a good firm to instruct;
- 92% felt proud of the work they delivered while at A&O;
- 79% would recommend A&O to colleagues, friends and family as a good place to work; and
- 31% saw themselves returning to work at A&O one day.

When you combine those positive sentiments with the size, scale and influence of an alumni network, it is a powerful indication of the potential the network can offer.

Added to this, as we said earlier, all top law firms compete with each other to recruit the best talent. An important part of making A&O attractive to potential recruits is what we can offer besides money. The 'employability for life' concept is a crucial part of this, and the alumni programme in all its aspects is positive evidence of A&O's commitment to existing staff, alumni and future employees.

There is certainly more that can be done to record and measure other benefits, such as talent referrals and the cost savings, in recruitment terms, of returning employees. But, in reality, it actually only takes a small team with a fairly conservative budget to manage a successful alumni programme (certainly in relation to the size of other support functions within a law firm), and the potential value, in many shapes and forms, is great.

12. Looking to the future

The process of convincing a partnership of the need for an 'employability for life' approach that supports people throughout their careers can be a hard task, particularly across different countries and cultures. However, there is a discernible shift happening in many partnerships.

It goes back to the unavoidable point that landing a training contract with a top law firm does not guarantee a long-term commitment from the generation Y (or even generation X) workforce. With far greater choice in their careers, and with only a small proportion ever likely to progress to partner, people today will stay on average for only four or five years. That is a big change from 20 years ago when it was commonly felt that leaving the firm signalled a failure in an individual's career. Law firms, it could be argued, lagged behind the big accountants and management consultants in how they managed human resources. Many firms, however, are working hard to address this. As the chief objectives of any partner are to build a long-term sustainable practice and to cross-sell the expertise of other partners to clients, it clearly makes sense not to alienate your alumni, many of whom will go on to be those clients.

Now, firms must create an environment where there is enough trust for people to have honest conversations about their careers while at the firm and when they consider moving on. As part of trying to create such an environment, A&O has introduced its mentoring programme as described above. The employment agreement is then extended through a strong alumni programme to continue to help people move in the right direction throughout their career – because a business that offers this will attract the best people.

The logical next step for alumni programmes could be to follow the example of other professional services firms, management consultants in particular, and start proactively to place leavers in roles within client organisations. However, this needs to be treated with caution by law firms, as the most important point is for trust to exist between the employee and employer, which means giving honest advice as to what steps an employee can take next. It may well be that another law firm, even a competitor, would be the appropriate next step. Not everyone is interested in, or suited to, an in-house role. Equally, the best option could be to help the person land a role with a client, and the law firm may be able to assist greatly with that. However, the crucial point is that it must be a case-by-case judgement. Fundamentally, the employee must be confident that he or she will receive genuine and honest advice, and not be pushed towards a potential client just because it suits the former employer.

There is still work to be done in law firms to embed the 'employability for life' approach and to realise the greatest value from alumni networks. However, to come back to the original point, underpinning all of this must be the goal, first and foremost, to see your people leave the firm with a strong sense of goodwill, pride and loyalty. That is the foundation of building strong relationships from which strong networks grow. It is, of course, not only good for business but actually the right thing to do.

Good relationships and networks are a crucial part of recruitment and retention in a 'people business', such as a law firm. They are the one, powerful thing that cannot be replicated. This is true at every stage of recruitment and retention: the initial attraction of going to work for a firm who will support and value you; the positive experience you have while working there; and the support you receive if and when you decide to move on and after you have left.

Every law firm wants to recruit the best people and retain them for as long as they add to the success of the business. However, most firms also recognise that it is harder to do this than ever before. The sensible firm will work hard to ensure that those leaving become alumni who retain a great sense of loyalty for their old firm and directly (as a client) or indirectly (by recommendation) continue to enhance the success of the firm. An alumni programme properly run can greatly assist in this crucial business objective. A&O's alumni programme includes:

- Ways to connect with A&O people past and present through a programme of events. Every year, all alumni are invited to at least one networking event; for example:
  - annual global alumni reunions across multiple A&O offices
  - 'class reunions' for trainees in specific intakes
  - access to A&O's global client seminar programme
  - retirees' summer party
  - former London partners' and directors' dinner
  - keynote speaker sessions
- Access to the dedicated Alumni Network website:
  - online people directory to find and connect with other members
  - A&O and alumni news
  - job vacancies
  - log-in using LinkedIn, Facebook, Google or Xing
  - share or add discussion items, photos, marketplace jobs and more
  - access to discount schemes
- Regular communications
  - monthly alumni newsletter
  - Alumni Yearbook, published in December each year
- Careers centre
  - A&O job vacancies as well as alumni advertising their own marketplace jobs
  - *pro bono* opportunities for alumni
- Alumni mentoring programme: open to all global alumni, A&O partners and staff
- Alumni referral scheme
  - A&O's employee referral scheme (which offers a financial reward to staff who successfully recommend people to A&O) extends to alumni, to encourage candidate referrals across our network of offices
- Office space for alumni in selected offices
- Opportunities to participate in the A&O choir and orchestra, who have put on performances at Glyndebourne Opera House, Sadler's Wells and Holland Park Opera House in the United Kingdom (see section 4 above)
- Opportunities to be involved in the firm's charity work

About the authors

Ida Abbott
President, Ida Abbott Consulting
IdaAbbott@aol.com

Ida helps employers manage, develop and retain legal talent, and serves as mentor and coach to high-achieving individuals seeking professional success. A former trial lawyer, she was also an early leader in efforts to promote talent management in the legal profession, for which she was elected a Fellow of the College of Law Practice Management.

Ida has particular expertise in mentoring, sponsorship and advancing women in business and the professions. She is on the Executive Committee of the National Legal Mentoring Consortium, vice-chair of the California State Bar Mentoring Task Force, and co-founder of the Hastings Leadership Academy for Women at Hastings Law School, where she is a Faculty Fellow. She is also a mentor in Law Without Walls, a unique worldwide programme focusing on law, business and innovation.

Ida is a prominent speaker and author whose most recent book is *Sponsoring Women: What Men Need to Know*.

Antonin Besse
Founder, Besse Executive Coaching and Training
antonin.besse@btinternet.com

Antonin combines a strong career history – over three decades as an international lawyer with Freshfields Bruckhaus Deringer LLP – with what clients describe as a natural ability to build empathy and trust, as well as respect. Others describe him variously as reflective, compassionate, mischievous, charming, creative, warm, caring, astute, focused and having huge natural curiosity. His coaching clients include leading law firms and financial institutions.

In addition to coaching, Antonin is a co-founder of Interview Advantage Ltd, which prepares undergraduates for the world of work. He also trains lawyers in leadership and how to manage complex international deals. His other activities include cabinet-making, and understanding as much about cosmology and quantum physics as it is possible for a recovering lawyer to do. Antonin is French, is qualified as a lawyer in both the UK and France, and lives in Oxford.

Heidi K Gardner
Harvard Law School
hgardner@law.harvard.edu

Heidi K Gardner is a Distinguished Fellow in Harvard Law School's Center on the Legal Profession and author of the book *Smart Collaboration: How Professionals and Their Firms Succeed by Breaking Down Silos* (Harvard Business Press, 2017). She was previously on the faculty at Harvard Business School.

Heidi's research focuses on leadership and collaboration in professional service firms, and she received the Academy of Management's prize for Outstanding Practical Implications for Management. She has authored or co-authored more than 50 book chapters, case studies, and articles in scholarly and practitioner journals. Her first book, *Leadership for Lawyers: Essential Strategies for Law Firm Success*, co-edited with Rebecca Normand-Hochman, was published in 2015.

Heidi has lived and worked on four continents, including positions with McKinsey & Co and Procter & Gamble, and as a Fulbright Fellow. She earned a master's degree from the London School of Economics and a PhD from London Business School.

Anna Grishchenkova
Partner, KIAP Attorneys at Law
ag@kiaplaw.ru

Anna leads the litigation and international arbitration practice at KIAP. Her core areas of specialisation include support for debt-recovery disputes, corporate conflicts, disputes with public authorities, and bankruptcy proceedings. She has been involved in over 300 legal proceedings, and has represented clients before Russian and international arbitration authorities.

Anna is recommended by *Chambers Europe*, *Chambers Global*, *Legal 500 EMEA* and *Best Lawyers*. In 2016 she was elected as the new regional representative of Russia in the IBA Litigation Committee (2016 to 2017).

She is on the list of arbitrators in Austria (VIAC) and Russia (RAA). She is a frequent speaker at major Russian and international law conferences.

Tony King
Training consultant and director, AGK PSF Training Ltd
tony.g.king888@gmail.com

After qualifying as a solicitor, Tony taught at the College of Law, London (now the University of Law) for several years and then joined one of the firms which merged to create Clifford Chance as a tax lawyer.

Tony was involved in education, training and professional development at Clifford Chance from 1988 until he retired as the director, Clifford Chance Academy, Clifford Chance LLP in July 2014. Over that time, he was involved in all aspects of learning and development for the firm's global workforce.

He has been involved in a range of national and international representative bodies, including the Legal Education and Training Group, the City of London Law Society, the Law Society of England and Wales, and the International Bar Association.

In addition to advising firms on learning and development issues, Tony's current roles include membership of the Queen's Counsel Selection Panel and a trusteeship of a charity.

Jean-Baptiste Lebelle
Head of HR, Allen & Overy, Paris
jean-baptiste.lebelle@allenovery.com

Jean-Baptiste is head of HR for the Paris office of Allen & Overy.

He has more than 15 years' experience on HR matters in the legal business sector and worked for major law firms in Paris as a headhunter, before starting a career as an HR professional. Before joining Allen & Overy, Jean-Baptiste was the head of HR of PwC tax and legal services in Paris.

Jean-Baptiste has been particularly involved in recruitment and retention issues for many years, and on several occasions has worked on the implementation of a new employer proposition.

He graduated from Sciences Po Paris and holds a master's degree in law from Panthéon University. He is also visiting lecturer on HR issues for different institutions, including Sorbonne University and HEC.

Mahmood Lone
Partner, Allen & Overy
mahmood.lone@allenovery.com

Mahmood is a partner in the litigation team in London. He advises on domestic and cross-border disputes and regulatory investigations and is particularly known for his expertise in disputes arising from complex derivatives and structured products. His contentious regulatory practice includes advising leading financial institutions on high-profile market abuse/manipulation issues including allegations of benchmark rate manipulation.

Mahmood was appointed co-chairman of the Alumni Network in April 2016.

Patrick J McKenna
Principal, McKenna Associates Inc
patrick@patrickmckenna.com

Patrick is an internationally recognised strategist, lecturer and seasoned adviser to the leaders of premier law firms and author of eight books, most notably his international business bestseller *First Among Equals*, currently in its sixth printing and translated into nine languages.

His three decades of experience led to being the subject of a Harvard Law Case Study entitled: *Innovations In Legal Consulting*. One example of that innovation was his launching the first instructional programme designed specifically to address the issues that new firm leaders of larger firms face in their first 100 days.

Patrick serves as contributing editor to *Of Counsel* based in New York City; he writes a regular thought leadership column for *Legal Executive Institute*; he is the first expert in professional services admitted to the Association of Corporate Executive Coaches, the #1 group for senior-level CEO coaches; and he is the recipient of an honorary fellowship from Leaders Excellence at Harvard Square.

Alison Nolan
Founder, Open Consulting
alison.nolan@openconsulting.global

Alison is an independent consultant and coach. She founded Open Consulting to help leaders in organisations work more effectively through people development, leadership and transformational change.

Formerly global head of partner development at Hogan Lovells, she set up the firm's people development team from scratch and led it for more than 10 years. During that time she advised the firm on all aspects of people development, focusing on leadership, cultural change, post-merger integration, career transitions, creating effective teams and personal development. She was responsible for a suite of award-winning programmes for senior associates and partners, including winning the *Financial Times* Innovative Lawyers 2016 award for innovation in human resources.

Alison has a wealth of experience designing and delivering successful change initiatives, development programmes, workshops and development centres for lawyers and partners, as well as individual coaching and group facilitation.

She has an MSc in People and Organisational Development, and is an accredited coach and Time to Think facilitator.

Rebecca Normand-Hochman
Partner, Venturis Consulting Group
Founder and director, Institute of Mentoring
rebecca.normand-
hochman@venturisconsulting.com

Rebecca Normand-Hochman is a partner in Venturis Consulting Group, a strategy and management consultancy based in several European countries – she heads the Paris office. She is also the founder and a director of the Institute of Mentoring which provides insight, research and advice to advance mentoring best practices in the legal profession.

Ms Normand-Hochman practised international finance law in London and Paris for a number of years. Her experience with Allen & Overy in Paris laid the foundation for her present work on talent and leadership for lawyers. She has carried out extensive research on law firm talent management, which draws on best practices and collaboration with leading experts in leadership, change management, coaching and mentoring.

Through her work with Venturis Consulting Group and the Institute of Mentoring, Ms Normand-Hochman researches, speaks, writes and consults on talent and leadership challenges and strategies that relate to the practice of law.

Since 2012 she has been leading the main talent management initiatives of the International Bar Association Law Firm Management Committee, including coordinating the books *Managing Talent for Success* and *Mentoring and Coaching for Lawyers* and leading the IBA Law Firm Mentoring Programme between 2012 and 2014. Ms Normand-Hochman is an officer and advisory board member of the Law Firm Management Committee, where she chairs the Talent and Leadership Working Group. She is also the consulting editor of related books in the series on the business of law: *Mentoring and Coaching for Lawyers; Managing Talent for Success* and co-consulting editor of *Leadership for Lawyers.*

Guillaume Pican
Associate director, Page Executive
GuillaumePican@pageexecutive.com

Guillaume specialises in selecting executive profiles with a flexible approach to talent attraction. Thanks to his long years of experience in screening highly qualified profiles, he has an in-depth knowledge of the needs and demands of companies in many sectors (eg, industry, consulting, legal departments).

Over the last 10 years he has worked for several businesses for the PageGroup across a number of different disciplines and two countries (France and the United States). Between 2011 and 2015, he was director of the tax and legal department in Michael Page France. There he ran a team dedicated to all legal sectors (ie, in-house – temporary or permanent contracts – and private practice). His current role focuses on the development of Page Executive in Paris.

Prior to his experience in PageGroup, Guillaume was an engineer in an international group in the food industry.

Alessandro Portolano
Partner, Chiomenti
alessandro.portolano@chiomenti.net

Alessandro is a partner at Chiomenti and, since 2015, he has been a co-managing partner in charge of the firm's associates. He assists banks, asset managers, insurers and other regulated entities in all areas of banking and financial services regulation. Between 1995 and 2003 he worked within the banking and finance supervision department of the Bank of Italy.

Alessandro holds a law degree from LUISS Guido Carli of Rome and a master of laws from the University of Chicago Law School.

Cecilia Poullain
Structurer, Natixis Asset Management
cecilia.poullain@am.natixis.com

Cecilia has 26 years' experience as a lawyer and structurer in major law firms and financial institutions in Australia, England and France. As a member of Natixis Asset Management's fixed income department, she currently specialises in structuring loan funds on various asset classes (corporate, aircraft, infrastructure, real estate), but has previously focused on structured finance products and derivatives. She is an active member of the ICMA Steering Committee on private placements and the French Euro private placement group. She is a fluent speaker of English and French. Outside working hours, she is a soprano and a writer.

Gerard J Tanja
Partner, Venturis Consulting Group
gerard.tanja@venturisconsulting.com

Gerard Tanja is a partner at Venturis. He holds LLM and PhD degrees in law, and has an MBA from the University of California. Before establishing Venturis, Gerard worked at the University of Leyden, was legal adviser to the minister of foreign affairs and was, before moving to Clifford Chance (World Firm Management Committee), general director of the TMC ASSER Institute for International Law.

At Clifford Chance, Gerard was responsible for HR development and know-how (KH) management.

At Venturis Consulting Group, Gerard specialises in strategy formulation, merger consulting and KH management projects. He has been involved in a number of international law firm mergers, has assisted several Anglo-American firms with the establishment of their European offices and has undertaken a series of strategic reviews of European offices. In addition, he has been heavily involved in a number of law firm restructuring and governance initiatives and KH implementation initiatives in Benelux and Germany.

Boyan Wells
Retired Allen & Overy partner, London
boyan.wells@allenovery.com

Boyan Wells joined A&O in 1979 and from 1981 he worked in the International Capital Markets (ICM) group. He became a partner in 1987 and was head of ICM from 1998 to 2006. He was on the firm's board from 2006 until his retirement in 2014.

Boyan was appointed co-chairman of the Alumni Network in April 2016.